Nuclear Disarmament

Key Statements of Popes, Bishops, Councils and Churches

EDITED BY ROBERT HEYER

BR
115
.A85
N79
1982

PAULIST PRESS
New York/Ramsey

Library of Congress
Catalog Card Number: 82-81631

ISBN: 0-8091-2456-4

Published by Paulist Press
545 Island Road, Ramsey, N.J. 07446

Printed and bound in the
United States of America

Contents

PART TWO:
NORTH AMERICAN
CATHOLIC BISHOPS' STATEMENTS

PART THREE:
ECUMENICAL STATEMENTS

Contents

FOREWORD

REFLECTIONS ON RECENT TEACHING

During 1981 a visible and vocal constituency arose in the American Catholic hierarchy in opposition to the direction and dynamic of the nuclear arms race. The response was evident in the score of individual bishops who addressed the arms race in sermons, articles or pastoral letters in their own dioceses. It crystallized in the annual meeting of the U.S. Bishops' Conference in November. Archbishop John R. Roach, President of the Conference, described the nuclear race as *"the most dangerous moral issue in the public order today."* The chairman of the recently established Committee on War and Peace, Archbishop Joseph L. Bernardin, provided the meeting with a substantive report of progress being made toward a 1982 pastoral letter on the topic.[1] The Bernardin report in turn stimulated a ninety minute discussion among the bishops on the need to address the moral questions of the arms race as a key element in their pastoral teaching ministry.

The vigorous Catholic engagement with the threat of the arms race is not limited to the bishops and it is not confined to the United States. Within our country other groups within the

---

1. Both the Roach and Bernardin addresses can be found in *Origins,* Vol. II, #25 (3 December 1981)

church, notably Pax Christi and the Catholic Peace Fellowship, have a sustained record of active engagement in the peace ministry. Most significantly, as Archbishop Bernardin noted in his report, strong well organized peace movements exist in the local churches of the Netherlands, West Germany and England. All of this, of course, is replicated in the Protestant and Jewish communities, but this is beyond my subject.

There are undoubtedly several stimuli to this coalescence of the Catholic response to the arms race, but one continuing reference is the papal and conciliar teaching of the last three decades. Although the moral problem of warfare has been a staple of Catholic moral theology from the New Testament and Patristic ages, the advent of nuclear weapons confronted the tradition with a new set of questions, providing a reassessment of what had been said and taught prior to World War II. It is this period of review and renewal of Catholic teaching on war and peace, running from Pius XII through John Paul II, that is the concern of this book.[2]

Development in Roman Catholic theology is always a mix of continuity and change. If present teaching simply mirrors the past we risk stagnation; if the present simply repudiates the past we may question its catholicity. Within these parameters, however, substantial change is possible, especially in Catholic moral teaching which addresses complex, contingent and changing questions. The post-World War II teaching on war and peace exhibits both continuity and change, but the dominant note is change, and therefore, development.

To illustrate the dynamic of development, I will examine three sources in the process, using other documents to fill in the picture. The three examples are Pius XII (1939–1957), Vatican II (1962–1965) and John Paul II.

Pius XII's teaching on war and peace has a double significance. First, he stands as a classical representative of the

---

2. A detailed analysis of Catholic teaching texts can be found in J.B. Hehir, *The Just-War Ethic and Catholic Theology: Dynamics of Change and Continuity,* in T. Shannon, ed., *War or Peace: The Search for New Answers* (N.Y.: Orbis Books, 1980) pp. 15-39

dominant voice in Catholic theology from St. Augustine to his pontificate: Pius XII articulates the just-war position. Second, Pius XII was the first Pope who had to assess the meaning of nuclear weapons for the just-war theory. There are three dominant characteristics to the very substantial corpus of Pius XII's writings on international affairs, most of which appeared in his Christmas Address from 1939–1956.[3]

The first was his conviction that the reconstruction of the international system after two world wars required a change in the political and legal structure of the system. Pius XII urged the idea which has remained a central thread in postwar papal teaching: the need for an international authority of some form to coordinate the interaction of sovereign states in an increasingly interdependent world. John XXIII elaborated this theme regarding political-military questions in *Peace on Earth* (1963); Paul VI specified the theme regarding political-economic questions in the *Development of Peoples* (1967).[4] Pius XII's fundamental contribution was to locate his espousal of the just-war theory within the wider framework of the classical "jus gentium" tradition of an ordered and organized world community.

Second, Pius XII's approach to nuclear weapons, found in a series of addresses he gave on atomic, biological and chemical warfare, was to try to incorporate them in the just-war framework. His teaching includes an unstated empirical premise and explicit moral judgment. The premise classified nuclear weapons as a quantitatively but not a qualitatively new development in the history of weaponry. The moral judgment flowed, in part, from this assessment. Pius XII did not rule out in principle the use of nuclear weapons; rather he as-

---

3. Cf. V. Yzermans, ed., *Major Addresses of Pius XII,* Vol. 2 (St. Paul: North Central Publishing Co. 1961). The best analysis of Pius XII's position is J.C. Murray, Remarks on the Moral Problem of War, *Theological Studies,* 20 (1959) p. 40–61.

4. Papal and conciliar teaching from John XXIII through Paul VI can be found in J. Gremillion, *The Gospel of Peace and Justice: Catholic Social Teaching Since Pope John* (N.Y.: Orbis Books, 1976). Here the texts will be referred to by paragraph numbers.

sessed their moral significance in terms of the principle of proportionality.[5] If their effects could not be contained, he
argued, they could not be used. This analysis set limits on
some nuclear weapons, but left open the debate about the morality of limited nuclear war.

Third, Pius XII refused to provide moral justification for a
Catholic position supporting conscientious objection. This ef-
fectively ruled out, in his teaching, a theoretical basis for a
Catholic pacifist position.

The writings of Pius XII close a period in the history of
Catholic theology of war and peace. This does not mean of
course that he had no influence on the future or that there is
no continuity with later teaching. Rather, it means that the
just-war themes found in Pius XII continue after him but with
modification. The prevailing model is based on the teaching of
Vatican II, contained in the *Pastoral Constitution on the
Church in the Modern World* (1965). This document is not the
most recent teaching on war and peace, but it establishes the
theological framework within which the more recent teaching
is situated. To move from Pius XII to Vatican II on war and
peace is to follow the dynamic of development in Catholic
thought. The development would not have been possible, however, without the contribution of John XXIII's encyclical
Peace on Earth.

Both the tone and the themes of *Peace on Earth* are different from Pius XII's analysis of the nuclear arms race. The
tone of the document is not simply a matter of style; it conveys
the substantive judgment that nuclear weapons present a
qualitatively new moral problem to Catholic teaching. The destructive capability of specific weapons, and the more general
conflict to which even limited use of nuclear weapons may
lead, challenge the underlying premise of just-war theory:
that the limited use of force can be a legitimate extension of
politics. The recognition of this challenge is contained in one
of the most publicized sentences of the encyclical: "Therefore,
in this age of ours, which prides itself on its atomic power, it is

5. Cf. Murray, p. 51

irrational to think that war is a proper way to obtain justice for violated rights."[6]

Without ever rejecting Pius XII's assessment of nuclear weapons in terms of the principle of proportionality, *Peace on Earth* conveys a much harsher judgment on the idea of nuclear war. It calls for the banning of nuclear weapons, a process of equal and simultaneous arms reduction and a displacement of the nuclear balance as the basis for peace.[7] In his proposals for arms control and international order, John XXIII reflects the earlier teaching of Pius XII. His specific treatment of nuclear war, however, is strikingly different, even to the point of omitting in the encyclical any reference to the standard principle that nations possess the right of legitimate defense. The absence of the principle is puzzling, since the apparent challenge it poses to the just-war position is not complemented by any alternative position.

In the movement from Pius XII to Vatican II, *Peace on Earth* serves as a transitional document. It changed the direction in Catholic thinking on nuclear war without specifying the categories for future debate or adopting specific conclusions. New categories and specific judgments are both contained in the *Pastoral Constitution;* it is the controlling text in Catholic moral teaching on war and peace to the present moment. Theologians, bishops and activists in the Catholic community have gone beyond the assertions of the *Pastoral Constitution* in what they have said and done, but their words and deeds reflect the change accomplished by the teaching of Vatican II.

The *Pastoral Constitution* has six basic points in its chapter on the "Fostering of Peace and the Establishment of a Community of Nations." First, both the title of the chapter and its contents place the document in line with the political-legal vision found in Pius XII and John XXIII. The work of peace is tied to the establishment of justice within and among nations. Peace, the council affirms, is not simply the absence

---

6. Peace on Earth, para. 127

7. Same, para. 112

of war, but the construction of a political-economic order which will meet the demands of both justice and love.[8]

Second, in light of this positive conception of peace, the council calls Catholics to "an evaluation of war with an entirely new attitude."[9] One does not find in the document an articulated design of what the new attitude should be, but there are examples in the text. A primary element is the stress placed upon the responsibility of personal conscience regarding warfare. A very significant move was made in Vatican II's teaching on conscience which is not recognized unless the history of the conciliar text is known. In classical just-war theory Catholic authors always acknowledged a responsibility of conscience on the part of citizens and soldiers. The logic of the moral decision, however, began with "the presumption of the law." This meant that the command of the state was to be considered to be legitimate and the burden of proof of the obligation to disobey rested with the individual. The first draft of the conciliar text contained that traditional formula about "presumption of the law" but the phrase was removed in the council's debate. In its place one finds a strong imperative requiring resistance to any command which violates the natural law.[10]

Third, growing out of the stress on conscience the conciliar document sets forth a justification for a nonviolent posture as a mode of discipleship, including the right of conscientious objection. The latter position is not set forth as a requirement, and it is balanced by a statement affirming military service as a genuine contribution to peace.[11] The doctrinal significance of the reference to conscientious objection is that it establishes, alongside the just-war position, an option of Catholic pacifism.

Fourth, the just-war position is reaffirmed by implication;

---

8. *The Pastoral Constitution on the Church in the Modern World,* para. 78

9. Same, para. 80

10. Same, para. 79

11. Same, para. 79

since the document asserts the right of states to legitimate defense, it opens the moral argument of what constitutes an act of legitimate defense. The purpose of just-war theory has been to answer that question for societies as a whole and for individuals.[12]

Fifth, the justification of the right to use force is sharply circumscribed when the council speaks of "scientific weapons." The clear referent here is nuclear weapons which "can inflict massive and indiscriminate destruction, thus going far beyond the bounds of legitimate defense."[13] Such a prospect moves the council to reaffirm previous papal condemnations of total war, and to make its own condemnation of attacks on civilian centers of population.[14]

Sixth, the potential *use* of weapons of mass destruction brought the council to an unequivocal condemnation of attacks on civilian centers, but the problem of *deterrence* produced a more circumspect judgment. While succinctly stating the moral dilemma posed by deterrence (the threat to use nuclear weapons *may* prevent use, but the declared intention to strike civilian centers *is* immoral), *the council chose not to make a final judgment on it.*[15]

These six assertions have structured the Catholic debate about nuclear weapons since Vatican II, even though they don't exhaust its contents. Indeed the substance of the Catholic argument has been sufficiently far reaching and pluralistic that a summary of it here would not be possible.[16] A more defined task is to comment on the role of Paul VI in the post-conciliar debate. Pope Paul's commitment to a ministry of peace was one of the most visible dimensions of his papacy. Surprisingly, however, he did not issue a major teaching document on war and peace in the style of Pius XII or John XXIII. His con-

----

12. Same, para. 79

13. Same, para. 80

14. Same, para. 80

15. Same, para. 81

16. A sense of the spectrum can be gained from comparing the Shannon book with J.J. O'Connor, *In Defense of Life* (Boston; St. Paul Editions, 1981)

tribution is found in his U.N. address of 1965 and the inauguration of the annual Day of Peace throughout the church, a practice which continues to the present.

The U.N. address was classical in structure and contemporary in tone. The contemporary note was a fervent appeal to banish war from human affairs: *"No more war, war never again!"* The *classical* character was the careful case made affirming the limited but real right of defense which nations retain in a still decentralized international system.[17] The Day of Peace messages maintained in a more pastoral tone this mix of the plea for peace and the acknowledgement of legitimate defense. At key moments Paul VI also reinforced Vatican II's legitimation of a nonviolent option for Catholics.

John Paul II brings his own distinctive style to the teaching on war and peace. His discourses on the topic thus far have been at the United Nations in New York, UNESCO in Paris, in Ireland and at Hiroshima.[18] On key ideas he stands in direct continuity with the previous papal teaching; these include *an unequivocal condemnation of the arms race* and the misallocation of resources it produces.

The distinguishing characteristics of his approach are found in three themes. First, the categories John Paul uses; until the 1982 Day of Peace message he had not employed the traditional categories of analysis. Specifically, he had neither affirmed in principle a nation's right to legitimate defense, as did Paul VI and Vatican II, nor had he endorsed in principle the position of conscientious objection as the *Pastoral Constitution* had. The Day of Peace message asserts the moral right and duty of a nation to defend its "existence and freedom by proportionate means against an unjust aggressor."[19] Even while acknowledging the right, he limited it severely because of the nature of modern warfare. The fact that John Paul had not used any of the classical categories before the 1982 state-

---

17. *Address at the United Nations,* para 5

18. Cf. *Origins,* Vol. 9 (10/11/79); Vol. 10 (3/12/81); Vol. 10 (6/12/80)

19. *Day of Peace Message* 1982, para. 12; 12/21/81

ment did not of course mean negation of them. It simply high-lights that analysts of the Pope's thought will have to examine it in light of traditional principles as well as John Paul's dis-tinctive categories which are indicated below.

Second, the Holy Father has consistently endorsed non-violent solutions to problems, most vigorously in his homily at Drogheda on the border of Northern Ireland.[20] In Brazil he stated his conviction that failure to address systematic pat-terns of injustice will lead to violence, but such a solution will be "without lasting result and without benefit for man."[20] It could be argued that both of these situations, Ireland and Bra-zil, are questions of internal order rather than interstate prob-lems, but the Pope has made a similar plea for nonviolent approaches to conflict at the international level, notably in his address at Hiroshima.[21]

Third, in his analysis of the nuclear arms race, the Pope has cast his argument in terms of the relationship of technol-ogy, ethics and politics. The theme is a central one in his thought, one he uses to address medical-moral questions as well as international relations. In his first encyclical, the *Re-deemer of Man,* and in his recent address at Hiroshima he used the prism of technology and ethics to analyze the mean-ing of the arms race.[22] John Paul II's analysis involves two steps. First, the nuclear arms race is depicted as the most visi-ble example of a larger question: how modern technology can move beyond both moral and political guidance thus *submit-ting the human person to an impersonal power.* The technologi-cal dynamic of the arms race fits this pattern—new improvements in weaponry are always one step ahead of the most recent attempts to control them.

Second, *this technological dynamic means that the chal-lenge for the human community is to reestablish the primacy of ethics and politics over technology.* In his address to scientists

20. *Origins,* Vol. 9 (10/11/79) p. 272–75

21. *Origins,* Vol. 10 (7/17/80) p. 127

22. *Origins,* Vol. 9 (10/11/79); Vol. 10 (3/12/79)

and intellectuals at Hiroshima, John Paul II stated his basic theme:

> In the past, it was possible to destroy a village, a town, a region, even a country. Now it is the whole planet that has come under threat. This fact should finally compel everyone to face a basic moral consideration: From now on, it is only through a conscious choice and through a deliberate policy that humanity can survive.[23]

The realm of moral choice on this issue lies ultimately, although not exclusively, in the political process. Scientists, journalists, educators and religious leaders prepare the atmosphere of choice, even shape the categories for choosing, but effective action on the arms race requires decisive political action. At the United Nations and at the White House in 1979, John Paul II acknowledged this and called for political measures to control and reverse the spiral of the arms race.[24]

As of 1981, these are the ideas which have shaped the Pope's view of war and peace, but it is still a new pontificate. John Paul II's religious vision, sophisticated sense of the interaction of technology, ethics and politics, and his capability to command world-wide attention for his ideas all point to an active engagement on this question. We will undoubtedly hear more from John Paul II on war and peace.

This article began with a comment about voices in the American church on the arms race. The universal teaching briefly summarized here has set the framework for the teaching of our local church. The universal teaching is general and often one step removed from specific examples. The local teaching, addressing the arms race within the public debate of one of the superpowers has a more specific, concrete and, at times, more complex character. This complementarity of the universal and local levels of Catholic social teaching fits the

---

23. *Origins,* Vol. 8 (3/22/79) p. 634; Vol. 10 (3/12/81)

24. *Origins,* Vol. 10 (3/12/81) p. 621

model outlined by Paul VI in his apostolic letter, *The Eighti-
eth Year* (1971):

> In the face of such widely varying situations it is diffi-
> cult for us to utter a unified message and to put for-
> ward a solution which has universal validity. . . . It is
> up to the Christian communities to analyze with ob-
> jectivity the situation which is proper to their own
> country, to shed on it the light of the Gospel's unal-
> terable words and to draw principles of reflection,
> norms of judgment and directives for action from the
> social teaching of the Church.[25]

25. *Origins,* Vol. 9 (10/11/79) p. 266; Vol. 9 (10/25/79) p. 300

PART ONE

CONCILIAR DOCUMENTS AND PAPAL STATEMENTS

[1] Pope Pius XII, Christmas Message, December 12, 1944

From the decisions already published by international commissions one may draw the conclusion that an essential point in any future international arrangement will be the formation of an organization for the maintenance of peace. This organization will be vested by common consent with supreme authority and with power to smother in its germinal stage any threat of isolated or collective aggression.

No one can hail this development with greater joy than he who has long upheld the principle that the idea of war as an apt and appropriate means of solving international conflicts is now out of date.

No one can wish success to this undertaking which is now being worked out more seriously and purposefully than ever before, with greater enthusiasm than he who has conscientiously striven to make the Christian and religious mentality reject modern war, with its monstrous means of conducting hostilities.

Unquestionably the progress of Man's inventions, which should have heralded the realization of greater well being for all mankind, has been employed instead to destroy all that had been built up through the ages.

By that very fact the immorality of wars of aggression has been patently demonstrated.

[2] Pope Pius XII, Address, September 30, 1954

... Is modern "all out warfare", especially ABC warfare (atomic, bacteriological, chemical warfare), permissible as a matter of principle? There can be no doubt, particularly in view of the untold horror and suffering induced by modern warfare, that to launch such a war other than on just grounds (that is to say, without it being imposed upon one by an obvious, extemely serious, and otherwise unavoidable violation of justice) could be an "offense" worthy of the most severe national and international sanctions. One cannot even in principle ask whether atomic, chemical and bacteriological warfare is lawful other than when it is deemed absolutely necessary as a means of self-defense under the condition previously stipulated. Even then, however, every possible effort must be made to avert it through international agreements, or to place upon its use such distinct and rigid limitation as will guarantee that its effects will be confined to the strict demands of defense. Moreover, should the use of this method of warfare entail such an extension of the existing evil as would render man wholly incapable of controlling it, its use should be rejected as immoral. In such an instance it would no longer be a question of "defense" against injustice, and of the necessary "safeguarding" of legitimate possessions, but of the pure and simple annihilation of all human life within the radius of action. Under no circumstances is this to be permitted.

[3] Pope John XXIII, *Pacem in Terris,* April 11, 1963

Disarmament

109. On the other hand, it is with deep sorrow that We note the enormous stocks of armaments that have been and still are being made in the more economically developed countries with a vast outlay of intellectual and economic resources. And so it happens that, while the people of these countries are loaded with heavy burdens, other countries as a result are deprived of the collaboration they need in order to make economic and social progress.

110. The production of arms is allegedly justified on the grounds that in present-day conditions peace cannot be preserved without an equal balance of armaments. And so, if one country increases its armaments, others feel the need to do the same. And if one country is equipped with nuclear weapons, other countries must produce their own, equally destructive.

111. Consequently, people live in constant fear lest the storm that threatens every moment should break upon them with dreadful violence. And with good reason, for the arms of war are ready at hand. Even though it is difficult to believe that anyone would deliberately take the responsibility for the appalling destruction and sorrow that war would bring in its train, it cannot be denied that the conflagration may be set off by some uncontrollable and unexpected chance. And one must bear in mind that, even though the monstrous power of modern weapons acts as a deterrent, it is to be feared that the mere continuance of nuclear tests, undertaken with war in mind, will have fatal consequences for life on earth.

112. Justice, right reason and humanity, therefore, urgently demand that the arms race should cease; that the stockpiles which exist in various countries should be reduced equally and simultaneously by the parties concerned; that nuclear weapons should be banned; and that a general agreement should eventually be reached about progressive disarmament and an effective method of control.

In the words of Pius XII, Our predecessor of happy memory: "The calamity of a world war, with the economic and social ruin and the moral excesses and dissolution that accompany it, must not be permitted to envelop the human race for a third time."

113. All must realize that there is no hope of putting an end to the building up of armaments, nor of reducing the present stocks, nor still less of abolishing them altogether, unless the process is complete and thorough and unless it proceeds from inner conviction; unless, that is, everyone sincerely co-operates to banish the fear and anxious expectation of war with which men are oppressed. If this is to come about, the fundamental principle on which our present peace depends must be replaced by another, which declares that the true and solid peace of nations can consist, not in equality of arms, but in mutual trust alone.

We believe that this can be brought to pass, and We consider that it is something which reason requires, that it is eminently desirable in itself and that it will prove to be the source of many benefits.

114. In the first place, it is an objective demanded by reason. There can be, or at least there should be, no doubt that relations between states, as between individuals, should be regulated, not by the force of arms, but by the light of reason, by the rule, that is, of truth, of justice and of active and sincere co-operation.

115. Secondly, We say that it is an objective earnestly to be desired in itself. Is there anyone who does not ardently yearn to see war banished, to see peace preserved and daily more firmly established?

116. And finally, it is an objective which will be a fruitful source of many benefits, for its advantages will be felt everywhere—by individuals, by families, by nations, by the whole human family. The warning of Pius XII still rings in our ears: "Nothing is lost by peace; everything may be lost by war."

117. Since this is so, We, the Vicar on earth of Jesus Christ, Saviour of the world and author of peace, as interpreter of the profound longing of the entire human family, follow-

ing the paternal impulse of Our heart and seized by anxiety for the good of all, feel it Our duty to beseech men, especially those who have the responsibility of public affairs, to spare no labor in order to insure that world events follow a reasonable and human course.

118. In the highest and most authoritative assemblies, let men give serious thought to the problem of a peaceful adjustment of relations between political communities on a world level—an adjustment founded on mutual trust, on sincerity in negotiations and on faithful fulfillment of obligations assumed. Let them study the problem until they find that point of agreement from which they can commence to go forward towards accords that will be sincere, lasting and fruitful.

119. We, for Our part, will not cease to pray God to bless these labors so that they may lead to fruitful results.

[4] *Gaudium et Spes,* Constitution on the Church in the Modern World, December 7, 1965

Section I: The Avoidance of War

79. Even though recent wars have wrought physical and moral havoc on our world, the devastation of battle still goes on day by day in some part of the world. Indeed, now that every kind of weapon produced by modern science is used in war, the fierce character of warfare threatens to lead the combatants to a savagery far surpassing that of the past. Furthermore, the complexity of the modern world and the intricacy of international relations allow guerrilla warfare to be drawn out by new methods of deceit and subversion. In many cases the use of terrorism is regarded as a new way to wage war.

Contemplating this melancholy state of humanity, the Council wishes, above all things else, to recall the permanent binding force of universal natural law and its all-embracing principles. Man's conscience itself gives ever more emphatic voice to these principles. Therefore, actions which deliberately conflict with these same principles, as well as orders commanding such actions, are criminal, and blind obedience cannot excuse those who yield to them. The most infamous among these are actions designed for the methodical extermination of an entire people, nation or ethnic minority. Such actions must be vehemently condemned as horrendous crimes. The courage of those who fearlessly and openly resist those who issue such commands merits supreme commendation.

On the subject of war, quite a large number of nations have subscribed to international agreements aimed at making military activity and its consequences less inhuman. Their stipulations deal with such matters as the treatment of wounded soldiers and prisoners. Agreements of this sort must be honored. Indeed they should be improved upon so that the frightfulness of war can be better and more workably held in check. All men, especially government officials and experts in these matters, are bound to do everything they can to effect these improvements. Moreover, it seems right that laws make humane provisions for the case of those who for reasons of conscience refuse to bear arms, provided, however, that they agree to serve the human community in some other way.

Certainly, war has not been rooted out of human affairs. As long as the danger of war remains and there is no competent and sufficiently powerful authority at the international level, governments cannot be denied the right to legitimate defense once every means of peaceful settlement has been exhausted. State authorities and others who share public responsibility have the duty to conduct such grave matters soberly and to protect the welfare of the people entrusted to their care. But it is one thing to undertake military action for the just defense of the people, and something else again to seek the subjugation of other nations. Nor, by the same token, does the mere fact that war has unhappily begun mean that all is fair between the warring parties.

Those, too, who devote themselves to the military service of their country should regard themselves as the agents of security and freedom of people. As long as they fulfill this role properly, they are making a genuine contribution to the establishment of peace.

80. The horror and perversity of war is immensely magni-

fied by the addition of scientific weapons. For acts of war involving these weapons can inflict massive and indiscriminate destruction, thus going far beyond the bounds of legitimate defense. Indeed, if the kind of instruments which can now be found in the armories of the great nations were to be employed to their fullest, an almost total and altogether reciprocal slaughter of each side by the other would follow, not to mention the widespread devastation that would take place in the world and the deadly aftereffects that would be spawned by the use of weapons of this kind.

All these considerations compel us to undertake an evaluation of war with an entirely new attitude. The men of our time must realize that they have to give a somber reckoning of their deeds of war for the course of the future will depend greatly on the decisions they make today.

With these truths in mind, this most holy synod makes its own the condemnations of total war already pronounced by recent popes, and issues the following declaration.

Any act of war aimed indiscriminately at the destruction of entire cities or of extensive areas along with their population is a crime against God and man himself. It merits unequivocal and unhesitating condemnation.

The unique hazard of modern warfare consists in this: it provides those who possess modern scientific weapons with a kind of occasion for perpetrating just such abominations; moreover, through a certain inexorable chain of events, it can catapult men into the most atrocious decisions. That such may never truly happen in the future, the bishops of the whole world gathered together, beg all men, especially government officials and military leaders, to give unremitting thought to their gigantic responsibility before God and the entire human race.

To be sure, scientific weapons are not amassed solely for use in war. Since the defensive strength of any nation is considered to be dependent upon its capacity for immediate retaliation, this accumulation of arms, which increases each year, likewise serves, in a way heretofore unknown, as deterrent to possible enemy attack. Many regard this procedure as the most effective way by which peace of a sort can be maintained between nations at the present time.

81.Whatever be the facts about this method of deterrence, men should be convinced that the arms race in which an already considerable number of countries are engaged is not a safe way to preserve a steady peace, nor is the so-called balance resulting from this race a sure and authentic peace. Rather than being eliminated thereby, the causes of war are in danger of being gradually aggravated. While extravagant sums are being spent for the furnishing of ever new weapons, an adequate remedy cannot be provided for the multiple miseries afflicting the whole modern world. Disagreements between nations are not really and radically healed; on the contrary, they spread the infection to other parts of the earth. New approaches based on reformed attitudes must be taken to remove this trap and to emancipate the world from its crushing anxiety through the restoration of genuine peace.

Therefore, we say it again: the arms race is an utterly treacherous trap for humanity, and one which ensnares the poor to an intolerable degree. It is much to be feared that if this race persists it will eventually spawn all the lethal ruin whose path it is now making ready. Warned by the calamities which the human race has made possible, let us make use of the interlude granted us from above and for which we are thankful, to become more conscious of our own responsibility and to find means for resolving our disputes in a manner more worthy of man. Divine Providence urgently demands of us that we free ourselves from the age-old slavery of war. If we refuse to make this effort, we do not know where we will be led by the evil road we have set upon.

It is our clear duty, therefore, to strain every muscle in working for the time when all war can be completely outlawed by international consent. This goal undoubtedly requires the establishment of some universal public authority acknowledged as such by all and endowed with the power to safeguard on the behalf of all, security, regard for justice, and respect for rights. But before this hope for authority can be set up, the highest existing international centers must devote themselves vigorously to the pursuit of better means for obtaining common security. Since peace must be born of mutual trust between nations and not be imposed on them through a fear of the available weapons, everyone must labor to put an end at last to the arms race, and to make a true beginning of disarmament, not unilaterally indeed, but proceeding at an equal pace according to agreement, and backed up by true and workable safeguards.

82. In the meantime, efforts which have already been made and are still underway to eliminate the danger of war are not to be underrated. On the contrary, support should be given to the good will of the very many leaders who work hard to do away with war, which they abominate. These men, although burdened by the extremely weighty preoccupations of their high office, are nonetheless moved by the very grave peacemaking task to which they are bound, even if they cannot ignore the complexity of matters as they stand. We should fervently ask God to give these men the strength to go forward perseveringly and to follow through courageously on this work of building peace with vigor. It is a work of supreme love for mankind. Today it certainly demands that they extend their thoughts and their spirit beyond the confines of their own nation, that they put aside national selfishness and ambition to dominate other nations, and that they nourish a profound reverence for the whole of humanity, which is already making its way so laboriously toward greater unity.

The problems of peace and of disarmament have already been the subject of extensive, strenuous and constant examination. Together with international meetings dealing with these problems, such studies should be regarded as the first steps toward solving these serious questions, and should be promoted with even greater urgency by way of yielding concrete results in the future.

Nevertheless, men should take heed not to entrust themselves only to the efforts of some, while not caring about their own attitudes. For government officials who must at one and the same time guarantee the good of their own people and promote the universal good are very greatly dependent on public opinion and feeling. It does them no good to work for peace as long as feelings of hostility, contempt and distrust, as well as racial hatred and unbending ideologies, continue to divide men and place them in opposing camps. Consequently there is above all a pressing need for a renewed education of attitudes and for new inspiration in public opinion. Those who are dedicated to the work of education, particularly of the young, or who mold public opinion, should consider it their most weighty task to instruct all in fresh sentiments of peace. Indeed, we all need a change of heart as we regard the entire world and those tasks which we can perform in unison for the betterment of our race.

But we should not let false hope deceive us. For unless enmities and hatred are put away and firm, honest agreements concerning world peace are reached in the future, humanity, which already is in the middle of a grave crisis, even though it is endowed with remarkable knowledge, will perhaps be brought to that dismal hour in which it will experience no peace other than the dreadful peace of death. But, while we say this, the Church of Christ, present in the midst of the anxiety of this age, does not cease to hope most firmly. She intends to propose to our age over and over again, in season and out of season, this apostolic message: "Behold, now is the acceptable time for a change of heart; behold! now is the day of salvation."

Section II: Setting Up an International Community

83. In order to build up peace above all, the causes of discord among men, especially injustice, which foment wars must be rooted out. Not a few of these causes come from excessive economic inequalities and from putting off the steps needed to remedy them. Other causes of discord, however, have their source in the desire to dominate and in a contempt for persons. And, if we look for deeper causes, we find them in human envy, distrust, pride, and other egotistical passions. Man can-

not bear so many ruptures in the harmony of things. Consequently, the world is constantly beset by strife and violence between men, even when no war is being waged. Besides, since these same evils are present in the relations between various nations as well, in order to overcome or forestall them and to keep violence once unleashed within limits it is absolutely necessary for countries to cooperate more advantageously and more closely together and to organize together international bodies and to work tirelessly for the creation of organizations which will foster peace.

[5] Pope Paul VI, Address to the General Assembly of the United Nations, October 4, 1965

Let weapons be dropped and total peace built up

19. And now We come to the most important point of Our message, which is, at first, a negative point. You are expecting Us to utter this sentence, and We are well aware of its gravity and solemnity: *not some peoples against others,* never again, never more! It was principally for this purpose that the Organisation of the United Nations arose: against war, in favour of peace! Listen to the lucid words of a great man, the late John Kennedy who proclaimed four years ago: "Mankind must put an end to war, or war will put an end to mankind". Many words are not needed to proclaim this loftiest aim of your institution. It suffices to remember that the blood of millions of men, that numberless and unheard of sufferings, useless slaughter and frightful ruin, are the sanction of the past which unites you with an oath which must change the future history of the world: No more war, war never again! Peace, it is peace which must guide the destinies of peoples and of all mankind.

20. Gratitude and high praise are due to you, who for twenty years have laboured for peace; gratitude and praise for the conflicts which you have prevented or have brought to an end. The results of your efforts in recent days in favour of

peace, even if not yet proved decisive, are such as to deserve that We, presuming to interpret the sentiments of the whole world, express to you both praise and thanks.

21. Gentlemen, you have performed and you continue to perform a great work: the education of mankind in the ways of peace. The U.N. is the great school where that education is imparted, and we are today in the assembly hall of that school. Everyone who takes his place here becomes a pupil and also a teacher in the art of building peace. When you leave this hall, the world looks upon you as the architects and constructors of peace.

22. Peace, as you know, is not built up only by means of politics or the balance of forces and of interests. It is constructed with the mind, with ideas, with works of peace. You are already working in this direction. But your work is still at the initial stages. Will the world ever succeed in changing that selfish and contentious mentality from which so much of its history has been woven? It is not easy to foresee. On the other hand, it is easy to affirm that we must resolutely march towards a new future, a future of truly human peace, that peace which God has promised to men of good will. The paths that lead to such a peace have already been marked out: the first is that of disarmament.

23. If you want to be brothers, let the weapons fall from your hands. You cannot love with weapons in your hands. Long before they mete out death and destruction, those terrible arms supplied by modern science foment bad feelings and cause nightmares, distrust, and dark designs. They call for enormous expenditures and hold up projects of human solidarity and of great usefulness. They lead astray the mentality of peoples. As long as man remains that weak, changeable and even wicked being he often shows·himself to be, defensive armaments will, alas, be necessary. But you, gentlemen, men of courage and outstanding merit, are seeking means to guarantee the stability of international relations without the need of recourse to arms. This is a goal worthy of your efforts; this is what the peoples of the world expect from you. This is what must be achieved! For that unchallenged confidence in this

Organisation must increase; its authority must be strengthened. Then your aim, it may be hoped, will be accomplished.
You will thus win the gratitude of all peoples, relieved of an
overburdening expenditure on armaments, and freed from the
nightmare of ever imminent war.

24. We are happy to know that many of you have given
favourable consideration to the appeal We addressed last December at Bombay to all nations, when We invited them in the
interests of peace to apply for the benefit of developing nations
a portion at least of the savings that would result from a reduction in armaments. We here renew that invitation, confident of your feelings of humanity and generosity.

[6]   Pope Paul VI, On the Development of Peoples, March 26, 1967

. . . When we were at Bombay to attend the international
Eucharistic Congress we asked the heads of states to use a
part of the expenditure for military equipment to establish a
World Fund for the purpose of giving aid to destitute peoples.
Though this fund is primarily intended to combat want, it also
serves to promote development. For only harmonious international cooperation, of which the Fund would be both a symbol
and an instrumentality, could succeed in putting an end to
senseless rivalries on the one hand, and on the other serve as
the beginning of mutual, peaceful, and beneficial dialogues between nations. [51]

Who does not see that in consequence of the World Fund
which we have mentioned an opportunity will be given to
make some deduction in expenditures suggested either by fear
or by arrogance? While so many people are going hungry,
while so many people spend their lives submerged in the darkness of ignorance, while so many schools, hospitals, homes
worthy of the name, are needed, every public or private squandering, every expenditure either of nations or individuals
made for the sake of pretentious parade, finally every financially depleting arms race—all these we say become a scandal-

ous and intolerable crime. The most serious obligation enjoined on us demands that we openly denounce it. Would that those in authority listened to us before it is too late. [53]

[7] Justice in the World, Synod of Bishops Second General Assembly November 30, 1971

9. The paradox lies in the fact that within this perspective of unity the forces of division and antagonism seem today to be increasing in strength. Ancient divisions between nations and empires, between races and classes, today possess new technological instruments of destruction. The arms race is a threat to man's highest good, which is life; it makes poor peoples and individuals yet more miserable, while making richer those already powerful; it creates a continuous danger of conflagration, and in the case of nuclear arms, it threatens to destroy all life from the face of the earth. At the same time new divisions are being born to separate man from his neighbour. Unless combatted and overcome by social and political action, the influence of the new industrial and technological order favours the concentration of wealth, power and decision-making in the hands of a small public or private controlling group. Economic injustice and lack of social participation keep a man from attaining his basic human and civil rights.

International Action

63. Since the Synod is of a universal character, it is dealing with those questions of justice which directly concern the entire human family. Hence, recognizing the importance of international cooperation for social and economic development, we praise above all else the inestimable work which has been done among the poorer peoples by the local Churches, the missionaries and the organizations supporting them; and we intend to foster those initiatives and institutions which are working for peace, international justice and the development of man. We therefore urge Catholics to consider well the following propositions:

64. (1) Let recognition be given to the fact that international order is rooted in the inalienable rights and dignity of the human being. Let the United Nations Declaration of Human Rights be ratified by all Governments who have not yet adhered to it, and let it be fully observed by all.

65. (2) Let the United Nations—which because of its unique purpose should promote participation by all nations—and international organizations be supported insofar as they are the beginning of a system capable of restraining the armaments race, discouraging trade in weapons, securing disarmament and settling conflicts by peaceful methods of legal action, arbitration and international police action. It is absolutely necessary that international conflicts should not be settled by war, but that other methods better befitting human nature should be found. Let a strategy of non-violence be fostered also, and let conscientious objection be recognized and regulated by law in each nation.

[8]   Pope Paul VI, Address to the Diplomatic Corps, January 10, 1972

... may we draw your attention for a few moments to what is perhaps the most disconcerting phenomenon of our time: the arms race. It is an epidemic phenomenon: no people now seems able to escape its contagion.

The result is that world expenditure on armaments today already adds up to astronomical figures: every country shares in it; Great Powers and medium ones, even the weak nations or those of the so-called "Third World."

What is most disconcerting is that this phenomenon is occurring at a time when men have become more aware of their own dignity and have a livelier sense of being members of the same human family; when individuals and peoples are more keenly aspiring to peace in justice, and when among the younger generation—for many of whom the human family is already a living unity—protests against the arms race are becoming ever more widespread.

What is the explanation for so deep-rooted and distressing a contradiction within the human family, a contradiction between the growing sincere desire for peace on the one hand and the growing fearsome production of instruments of war on the other?

There are some who see in armaments, at least for the great and medium Powers, as it were a necessity of their economic system, which is based on their production, if they are to avoid economic imbalance and mass unemployment. But such motivation is radically opposed to the spirit of civilization and still more to that of Christianity. How can it be admitted that there is no way of finding work for hundreds of thousands of workers other than setting them to make instruments of death? [*1143–1147*]

It is further observed that there continues to be a widespread conviction that, while the policy of armaments cannot be justified in itself, it can however be explained by the fact that, if peace is possible today it can only be one based on a balance of Armed Forces. "Whatever is to be thought of this method of deterrence", declares the Constitution *Gaudium et Spes*, "men should be convinced that the arms race in which so many countries are engaged is not a safe way to preserve a ready peace. Nor is the so-called balance resulting from this race a sure and authentic peace." (Gaudium et Spes, 81) [*1149–1150*]

For this reason the realization of peace in justice demands—and attempts to attain this are already being carried out with courageous and wise initiatives—that the opposite road be followed: that of progressive disarmament. . . . [*1151*]

[9] Pope Paul VI, Annual Message for Day of Peace, January 1, 1976

Arms and wars are, in a word, to be excluded from civilization's programs. Judicious disarming is another weapon of peace. As the prophet Isaiah said: "He will wield authority over the nations and adjudicate between many peoples; these will hammer their swords into plough-shares, their spears into sickles" (Is. 2:4). Then let us listen to the word of Christ: "Put your sword back for all who draw the sword will die by the sword" (Mt. 26:52). Is this utopia? For how much longer?

Here we enter into the speculative world of ideal human-ity, of the new mankind still to be born, still to be educated—mankind stripped of its grievous weight of murderous military weaponry, and rather clothed and strengthened by moral principles which are natural to it. These are principles which already exist, but still in a theoretical and in practice imma-ture, weak and tender state, only at the beginning of their penetration into the profound and operative consciousness of peoples.

Their weakness, which seems incurable to the diagnosti-cians, the so-called realists of historical and anthropological studies, comes especially from the fact that military dis-armament, if it is not to constitute an unforgivable error of impossible optimism, of blind ingenuousness, of a tempting op-portunity for others' oppression, should be common and gener-al. Disarmament is either for everyone, or it is a crime of neglect to defend oneself. Does not the sword, in the concert of historical and concrete life in society, have its own *raison d'etre*, for justice and peace? (cf. Rom. 13:4). Yes, we must ad-mit it.

But has there not come into the world a transforming dy-namism, a hope which is no longer unlikely, a new and effec-tive progress, a future and longed-for history which can make itself present and real, ever since the master, the prophet of the New Testament, proclaimed the decline of the archaic, primitive and instinctive tradition, and, with a word having in itself power not only to denounce and to announce, but also to generate, under certain conditions, a new mankind, declared: "Do not imagine that I have come to abolish the law or the prophets. I have come not to abolish but complete them. . . You have learnt how it was said to our ancestors: 'You must not kill'; and if anyone does kill he must answer for it before the court. But I say this to you: Anyone who is angry with his brother will answer for it before the court" (Mt. 5:17, 21–22).

It is no longer a simple, ingenuous and dangerous utopia. It is the new law of mankind which goes forward, and which arms peace with a formidable principle: "You are all brethren" (Mt. 23:8). If the consciousness of universal brotherhood truly penetrates into the hearts of men, will they still need to arm themselves to the point of becoming blind and fanatic killers of their brethren who in themselves are innocent, and of perpetrating, as a contribution to peace, butchery of untold magnitude, as at Hiroshima on August 6, 1945? In fact has not our own time had an example of what can be done by a weak man, Gandhi—armed only with the principle of non-violence—to vindicate for a nation of hundreds of millions of human beings the freedom and dignity of a new people?

Civilization walks in the footsteps of peace armed only with an olive branch. Civilization is followed by the doctors with the weighty volumes on the law which will lead to the ideal human society; there follow the politicians, expert not so much in the calculation of all-conquering armies for winning wars and repressing the defeated and demoralized, but rather in assessing the resources of the psychology of goodness and friendship.

[10] Pope Paul VI, World Day of Peace Message, January 1, 1977

Do we want peace? Then let us defend life!

The phrase "peace and life" may seem almost tautological, a rhetorical slogan. It is not so. The combination of the two terms in the phrase represents a hard-won conquest in the onward march of human progress—a march still short of its final goal. How many times in the drama of human history the phrase "peace and life" has involved a fierce struggle of the two terms, not a fraternal embrace. Peace is sought and won through conflict, like a sad doom necessary for self-defense.

The close relationship between peace and life seems to spring from the nature of things, but not always, not yet from the logic of people's thought and conduct. This close relationship is the paradoxical novelty that we must proclaim for this year of grace 1977 and henceforth forever, if we are to understand the dynamics of progress.

To succeed in doing so is no easy and simple task: we shall meet the opposition of too many formidable objections, which are stored in the immense arsenal of pseudo-convictions, empirical and utilitarian prejudices, so-called reasons of state, and habits drawn from history and tradition. Even today, these objections seem to constitute insurmountable obstacles.

The tragic conclusion is that if, in defiance of logic, peace and life can in practice be dissociated, there looms on the horizon of the future a catastrophe that in our days could be immeasurable and irreparable both for peace and life. Hiroshima is a terribly eloquent proof and a frightening prophetic example of this. In the reprehensible hypothesis that peace were thought of in unnatural separation from its relationship with life, peace could be imposed as the sad triumph of death. The words of Tacitus come to mind: "They make a desert and call it peace" (*ubi solitudinem faciunt, pacem appellant. Agricola*, 30). Again, in the same hypothesis, the privileged life of some can be exalted, can be selfishly and almost idolatrously preferred, at the expense of the oppression or suppression of others. Is that peace?

This conflict is thus seen to be not merely theoretical and moral but tragically real. Even today it continues to desecrate and stain with blood many a page of human society. The key to truth in the matter can be found only by recognizing the primacy of life as a value and as a condition for peace. The formula is: "If you want peace, defend life." Life is the crown of peace. If we base the logic of our activitiy on the sacredness of life, war is virtually disqualified as a normal and habitual means of asserting rights and so of ensuring peace. Peace is but the incontestable ascendancy of right, in the final analysis, the joyful celebration of life.

Here the number of examples is endless, as is the case history of the adventures, or rather the misadventures, in which life is put at peril in the face of peace. We make our own the classification which, in this regard, has been presented according to "three essential imperatives." According to these imperatives, in order to have authentic and happy peace, it is necessary "to defend life, to heal life, to promote life."

The policy of massive armaments is immediately called into question. The ancient saying, which has taught politics and still does so—"if you want peace, prepare for war" (si vis pacem, para bellum)—is not acceptable without radical reservation (cf. Lk 14:3). With the forthright boldness of our principles, we thus denounce the false and dangerous program of the "arms race," of the secret rivalry between peoples for military superiority.

Even if through a surviving remnant of happy wisdom, or through a silent yet tremendous contest in the balance of hostile deadly powers, war (and what a war it would be!) does not break out, how can we fail to lament the incalculable outpourings of economic resources and human energies expended in order to preserve for each individual state its shield of ever more costly, ever more efficient weapons, and this to the detriment of resources for schools, culture, agriculture, health and civic welfare? Peace and life support enormous and incalculable burdens in order to maintain a peace founded on a perpetual threat to life, as also to defend life by means of a constant threat to peace.

People will say: it is inevitable. This can be true within a concept of civilization that is still so imperfect. But let us at least recognize that this constitutional challenge which the arms race sets up between life and peace is a formula that is fallacious in itself and which must be corrected and superseded. We therefore praise the effort already begun to reduce and finally to eliminate this senseless cold war resulting from the progressive increase of the military potential of the various nations, as if these nations should necessarily be enemies of each other, and as if they were incapable of realizing that such a concept of international relations must one day be resolved in the ruination of peace and of countless human lives.

[11]   Pope Paul VI, World Day of Peace Message, January 1, 1978

It seems to us that two main phenomena claim the attention of all of us in the evaluation of peace itself.

The first phenomenon is magnificently positive, and is constituted by the developing progress of peace. It is an idea that is gaining prestige in the conscience of humanity; it advances, and precedes and accompanies the idea of progress, which is the idea of the unity of the human race. The history of our time—let it be said for its glory—is studded with the flowers of a splendid documentation in favor of peace, one that has been carefully thought out, desired, organized, celebrated and defended: Helsinki teaches this. And these hopes are confirmed by the next special session of the General Assembly of the United Nations organization, devoted to the problem of disarmament, and also by the numerous efforts of both great and humble workers for peace.

No one today dares to defend as principles of well-being and of glory, deliberate programs of murderous strife between men, that is, programs of war. Even where the community expressions of legitimate national interest, supported by motives that seem to coincide with the prevailing reasons of law, do not succeed in affirming themselves through war as a means of solution, one still has confidence that there can be avoided the desperate recourse to the use of arms, which today as never before is insanely murderous and destructive. But now the conscience of the world is horrified by the hypothesis that our peace is nothing but a truce, and that an uncontrollable conflagration can be suddenly unleashed.

We would like to be able to dispel this threatening and terrible nightmare by proclaiming at the top of our voice the absurdity of modern war and the absolute necessity of peace—peace not founded on the power of arms that today are endowed with an infernal destructive capacity (let us recall the tragedy of Japan), nor founded on the structural violence of some political regimes, but founded on the patient, rational and loyal method of justice and freedom, such as the great in-

ternational institutions of today are promoting and defending.
We trust that the magisterial teachings of our great predecessors Pius XII and John XXIII will continue to inspire on this
fundamental theme the wisdom of modern teachers and contemporary politicians.

[12] Pope Paul VI, Message to the General Assembly of the U.N. for Its Session on Disarmament, May 24, 1978

On the occasion of the Special Session which the General
Assembly of the United Nations has decided to devote to the
problem of disarmament, there exists a widespread expectation, and its echo has reached us. Does not the Holy See have
something to say on a subject of such burning relevance and
such vital importance for the future of the world?

Without being a member of your organization, the Holy
See follows its many activities with the greatest attention and
with a profound understanding, sharing its preoccupations
and its generous intentions. We cannot remain insensitive to
an expectation such as this.

We therefore very willingly accept the opportunity that
has been given to us to address once again a message to the
General Assembly of the United Nations, as we had the honor
to do, in person, in that already distant October of 1965. The
present circumstance is in effect absolutely exceptional in the
life of your organization and for the whole of humanity.

We come to you once again today, in the spirit and with
the sentiments of our first meeting, the remembrance of
which is always vivid and dear to our heart. Please accept our
respectful and cordial greeting.

We come to you as the representative of a church that is
made up of hundreds of millions of people spread throughout
all the continents. But at the same time we have the consciousness of giving a voice to the aspirations and hopes of
other hundreds of millions of people, Christians and non-Christians, believers and non-believers: We would like to gath-

er them together, as in an immense choir ascending toward God and toward those who have received from God the responsibility for the destiny of the nations.

Our message is meant to be, first of all, a message of congratulations for your having resolved to confront decisively, in this lofty forum, the problem of disarmament. Yours is an act of courage and wisdom. It is the response to an extremely grave and urgent need.

Our message is also a message of understanding. We know the exceptional difficulties that you must face, and we fully realize the weight of your responsibilities, but we have confidence in the seriousness and sincerity of your commitment.

Our message is meant to be above all—if you permit us to say so—a message of encouragement.

The peoples are manifesting such interest in the theme of your discussion because they believe that to disarm is, first of all, to deprive war of its means: Peace is their dream, their deepest aspiration.

The desire for peace is also the noble and profound motive that has brought you to this assembly. But, in the eyes of statesmen, the problem of disarmament presents itself under a much more articulated and much more complex form.

Faced with the situation as it is, the statesman asks himself, not without reason, if it is just and if it is possible not to recognize the right of the members of the international community to make their own provisions for their legitimate defense, and hence to procure the means necessary for such a goal.

And the temptation is strong to ask oneself if the best possible protection for peace does not in fact continue to be ensured, basically, by the old system of the balance of forces between the different states or groups of states. A disarmed peace is always exposed to danger; its very weakness is an incentive to attack it.

Against this background one can and must—it is said— develop, in a parallel way, efforts aimed on the one hand at perfecting the methods and bodies for preventing and resolving peacefully conflicts and confrontations; and on the other

hand to render less inhuman those wars that are not successfully avoided. At the same time, one can and must endeavor to
reduce mutually the arsenals of war, in a way that does not
destroy the existing balances, but lessens the temptations to
have recourse to weapons and lightens the enormous military
budgets.

Such seems to be the path of political realism. It claims
justification in reason and experience. To go further seems to
many people a useless or indeed dangerous effort.

Let us say at once that all substantial progress toward improving the mechanism of preventing conflicts, toward eliminating particularly dangerous and inhumane weapons, and
toward lowering the level of armaments and military expenditure, will be hailed by us as an extremely valuable and beneficial result.

But this is still not enough. The question of war and
peace, in fact, presents itself today in new terms.

It is not that the principles have changed. Aggression by
one state against another was illicit yesterday just as it is today. Even in the past, an "act of war directed to the indiscriminate destruction of whole cities or vast regions with their
inhabitants" was "a crime against God and humanity itself"
(*Gaudium et Spes*, 80). And war—although one must honor the
heroism of those who sacrifice their very lives to the service of
their native land or of some other noble cause—has always
been, in itself, a supremely irrational and morally unacceptable means of regulating the relationships between states,
though without prejudice to the right of legitimate defense.

But today, war has at its disposal means which have "immeasurably magnified its horrors and wickedness" (ibid.).

The logic underlying the quest for the balances of power
impels each of the adversaries to seek to ensure a certain margin of superiority, for fear of being left at a disadvantage. This
logic, in conjunction with the amazing progress of humanity in
the spheres of science and technology, has led to the discovery
of ever more sophisticated and powerful instruments of destruction. These instruments have accumulated and, by virtue
of an almost autonomous process, they tend to self-perpetuate

unendingly, in a continual escalation both in quantity and quality, with an immense expenditure of men and means, to the point of reaching today a potential amply capable of wiping out all life on the planet.

Developments in nuclear armament make up a special chapter, and certainly the most typical and striking one, of this quest for security through the balance of power and fear. But can one forget the "progress" that has also been made and that, alas, might still be made in the sphere of other arms of mass destruction or with the capacity to produce particularly damaging effects—arms that are considered to have, for that very reason, a special power of "dissuasion"?

But even though the "balance of terror" has been able to avoid the worst and may do so for some time more, to think that the arms race can thus go on indefinitely, without causing a catastrophe, would be a tragic illusion.

Certainly, the subject above all concerns, at least directly, the great powers and the countries forming their blocs, but it would be very hard for the other countries not to feel concerned.

Humanity therefore finds itself forced to turn back on itself and ask itself where it is going, or rather, what it is plunging into. It is forced above all to ask whether the point of departure is not mistaken and should therefore be radically altered.

The reasons for a change of this kind—whether moral reasons, or reasons of security or of particular and general interest—are certainly not lacking.

But, is it possible to find a substitute for the security—however uncertain and costly it may be—that each is trying to ensure by acquiring the means of his own defense?

Few problems appear today so inevitable and difficult as the problem of disarmament. Few problems respond so much to the needs and expectations of the people, and at the same time so readily provoke mistrust, skepticism and discouragement. Few problems demand, on the part of those who must face them, such great resources of idealism and such an acute sense of reality. It seems to be a problem situated at the level of a prophetic vision open to the hopes of the future. And yet one cannot really face this problem without remaining solidly based upon the hard and concrete reality of the present.

Disarmament therefore calls for an extraordinary effort of intelligence and political will on the part of all the members of the great family of nations, in order to reconcile demands that seem to contradict one another and cancel one another out.

The problem of disarmament is substantially a problem of mutual trust. It would therefore be largely useless to seek possible solutions of the technical aspects of disarmament if one were to fail to cure at its source the situation that serves as fertile soil for the proliferation of armaments.

Even the terror of new weapons runs the risk of being ineffective, to the extent that other guarantees are not found for the security of states and for the solution of the problems capable of bringing those states into confrontation on points vital to them.

If one wishes—as one must—to make substantial progress along the road to disarmament, it is therefore essential to find the means of replacing "the balance of terror" by "the balance of trust."

But, in practice, is this possible? And to what extent?

Certainly, a first step consists in trying to improve with good faith and good will the atmosphere and the reality of international relations, especially between the great powers and the blocs of states. In this way the fears and suspicions that today divide them can lessen, and it will be easier for them to believe in the real desire for mutual peace. It involves a long and complicated effort, but one that we would like to encourage with all our power.

Detente in the real sense, that is to say, founded upon a proven willingness to exercise mutual respect, is a condition for setting in motion a true process of disarmament. In turn, balanced and properly supervised disarmament measures assist detente to progress and grow stronger.

However, the international situation is too exposed to the ever possible changes and caprices of tragically free wills. Solid international trust therefore also presupposes structures that are objectively suitable for guaranteeing by peaceful means security and respect for, or recognition of, everyone's rights, against always possible bad will. In other words, such trust presupposes an international order capable of giving everyone what each is today seeking to ensure for himself by the possession and threat of arms, if not by their use.

But is there not a risk of thus slipping into utopianism?

We think that we can and must resolutely answer no. It is true that the task in question is extremely arduous, but it is not beyond the tenacity and wisdom of people who are aware of their own responsibilities before humanity and history—above all before God. This means the need for a higher religious awareness. Even those who do not take God into account can and must recognize the fundamental exigencies of the moral law that God has written in the depths of human hearts and that must govern people's mutual relationships on the basis of truth, justice and love.

At a time when humanity's horizons are widening far beyond the confines of our planet, we refuse to believe that man, animated by such an awareness, is not capable of exorcising the demon of war which threatens to destroy him, even if this demands of him immense efforts and a reasonable renunciation of old-fashioned concepts that continue to set peoples and nations at odds.

In making our own and expressing to you anew the hope and anguish of humanity aspiring to the peace it needs, we are aware that the path which must lead to the coming of a new international order capable of eliminating wars and the causes of wars and thus making arms superfluous cannot in any case be as short as we would like it to be.

It will therefore be indispensable in the meantime to plan and promote a strategy of peace and disarmament—a step-by-step strategy but one that is at the same time almost impatient, a strategy that is balanced yet courageous—always keeping our eyes and our wills fixed on the final goal of general and complete disarmament.

We do not have the competence or authority to indicate to

you the methods and mechanisms for such a strategy, which in any case presupposes the setting up of reliable and effective international control systems. We believe however that there is common agreement with you on the need to lay down some priorities in the effort aimed at halting the arms race and reducing the amount of existing arms.

A. Nuclear weapons certainly have first place: They are the most fearsome menace with which mankind is burdened. We appreciate very much the initiatives that have already been taken in this area, but we must encourage all countries, particularly those which have the chief responsibility for it, to continue to develop these initiatives, with the final goal of completely eliminating the atomic arsenal. At the same time means must be found for giving all peoples access to the immense resources of nuclear energy for their peaceful use.

B. Next come already existing or possible weapons of mass destruction, such as chemical, radiological and all other such weapons, and those that strike indiscriminately or, to use an expression that is itself rather cruel, weapons with excessively and needlessly cruel effects.

C. Mention must also be made of trade in conventional weapons, which are, so to speak, the principal fuel for local or limited wars. In comparison with the immensity of the catastrophe that a war resorting to the whole arsenal of strategic and other weapons would mean for the world or for whole continents, such conflicts may seem of minor importance, if not negligible.

But the destruction and suffering that they cause to the people that are their victims are no less than those that would be brought about on quite a different scale by a general conflict. Furthermore, the increase in arms budgets can stifle the economy of countries that are often still at the developing stage. Besides, account must be taken of the danger that, in a world which has grown small and in which different interests interfere and clash, a local conflict could gradually provoke much wider conflagrations.

The arms race is a matter of scandal; the prospect of disarmament is a great hope. The scandal concerns the crying disproportion between the resources in money and intelligence devoted to the service of death and the resources devoted to the service of life. The hope is that, by cutting down on military expenditure, a substantial part of the immense resources that it now absorbs can be employed in a vast world development project.

We feel the scandal. We make the hope our own.

In this same hall where you are gathered today we renewed on Oct. 4, 1965 the appeal we made to all states on the occasion of our journey to Bombay the previous December: "to devote to the benefit of developing nations at least a part of the money that could be saved through a reduction of armaments."

We now repeat this appeal with still more force and insistence, calling on all countries to study and put into operation an organic plan within the framework of the programs for the fight against inequality, underdevelopment, hunger, disease and illiteracy. Justice demands it; the general interest recommends it. For progress by each of the members of the great human family will be to the advantage of progress by all and will serve to give a more solid foundation to peace.

Disarmament, a new world order and development are three obligations that are inseparably bound together and that by their essence presuppose a renewal of public outlook.

We know and understand the difficulties presented by these obligations. But it is our will and our duty to remind you strongly, as people who are conscious of responsibility for the destiny of mankind, of the very serious reasons that make it necessary to find means of overcoming these difficulties. Do not depart without having laid the foundations and given the indispensable impulse to the solution of the problem that has brought you here together. Tomorrow may be too late.

But, you will ask, what contributions can and will the Holy See make to this immense common effort for disarmament and peace?

It is a question you have a right to ask. It places us in our turn face to face with our responsibilities, with respect to which our means are much inferior to our will.

The Holy See is not a world power, nor has it political power. It has declared in a solemn treaty that "it wishes to remain and will remain extraneous to all temporal disputes between states and to international congresses held for such objects, unless the contending parties make concordant appeal to its mission of peace; at the same time reserving the right to exercise its moral and spiritual power" (Lateran Treaty, Article 24).

Sharing your problems, conscious of your difficulties, and strong by our very weakness, we accordingly say to you with great simplicity: If you ever think that the Holy See can help overcome the obstacles blocking the way to peace, it will not hide behind the argument of its "non-temporal" character nor shy away from the responsibilities that could be involved in interventions that have been desired and asked for. For the Holy See greatly esteems peace and greatly loves it.

In any case, we shall continue to proclaim aloud, untiringly and without losing courage, the duty of peace, the principles that govern its dynamism, and the means of gaining and defending it through renouncing by common accord the weapons that threaten to kill it while claiming to serve it.

We know the strength of public opinion when it is upheld by solid, ideal convictions firmly rooted in consciences. We shall therefore continue to cooperate in order to educate dynamically for peace the new humanity. We shall continue to recall that there will be no disarmament of weapons if there is no disarmament of hearts.

We shall continue to pray for peace.

Peace is the fruit of the good will of men and women, but it remains continually exposed to perils that good will does not always succeed in controlling. That is why peace has always appeared to mankind as above all else a gift from God. We shall ask him for it: Grant us peace. And we shall ask him to guide your work, in order that its results, both immediate and future, will not disappoint the hope of the people.

[13] Pope John Paul II, *Redemptor Hominis*, March 4, 1979

This difficult road of the indispensable transformation of the structures of economic life is one on which it will not be easy to go forward without the intervention of a true conversion of mind, will and heart. The task requires resolute commitment by individuals and peoples that are free and linked in solidarity. All too often freedom is confused with the instinct for individual or collective interest or with the instinct for combat and domination, whatever be the ideological colors with which they are covered. Obviously these instincts exist and are operative, but no truly human economy will be possible unless they are taken up, directed and dominated by the deepest powers in man, which decide the true culture of peoples. These are the very sources for the effort which will express man's true freedom and which will be capable of ensuring it in the economic field also. Economic development, with every factor in its adequate functioning, must be constantly programed and realized within a perspective of universal joint development of each individual and people, as was convincingly recalled by my predecessor Paul VI in *Populorum Progressio*. Otherwise, the category of "economic progress" becomes in isolation a superior category subordinating the whole of human existence to its partial demands, suffocating man, breaking up society, and ending by entangling itself in its own tensions and excesses.

It is possible to undertake this duty. This is testified by certain facts and results, which it would be difficult to mention more analytically here. However, one thing is certain: At the basis of this gigantic sector it is necessary to establish, accept and deepen the sense of moral responsibility, which man must undertake. Again and always man.

This responsibility becomes especially evident for us Christians when we recall—and we should always recall it—the scene of the last judgment according to the words of Christ related in Matthew's Gospel.

This eschatological scene must always be "applied" to

man's history; it must always be made the "measure" for human acts as an essential outline for an examination of conscience by each and every one: "I was hungry and you gave me no food . . . naked and you did not clothe me . . . in prison and you did not visit me." These words become charged with even stronger warning, when we think that, instead of bread and cultural aid, the new states and nations awakening to independent life are being offered, sometimes in abundance, modern weapons and means of destruction placed at the service of armed conflicts and wars that are not so much a requirement for defending their just rights and their sovereignty but rather a form of chauvinism, imperialism, and neocolonialism of one kind or another. We all know well that the areas of misery and hunger on our globe could have been made fertile in a short time, if the gigantic investments for armaments at the service of war and destruction had been changed into investments for food at the service of life.

This consideration will perhaps remain in part an "abstract" one. It will perhaps offer both "sides" an occasion for mutual accusation, each forgetting its own faults. It will perhaps provoke new accusations against the church. The church, however, which has no weapons at her disposal apart from those of the spirit, of the word and of love, cannot renounce her proclamation of "the word . . . in season and out of season." For this reason she does not cease to implore each side of the two and to beg everybody in the name of God and in the name of man: Do not kill! Do not prepare destruction and extermination for men! Think of your brothers and sisters who are suffering hunger and misery! Respect each one's dignity and freedom!

17. Human Rights: "Letter" or "Spirit"

This century has so far been a century of great calamities for man, of great devastations, not only material ones but also moral ones, indeed perhaps above all moral ones. Admittedly it is not easy to compare one age or one century with another under this aspect, since that depends also on changing historical standards. Nevertheless, without applying these comparisons, one still cannot fail to see that this century has so far been one in which people have provided many injustices and sufferings for themselves. Has this process been decisively curbed? In any case, we cannot fail to recall at this point, with esteem and profound hope for the future, the magnificent effort made to give life to the United Nations organization, an effort conducive to the definition and establishment of man's objective and inviolable rights, with the member states obliging each other to observe them rigorously. This commitment has been accepted and ratified by almost all present-day states, and this should constitute a guarantee that human rights will become throughout the world a fundamental principle of work for man's welfare.

There is no need for the church to confirm how closely this problem is linked with her mission in the modern world. Indeed it is at the very basis of social and international peace, as has been declared by John XXIII, the Second Vatican Council, and later Paul VI, in detailed documents. After all, peace comes down to respect for man's inviolable rights—*Opus iustitiae pax*—while war springs from the violation of these rights and brings with it still graver violations of them. If human rights are violated in time of peace, this is particularly painful and from the point of view of progress it represents an incomprehensible manifestation of activity directed against man, which can in no way be reconciled with any program that describes itself as "humanistic." And what social, economic, political or cultural program could renounce this description? We are firmly convinced that there is no program in today's world in which man is not invariably brought to the fore, even when the platforms of the programs are made up of conflicting ideologies concerning the way of conceiving the world.

[14] Pope John Paul II, Address to the XXXIV General Assembly of the U.N., October 2, 1979

Paul VI was a tireless servant of the cause of peace. I wish to follow him with all my strength and continue his service.

The Catholic Church in every place on earth proclaims a message of peace, prays for peace, *educates for peace.* . . .

We are troubled also by reports of the development of weaponry exceeding in quality and size the means of war and destruction ever known before. In this field we applaud the decisions and agreements aimed at reducing the arms race. Nevertheless, the life of humanity today is seriously endangered by the threat of destruction and by the risk arising even from accepting certain "tranquillizing" reports. And the resistance to actual concrete proposals of real disarmament, such as those called for by this Assembly in a special session last year shows that together with the will for peace that all profess and that most desire there is also in existence—perhaps in latent or conditional form but nonetheless real—the contrary and the negation of this will. The continual *preparations for war* demonstrated by the production of ever more numerous, powerful and sophisticated weapons in various countries show that there is a desire to be ready for war, and *being ready* means *being able to start it*; it also means taking the risk that sometime, somewhere, somehow, someone can set in motion the terrible mechanism of general destruction. [10]

. . . in this perspective we must ask ourselves whether there will continue to accumulate over the heads of this new generation of children the threat of common extermination for which the means are in the hands of the modern states, especially the major world powers. Are the children to receive the arms race from us as a necessary inheritance? How are we to explain this unbridled race?

The ancients said: *Si vis pacem, para bellum.* But can our age still really believe that the breathtaking spiral of armaments is at the service of world peace? In alleging the threat of a potential enemy, is it really not rather the intention to keep for oneself a means of threat, in order to get the upper hand with the aid of one's own arsenal of destruction? Here too it is the human dimension of peace that tends to vanish in favor of ever new possible forms of imperialism. [22]

[15] Pope John Paul II, World Day of Peace Message, December 18, 1979

Truth Strengthens the Means of Peace

8. The path from a less human to a more human situation, both in national and in international life, is a long one, and it has to be traveled in stages. The man of peace knows this, he says so and he finds in the efforts for truth that I have just described the light he needs to keep his course set correctly. The man of violence knows it also, but he does not say so, and he deceives public opinion by holding up the glittering prospect of a radical and speedy solution, and then settles into his lie and explains away the constantly repeated delays in the arrival of the freedom that had been promised and the abundance that had been assured.

There is no peace without readiness for sincere and continual dialogue. Truth too requires dialogue, and therefore reinforces this indispensable means for attaining peace. Truth has no fear, either, of honorable agreements, because truth brings with it the light that enables it to enter into such an agreement without sacrificing essential convictions and values. Truth causes minds to come together. It shows what already unites the parties that were previously opposed. It causes the mistrust of yesterday to decrease, and prepares the ground for fresh advances in justice and brotherhood and in the peaceful co-existence of all human beings.

In this context I cannot fail to say a word about the arms race. The situation in which humanity is living today seems to include a tragic contradiction between the many fervent declarations in favor of peace and the no less real vertiginous escalation in weaponry. The very existence of the arms race can even cast a suspicion of falsehood and hypocrisy on certain declarations of the desire for peaceful coexistence. What is worse, it can often even justify the impression that such declarations serve only as a cloak for opposite intentions.

[16]   Pope John Paul II, *Dives in Misericordia*, November 30, 1980

The pastoral constitution *Gaudium et Spes* of the Second Vatican Council is certianly not the only document that deals with the life of this generation, but it is a document of particular importance. "The dichotomy affecting the modern world," we read in it, "is, in fact, a symptom of a deeper dichotomy that is in man himself. He is the meeting point of many conflicting forces. In his condition as a created being he is subject to a thousand shortcomings, but feels untrammeled in his inclinations and destined for a higher form of life. Torn by a welter of anxieties he is compelled to choose between them and repudiate some among them. Worse still, feeble and sinful as he is, he often does the very thing he hates and does not do what he wants. And so he feels himself divided, and the result is a host of discords in social life."

Toward the end of the introductory exposition we read: "In the face of modern developments there is a growing body of men who are asking the most fundamental of all questions or are glimpsing them with a keener insight: What is man? What is the meaning of suffering, evil, death, which has not been eliminated by all this progress? What is the purpose of these achievements, purchased at so high a price?"

In the span of the 15 years since the end of the Second Vatican Council has this picture of tensions and threats that mark our epoch become less disquieting? It seems not. On the contrary, the tensions and threats that in the council document seem only to be outlined and not to manifest in depth all the dangers hidden within them have revealed themselves more clearly in the space of these years; they have in a different way confirmed that danger, and do not permit us to cherish the illusions of the past.

11. Sources of Uneasiness
Thus, in our world the feeling of being under threat is increasing. There is an increase of that existential fear connected especially, as I said in the encyclical *Redemptor Hominis*,

with the prospect of a conflict that in view of today's atomic stockpiles could mean the partial self-destruction of humanity. But the threat does not merely concern what human beings can do to human beings through the means provided by military technology; it also concerns many other dangers produced by a materialistic society which—in spite of "humanistic" declarations—accepts the primacy of things over persons.

Contemporary man, therefore, fears that by the use of the means invented by this type of society, individuals and the environment, communities, societies and nations can fall victim to the abuse of power by other individuals, environments and societies. The history of our century offers many examples of this. In spite of all the declarations on the rights of man in his integral dimension, that is to say in his bodily and spiritual existence, we cannot say that these examples belong only to the past.

Man rightly fears falling victim to an oppression that will deprive him of his interior freedom, of the possibility of expressing the truth of which he is convinced, of the faith that he professes, of the ability to obey the voice of conscience that tells him the right path to follow. The technical means at the disposal of modern society conceal within themselves not only the possibility of a "peaceful" subjugation of individuals, of environments, of entire societies and of nations, that for one reason or another might prove inconvenient for those who possess the necessary means and are ready to use them without scruple. An instance is the continued existence of torture, systematically used by authority as a means of domination and political oppression and practiced by subordinates with impunity.

Together with awareness of the biological threat, therefore, there is a growing awareness of yet another threat, even more destructive of what is essentially human, what is intimately bound up with the dignity of the person and his or her right to truth and freedom.

All this is happening against the background of the gigantic remorse caused by the fact that, side by side with wealthy and surfeited people and societies, living in plenty and ruled by consumerism and pleasure, the same human family contains individuals and groups that are suffering from hunger. There are babies dying of hunger under their mothers' eyes. In various parts of the world, in various socio-economic systems, there exist entire areas of poverty, shortage and underdevelopment. This fact is universally known.

The state of inequality between individuals and between nations not only still exists; it is increasing. It still happens that side by side with those who are wealthy and living in plenty there exist those who are living in want, suffering misery and often actually dying of hunger; and their number reaches tens, even hundreds of millions. This is why moral uneasiness is destined to become even more acute. It is obvious that a fundamental defect, or rather a series of defects, indeed a defective machinery is at the root of contemporary economics and materialistic civilization, which does not allow the human family to break free from such radically unjust situations.

This picture of today's world in which there is so much evil, both physical and moral, so as to make it a world entangled in contradictions and tensions, and at the same time full of threats to human freedom, conscience and religion—this picture explains the uneasiness felt by contemporary man. This uneasiness is experienced not only by those who are disadvantaged or oppressed, but also by those who possess the privileges of wealth, progress and power.

And, although there is no lack of people trying to understand the causes of this uneasiness, or trying to react against it with the temporary means offered by technology, wealth or power, still in the very depth of the human spirit this uneasiness is stronger than all temporary means. This uneasiness concerns—as the analyses of the Second Vatican Council rightly pointed out—the fundamental problems of all human existence. It is linked with the very sense of man's existence in the world, and is an uneasiness for the future of man and all humanity; it demands decisive solutions, which now seem to be forcing themselves upon the human race.

[17] Pope John Paul II, War Is Death, Address at Memorial Park, Hiroshima, Japan, February 25, 1981

War is the work of man. War is destruction of human life. War is death.

Nowhere do these truths impose themselves upon us more forcefully than in this city of Hiroshima, at this peace memorial. Two cities will forever have their names linked together, two Japanese cities, Hiroshima and Nagasaki, as the only cities in the world that have had the ill fortune to be a reminder that man is capable of destruction beyond belief. Their names will forever stand out as the names of the only cities in our time that have been singled out as a warning to future generations that war can destroy human efforts to build a world of peace.

Mr. Mayor, dear friends here present and all of you who are listening to my voice and whom my message will reach.

1. It is with deep emotion that I have come here today as a pilgrim of peace. I wanted to make this visit to the Hiroshima Peace Memorial out of a deep personal conviction that to remember the past is to commit oneself to the future.

Together we recall that it is one of humanity's sad achievements that all across the face of the earth the names of very many—too many—places are remembered mainly because they have witnessed the horror and suffering produced by war: war memorials that with the victory of one side also recall the suffering and death of countless human beings; cemeteries where rest those who sacrificed their very lives in the service of their country or in the service of a noble cause and cemeteries where lie the innocent civilian victims of war's destructive fury; the remains of concentration and extermination camps where contempt for man and for his inviolable rights reached its most base and cruel expression; battlefields where nature has mercifully healed the earth's scars, but without being able to blot out past human history of hate and enmity. Hiroshima and Nagasaki stand out from all those other places and monuments as the first victims of nuclear war.

I bow my head as I recall the memory of thousands of men, women and children who lost their lives in that one terrible moment, or who for long years carried in their bodies and minds those seeds of death which inexorably pursued their process of destruction. The final balance of the human suffering that began here has not been fully drawn up nor has the total human cost been tallied, especially when one sees what nuclear war has done—and could still do—to our ideas, our attitudes and our civilization.

2. To remember the past is to commit oneself to the future. I cannot but honor and applaud the wise decision of the authorities of this city that the memorial recalling the first nuclear bombing should be a monument to peace. By so doing, the city of Hiroshima and the whole people of Japan have forcefully expressed their hope for a peaceful world and their conviction that man who wages war can also successfully make peace. From this city and from the event its name recalls, there has originated a new worldwide consciousness against war and a fresh determination to work for peace.

Some people, even among those who were alive at the time of the events that we commemorate today, might prefer not to think about the horror of nuclear war and its dire consequences. Among those who have never personally experienced the reality of armed conflict between nations, some might wish to abandon the very possibility of nuclear war. Others might wish to regard nuclear capacity as an unavoidable means of maintaining a balance of power through a balance of terror. But there is no justification for not raising the question of the responsibility of each nation and each individual in the face of possible wars and of the nuclear threat.

3. To remember the past is to commit oneself to the future. I evoke before you the memory of Aug. 6, 1945, so that we may better grasp the meaning of the present challenge. Since that fateful day, nuclear stockpiles have grown in quantity and in destructive power. Nuclear weaponry continues to be built, tested and deployed. The total consequences of full-scale nuclear war are impossible to predict, but even if a mere frac-

tion of the available weapons were to be used, one has to ask whether the inevitable escalation can be imagined and whether the very destruction of humanity is not a real possibility. I wish to repeat here what I said to the U.N. General Assembly:

> The continual preparations for war demonstrated by the production of ever more numerous, powerful and sophisticated weapons in various countries show that there is a desire to be ready for war, and being ready means being able to start it. It also means taking the risk that sometime, somewhere, somehow, someone can set in motion the terrible mechanism of general destruction (no. 10).

4. To remember the past is to commit oneself to the future. To remember Hiroshima is to abhor nuclear war. To remember Hiroshima is to commit oneself to peace. To remember what the people of this city suffered is to renew our faith in man, in his capacity to do what is good, in his freedom to choose what is right, in his determination to turn disaster into a new beginning. In the face of the man-made calamity that every war is, one must affirm and reaffirm, again and again, that the waging of war is not inevitable or unchangeable. Humanity is not destined to self-destruction.

Clashes of ideologies, aspirations and needs can and must be settled and resolved by means other than war and violence. Humanity owes it to itself to settle differences and conflicts by peaceful means. The great spectrum of problems facing the many peoples in varying stages of cultural, social, economic and political development gives rise to international tension and conflict. It is vital for humanity that these problems should be solved in accordance with ethical principles of equity and justice enshrined in meaningful agreements and institutions. The international community should thus give itself a system of law that will regulate international relations and maintain peace, just as the rule of law protects national order.

5. Those who cherish life on earth must encourage governments and decision makers in the economic and social fields to

act in harmony with the demands of peace rather than out of narrow self-interest. Peace must always be the aim: peace pursued and protected in all circumstances. Let us not repeat the past, a past of violence and destruction. Let us embark upon the steep and difficult path of peace, the only path that befits human dignity, the only path that leads to the true fulfillment of the human destiny, the only path to a future in which equity, justice and solidarity are realities and not just distant dreams.

6. And so, on this very spot where 35 years ago the life of so many people was snuffed out in one fiery moment, I wish to appeal to the whole world on behalf of life, on behalf of humanity, on behalf of the future.

To the heads of state and of government, to those who hold political and economic power, I say: Let us pledge ourselves to peace through justice; let us take a solemn decision now, that war will never be tolerated or sought as a means of resolving differences; let us promise our fellow human beings that we will work untiringly for disarmament and the banishing of all nuclear weapons; let us replace violence and hate with confidence and caring.

To every man and woman in this land and in the world I say: Let us assume responsibility for each other and for the future without being limited by frontiers and social distinctions; let us educate ourselves and educate others in the ways of peace; let humanity never become the victim of a struggle between competing systems; let there never be another war.

To young people everywhere I say: Let us together create a new future of fraternity and solidarity; let us reach out toward our brothers and sisters in need, feed the hungry, shelter the homeless, free the downtrodden, bring justice where injustice reigns and peace where only weapons speak. Your young hearts have an extraordinary capacity for goodness and love. Put them at the service of your fellow human beings.

To everyone I repeat the words of the prophet: "They shall beat their swords into plowshares and their spears into pruning hooks. Nation shall not lift up sword against nation, neither shall they learn war any more" (Is. 2:4).

To those who believe in God I say: Let us be strong in his strength that infinitely surpasses our own; let us be united in the knowledge that he calls us to unity; let us be aware that love and sharing are not faraway ideals but the road to enduring peace—the peace of God.

7. And to the Creator of nature and man, of truth and beauty I pray:

Hear my voice, for it is the voice of the victims of all wars and violence among individuals and nations.

Hear my voice, for it is the voice of all children who suffer and will suffer when people put their faith in weapons and war.

Hear my voice when I beg you to instill into the hearts of all human beings the wisdom of peace, the strength of justice and the joy of fellowship.

Hear my voice, for I speak for the multitudes in every country and in every period of history who do not want war and are ready to walk the road of peace.

Hear my voice and grant insight and strength so that we may always respond to hatred with love, to injustice with total dedication to justice, to need with the sharing of self, to war with peace.

O God, hear my voice and grant unto the world your everlasting peace.

[18]   Pope John Paul II, Moral Choices for the Future, Address at United Nations University, Hiroshima, Japan, February 25, 1981

1. How can I express my feelings at this unique meeting in Hiroshima with the distinguished representatives of science, culture and higher learning? First of all, I would like to say that I feel very honored to be among a group of such highly qualified men and women who devote their energies to the business of government and to research, intellectual reflection

and teaching. I am very grateful to the city and prefecture of Hiroshima for welcoming me here today. I thank you sincerely for your cordial and benevolent welcome.

I would like to offer a particular greeting to the representatives of the University of the United Nations, represented here by its rector, Mr. Soedjatmoko, the vice-rectors, members of the council, and the principal collaborators of the university. Your institution, which by its statutes is linked to the United Nations and to UNESCO, is a completely original creation, founded to promote the lofty aims of the United Nations at the levels of research, advanced training and the dissemination of knowledge; it was deliberately established as a global and worldwide institution. My predecessor Paul VI and I have on more than one occasion expressed our esteem for this noble enterprise and our hopes for its future. It seeks to place science and research at the service of the great humanitarian ideals of peace, development, the improvement of natural resources and cooperation between the nations.

2. Ladies and gentlemen, we have gathered here today at Hiroshima: and I would like you to know that I am deeply convinced that we have been given a historic occasion for reflecting together on the responsibility of science and technology at this period, marked as it is by so much hope and so many anxieties. At Hiroshima, the facts speak for themselves in a way that is dramatic, unforgettable and unique. In the face of an unforgettable tragedy, which touches us all as human beings, how can we fail to express our brotherhood and our deep sympathy at the frightful wound inflicted on the cities of Japan that bear the names of Hiroshima and Nagasaki?

That wound affected the whole of the human family. Hiroshima and Nagaski: Few events in history have had such an effect on man's conscience. The representatives of the world of science were not the ones least affected by the moral crisis caused throughout the world by the explosion of the first atomic bomb. The human mind had in fact made a terrible discovery. We realized with horror that nuclear energy would henceforth be available as a weapon of devastation; then we learned that this terrible weapon had in fact been used, for the first time, for military purposes. And then there arose the question that will never leave us again: Will this weapon, perfected and multiplied beyond measure, be used tomorrow? If so, would it not probably destroy the human family, its members and all the achievements of civilization?

3. Ladies and gentlemen, you who devote your lives to the modern sciences, you are the first to be able to evaluate the disaster that a nuclear war would inflict on the human family. And I know that ever since the explosion of the first atomic bomb many of you have been anxiously wondering about the responsibility of modern science and of the technology that is the fruit of that science. In a number of countries, associations of scholars and research workers express the anxiety of the scientific world in the face of an irresponsible use of science, which too often does grievous damage to the balance of nature or brings with it the ruin and oppression of man by man. One thinks in the first place of physics, chemistry, biology and the genetical sciences, of which you rightly condemn those applications or experimentations which are detrimental to humanity.

But one also has in mind the social sciences and the human behavioral sciences when they are utilized to manipulate people, to crush their minds, souls, dignity and freedom. Criticism of science and technology is sometimes so severe that it comes close to condemning science itself. On the contrary, science and technology are a wonderful product of a God-given human creativity, since they have provided us with wonderful possibilities and we all gratefully benefit from them. But we know that this potential is not a neutral one: It can be used either for man's progress or for his degradation. Like you, I have lived through this period, which I would call the "post-Hiroshima period," and I share your anxieties. And today I feel inspired to say this to you: Surely the time has come for our society and especially for the world of science to realize that the future of humanity depends as never before on our collective moral choices.

4. In the past, it was possible to destroy a village, a town, a region, even a country. Now it is the whole planet that has

come under threat. This fact should finally compel everyone to face a basic moral consideration: From now on, it is only through a conscious choice and through a deliberate policy that humanity can survive. The moral and political choice that faces us is that of putting all the resources of mind, science and culture at the service of peace and of the building up of a new society, a society that will succeed in eliminating the causes of fratricidal wars by generously pursuing the total progress of each individual and of all humanity.

Of course, individuals and societies are always exposed to the passions of greed and hate; but, as far as within us lies, let us try effectively to correct the social situations and structures that cause injustice and conflict. We shall build peace by building a more humane world. In the light of this hope, the scientific, cultural and university world has an eminent part to play. Peace is one of the loftiest achievements of culture and for this reason it deserves all our intellectual and spiritual energy.

5. As scholars and researchers you represent an international community with a task that can be decisive for the future of humanity. But on one condition: that you succeed in defending and serving man's true culture as a precious possession. Your role is a noble one when you work toward man's growth in his being and not just in his possessions or his knowledge or his power. It is in the depths of his being that man's true culture lies.

I tried to express this fundamental aspect of our civilization in an address that I gave to UNESCO June 2, 1980:

> Culture is a specific way of man's 'existing' and 'being' ... Culture is that through which man, as man, becomes more man, 'is' more, has more access to 'being.' The fundamental distinction between what man is and what he has, between being and having, has its foundation there too ... All man's 'having' is important for culture, is a factor creative of culture, only to the extent to which man, through his 'having,'

can at the same time 'be' more fully as a man, become more fully a man in all the dimensions of his existence, in everything that characterizes his humanity.

This concept of culture is based upon a total view of man, body and spirit, person and community, a rational being and one ennobled by love: "Yes! The future of man depends on the primacy of spirit! Yes! The peaceful future of mankind depends on love!" (*Ibid.*). In truth, our future, our very survival are linked to the image that we will make of man.

6. Our future on this planet, exposed as it is to nuclear annihilation, depends upon one single factor: Humanity must make a moral about-face. At the present moment of history there must be a general mobilization of all men and women of good will. Humanity is being called upon to take a major step forward in civilization and wisdom. A lack of civilization, an ignorance of man's true values, brings the risk that humanity will be destroyed. We must become wiser. Pope Paul VI, in his encyclical titled "The Development of Peoples" (March 26, 1967, 20), several times stressed the urgent need to have recourse to the wise in order to guide the new society in its development. In particular, he said that "if further development calls for the work of more and more technicians, even more necessary is the deep thought and reflection of wise men in search of a new humanism which will enable modern man to find himself anew by embracing the higher values of love and friendship, of prayer and contemplation."

Above all in this country of Japan, renowned for its creativity, both cultural and technological, a country with so many scientists, scholars, writers and religious thinkers, I take the liberty of making a very special appeal. I wish to address myself to the wise men and women of Japan, and through them to the wise men and women of the whole world, in order to encourage them to pursue ever more effectively the task of social and moral reconstruction which our world so ardently awaits. Work together to defend and promote among all the people of your nation and of the world the idea of a just world, a world made to man's scale, a world that enables human beings to fulfill their capacities, a world that sustains them in their material, moral and spiritual needs.

7. Men and women dedicated to research and culture: Your work has taken on a completely new importance in this age marked by the rise of science and technology. What an achievement for our time, what intellectual and moral power, what a responsibility toward society and humanity! Shall we be able to join in placing this scientific and cultural heritage at the service of the true progress of humanity, for the building of a world of justice and dignity for all? The task is enormous; some will call it a utopian one. But how can we fail to sustain the trust of modern man against all the temptations to fatalism, to paralyzing passivity and to moral dejection? We must say to the people of today: Do not doubt, your future is in your own hands. The building of a more just humanity or a more united international community is not just a dream or a vain ideal. It is a moral imperative, a sacred duty, one that the intellectual and spiritual genius of man can face, through a fresh mobilization of everybody's talents and energies, through putting to work all the technical and cultural resources of man.

8. The people of our time possess, in the first place, tremendous scientific and technological resources. And we are convinced that these resources could be far more effectively used for the development and growth of peoples; let us envisage the progress made in agriculture, biology, medicine, the social communications media applied to education; then there are the social and economic sciences, and the science of planning, all of which could combine to direct in a more humane and effective way the process of industrialization and urbanization and promote the new models of international cooperation.

If all the rich nations of the world wanted to, they could call in an impressive number of specialists for the tasks of development. All of this obviously presupposes political choices and, more fundamentally, moral options. The moment is approaching when priorities will have to be redefined. For example, it has been estimated that about half of the world's research workers are at present employed for military purposes. Can the human family morally go on much longer in this direction?

There is also the question of the economic resources needed for giving a decisive impulse to the integral advancement of the human family. Here too we are faced with choices. Can we remain passive when we are told that humanity spends immensely more money on arms than on development and when we learn that one soldier's equipment costs many times more than a child's education?

9. Science and technology have always formed part of man's culture, but today we are witnessing the speedily increasing growth of a technology which seems to have destroyed its equilibrium with the dimensions of culture by acting as an element of division. Such is the great problem facing modern society. Science and technology are the most dynamic factors of the development of society today, but their intrinsic limitations do not make them capable, by themselves, of providing a power that will bind culture together. How then can a culture absorb science and technology, with their dynamism, without losing its own identity?

There are three temptations to be avoided in this regard. The first is the temptation to pursue technological development for its own sake, the sort of development that has for its only norm that of its own growth and affirmation, as if it were a matter of an independent reality in between nature and a reality that is properly human, imposing on man the inevitable realization of his ever new possibilities, as if one should always do what is technically possible. The second temptation is that of subjecting technological development to economic usefulness in accordance with the logic of profit or non-stop economic expansion, thus creating advantages for some while leaving others in poverty, with no care for the true common good of humanity, making technology into an instrument at the service of the ideology of "having." Third, there is also the temptation to subject technological development to the pursuit or maintenance of power, as happens when it is used for military purposes and whenever people are manipulated in order that they may be dominated.

10. As men and women dedicated to culture, you enjoy immense moral credibility for acting upon all the centers of decision making, whether private or public, that are capable of influencing the politics of tomorrow. Using all honest and effective means, make sure that a total vision of man and a generous idea of culture prevail. Work out persuasive arguments so that everyone will be brought to understand that peace or the survival of the human race is henceforth linked indissolubly with progress, development and dignity for all people.

You will succeed in your task if you restate with conviction that "science and technology find their justification in the service that they render to man and to humanity"; and that rational science must be linked with a series of spheres of knowledge open wide to spiritual values. I urge all scientists, centers of research and universities to study more deeply the ethical problems of the technological society, a subject which is already engaging the attention of a number of modern thinkers. It is a question that is closely connected with the problems of the just sharing of resources, the use of techniques for peaceful purposes, the development of nations.

11. The construction of a new social order presupposes, over and above the essential technological skills, a lofty inspiration, a courageous motivation, belief in man's future, in his dignity, in his destiny. It is man's heart and spirit that must be reached, beyond the divisions spawned by individual interests, selfishness and ideologies. In a word, man must be loved for his own sake. This is the supreme value that all sincere humanists, generous thinkers and all the great religions want to promote. Love for man as such is at the center of the message of Christ and his church: This relationship is indissoluble. In my speech to UNESCO, I stressed the fundamental link between the Gospel and man in his very humanity:

> This link is in fact a creator of culture in its very
> foundation. . . . Man must be affirmed for himself . . .
> What is more, man must be loved because he is man;

love must be claimed for man by reason of the particular dignity he possesses. The whole of the affirmations concerning man belongs to the very substance of Christ's message and of the mission of the church (10).

All those who desire the defense and progress of man must therefore love man for his own sake; and for this it is essential to count upon the values of the spirit, which are alone capable of transforming hearts and deeply rooted attitudes. All of us who bear in our hearts the treasure of a religious faith must share in the common work of man's development and we must do it with clear-sightedness and courage. All Christians, all those who call upon God, all spiritual families should be invited to join in a common effort to sustain, spiritually and culturally, all those men and women who devote themselves to the total growth of man.

12. In this country, one could not fail to evoke the great spiritual and religious traditions of Asia, traditions that have so enriched the worldwide heritage of man. Nor could one fail to wish for closer dialogue and effective collaboration between all those who believe in man's spiritual calling, his search for the absolute, for justice, for fraternity and, as we express it in our own faith, his thirst for redemption and immortality.

Rational science and man's religious knowledge need to be linked together. You who devote yourselves to the sciences, are you not invited to study the link which must be established between scientific and technological knowledge and man's moral knowledge? Knowledge and virtue were cultivated together by the ancients, in the East as well as in the West. Even today, I know well, many scholars, even though they do not all profess one particular religion, are searching for an integration between their science and their desire to serve the whole man. Through their intellectual honesty, their quest for what is true, their self-discipline as scholars, and through their objectivity and respect before the mysteries of the universe, these people make up a great spiritual family. All those who generously dedicate their knowledge to the progress of the people and all those who have faith in man's spiritual calling are invited to a common task: to constitute a real science of the total advancement of man.

13. In a word, I believe that our generation is faced by a great moral challenge, one which consists in harmonizing the values of science with the values of conscience. Speaking to UNESCO June 2, 1980, I made an appeal that I put before you again today:

> A conviction, which is at the same time a moral imperative, forces itself upon anyone who has become aware of the situation ... Consciences must be mobilized! The efforts of human consciences must be increased in proportion to the tension between good and evil to which people at the end of the 20th century are subjected. We must convince ourselves of the priority of ethics over technology, of the primacy of the person over things. Of the superiority of the spirit over matter (cf. *Redemptor Hominis,* 16). The cause of man will be served if science forms an alliance with conscience. The man of science will really help humanity if he keeps 'the sense of man's transcendence over the world and of God's transcendence over man' (Speech to the Pontifical Academy of Sciences, Nov. 10, 1979, 4).

Ladies and gentlemen, it is for you to take up this noble challenge.

[19] Pope John Paul II, World Day of Peace Message, January 1, 1982

To the young who in the world of tomorrow will make the great decisions,

To the men and women who today bear responsibility for life in society,

To families and teachers,

To individuals and communities,
To heads of state and government leaders:

It is to all of you that I address this message at the dawn of the year 1982. I invite you to reflect with me on the theme of the new world day: Peace is a gift of God entrusted to us.

1. This truth faces us when we come to decide our commitments and make our choices. It challenges the whole of humanity, all men and women who know that they are individually responsible for one another, and together responsible for the world.

At the end of the First World War my predecessor Pope Benedict XV devoted an encyclical to this theme. Rejoicing at the cessation of hostilities and insisting on the need to remove hatred and enmity through reconciliation inspired by mutual charity, he began his encyclical with a reference to "Peace, that magnificent gift from God: As Augustine says, 'even understood as one of the fleeting things of earth, no sweeter word is heard, no more desirable wish is longed for, and no better discovery can be made than this gift' (*De Civitate Dei*, Lib. XIX, c. XI)" (*Pacem Dei Munus: AAS* 12 [1920], p. 209).

Efforts for Peace in a Divided World

2. Since then my predecessors have often had to recall this truth in their constant endeavors to educate for peace and to encourage work for a lasting peace. Today peace has become, throughout the world, a major preoccupation not only for those responsible for the destiny of nations but even more so for broad sections of the population and innumerable individuals who generously and tenaciously dedicate themselves to creating an outlook of peace and to establishing genuine peace between peoples and nations.

This is comforting. But there is no hiding the fact that, in spite of the efforts of all men and women of good will, there are still serious threats to peace in the world. Some of these threats take the form of divisions within various nations; others stem from deep-rooted and acute tensions between opposing nations and blocs within the world community.

In reality, the confrontations that we witness today are distinguished from those of past history by certain new characteristics. In the first place they are worldwide: Even a local conflict is often an expression of tensions originating elsewhere in the world. In the same way, it often happens that a conflict has profound effects far from where it broke out.

Another characteristic is totality: Present-day tensions mobilize all the forces of the nations involved; moreover, selfish monopolization and even hostility are to be found today as much in the way economic life is run and in the technological application of science as in the way that the mass media or military resources are utilized.

Third, we must stress the radical character of modern conflicts: It is the survival of the whole human race that is at stake in them, given the destructive capacity of present-day military stockpiles.

In short, while many factors could contribute to uniting it, human society appears as a divided world: the forces for unity give way before the divisions between East and West, North and South, friend and enemy.

An Essential Problem

3. The causes of this situation are of course complex and of various orders. Political reasons are naturally the easiest to distinguish. Particular groups abuse their power in order to impose their yoke on whole societies. An excessive desire for expansion impels some nations to build their prosperity with a disregard for—indeed at the expense of—others' happiness.

Unbridled nationalism thus fosters plans for domination, which leave other nations with the pitiless dilemma of having to make the choice: either accepting satellite status and dependence or adopting an attitude of competition and hostility. Deeper analysis shows that the cause of this situation is the application of certain concepts and ideologies that claim to offer the only foundation of the truth about man, society and history.

When we come up against the choice between peace and war, we find ourselves face to face with ourselves, with our nature, with our plans for our personal and community lives, with the use we are to make of our freedom. Are relationships between people to continue inexorably along lines of incomprehension and merciless confrontation, because of a relentless law of human life? Or are human beings—by comparison with the animal species which fight one another according to the "law" of the jungle—specifically called upon and given the fundamental capability to live in peace with their fellows and to share with them in the creation of culture, society and history?

In the final analysis, when we consider the question of peace, we are led to consider the meaning and conditions of our own personal and community lives.

Peace, A Gift of God

4. Peace is not so much a superficial balance between diverging material interests—a balance pertaining to the order of quantity, of things. Rather it is, in its inmost reality, something that belongs to the essentially human order, the order of human subjects; it is thus of a rational and moral nature, the fruit of truth and virtue. It springs from the dynamism of free wills guided by reason toward the common good that is to be attained in truth, justice and love.

This rational and moral order is based on a decision by the consciences of human beings seeking harmony in their mutual relationships, with respect for justice for everybody, and therefore with respect for the fundamental human rights inherent in every person. One cannot see how this moral order could ignore God, the first source of being, the essential truth and the supreme good.

In this very sense peace comes from God as its foundation: It is a gift of God. When claiming the wealth and resources of the universe worked on by the human mind—and it is often on their account that conflicts and wars have sprung up—"man comes up against the leading role of the gift made by 'nature,' that is to say, in the final analysis, by the creator" (*Laborem Exercens*, 12). And God does more than give creation to humanity to administer and develop jointly at the service of all human beings without any discrimination: He also inscribes in the human conscience the laws obliging us to respect in numerous ways the life and the whole person of our fellow human beings, created like us in the image and after the likeness of God.

God is thus the guarantor of all these fundamental human rights. Yes, indeed, God is the source of peace; He calls to peace, he safeguards it and he grants it as the fruit of justice.

Moreover, God helps us interiorly to achieve peace or to recover it. In our limited life, which is subject to error and evil, we human beings go gropingly in search of peace amid many difficulties. Our faculties are darkened by mere appearances of truth, attracted by false gods and led astray by irrational and selfish instincts. Hence we need to open ourselves to the transcendent light of God that illuminates our lives, purifies them from error and frees them from aggressive passion.

God is not far from the heart of those who pray to him and try to fulfill his justice: When they are in continual dialogue with him, in freedom, God offers them peace as the fullness of the communion of life with God and with their brothers and sisters. In the Bible the word "peace" recurs again and again in association with the idea of happiness, harmony, well-being, security, concord, salvation and justice, as the outstanding blessing that God, "the Lord of peace" (2 Thess. 3:16), already gives and promises in abundance: "Now toward her I send flowing peace, like a river" (Is. 66:12).

A Gift of God Entrusted to Us

5. While peace is a gift, man is never dispensed from responsibility for seeking it and endeavoring to establish it by individual and community effort throughout history. God's gift of peace is therefore also at all times a human conquest and achievement since it is offered to us in order that we may accept it freely and put it progressively into operation by our creative will.

Furthermore, in his love for man, God never abandons us but even in the darkest moments of history drives us forward or leads us back mysteriously along the path of peace. Even the difficulties, failures and tragedies of the past and the present must be studied as providential lessons from which we may draw the wisdom we need in order to find new ways, more rational and courageous ways, for building peace.

It is by drawing inspiration from the truth of God that we are given the ideal and the energy we require in order to overcome situations of injustice, to free ourselves from ideologies of power and domination, and to make our way toward true universal fraternity.

Christians, faithful to Christ who proclaimed "the good news of peace" and established peace within hearts by reconciling them with God, have still more decisive reasons—as I shall stress at the end of this message—for looking on peace as a gift of God, and for courageously helping to establish it in this world, in accordance with this longing for its complete fulfillment in the kingdom of God. They also know that they are called upon to join their efforts with those of believers in other religions who tirelessly condemn hatred and war and who devote themselves, using different approaches, to the advancement of justice and peace.

We should first consider in its natural basis this deeply hopeful view of humanity as directed toward peace, and stress moral responsibility in response to God's gift. This illuminates and stimulates man's activity on the level of information, study and commitment for peace, three sectors that I would now like to illustrate with some examples.

Information

6. At a certain level, world peace depends on better self-knowledge on the part of both individuals and societies. This self-knowledge is naturally conditioned by information and by the quality of the information. Those who seek and proclaim the truth with respect for others and with charity are working for peace. Those who devote themselves to pointing out the values in the various cultures, the individuality of each society and the human riches of individual peoples, are working for peace. Those who by providing information remove the barrier of distance so that we feel truly concerned at the fate of far-

away men and women who are victims of war or injustice are working for peace.

Admittedly, the accumulation of such information, especially if it concerns catastrophes over which we have no control, can in the end produce indifference and surfeit in those who remain mere receivers of the information without ever doing whatever is within their power. But in itself, the role of the mass media continues to be a positive one: Each one of us is now called upon to be the neighbor of all his or her brothers and sisters of the human race (cf. Lk. 10:29-37).

High-quality information even has a direct influence upon education and political decisions. If the young are to be made aware of the problems of peace and if they are to prepare to become workers for peace, educational programs must necessarily give a special place to information about actual situations in which peace is under threat, and about the conditions needed for its advancement.

Peace cannot be built by the power of rulers alone. Peace can be firmly constructed only if it corresponds to the resolute determination of all people of good will. Rulers must be supported and enlightened by a public opinion that encourages them or, where necessary, expresses disapproval. Consequently it is also right that rulers should explain to the public those matters that concern the problems of peace.

Studies That Help to Build Peace

7. Building peace also depends upon the progress of research about it. Scientific studies on war, its nature, causes, means, objectives and risks, have much to teach us on the conditions for peace. Since they throw light on the relationships between war and politics, such studies show that there is a greater future in negotiation than in arms for settling conflicts.

It follows that the role of law in preserving peace is called upon to expand. It is well known that within individual states the work of jurists contributes greatly to the advancement of justice and respect for human rights. But their role is just as great for the pursuit of the same objectives on the international level and for refining the juridical instruments for building and preserving peace.

However, since concern for peace is inscribed in the inmost depths of our being, progress along the path of peace also benefits from the research of psychologists and philosophers. Admittedly, the science of war has already been enriched by studies on human aggressiveness, death-impulses and the herd instinct that can suddenly take possession of whole societies.

But much remains to be said about the fear we human beings have of taking possession of our freedom, and about our insecurity before ourselves and others. Better knowledge of life-impulses, of instinctive sympathy with other people, of readiness to love and share undoubtedly helps us to grasp better the psychological mechanisms that favor peace.

By this research psychology is thus called upon to throw light on and to complement the studies of the philosophers. Philosophers have always pondered the questions of war and peace. They have never been without responsibility in this matter. The memory is all too much alive of those famous philosophers who saw man as "a wolf for his fellow man" and war a historical necessity. However, it is also true that many of them wished to lay the foundation for a lasting or even everlasting peace by, for instance, setting forth a solid theoretical basis for international law.

All these efforts deserve to be resumed and intensified. The thinkers who devote themselves to such endeavors can benefit from the copious contribution of a present-day philosophical current that gives unique prominence to the theme of the person and devotes itself in a singular manner to an examination of the themes of freedom and responsibility. This can provide light for reflection on human rights, justice and peace.

Indirect Action

8. While the advancement of peace in a sense depends on information and research, it rests above all on the action that people take in its favor. Some forms of action envisaged here

have only an indirect relationship with peace. However, it would be wrong to think of them as unimportant: As we shall briefly indicate through some examples, almost every section of human activity offers unexpected occasions for advancing peace.

Such is the case of cultural exchanges in the broadest sense. Anything that enables people to get to know each other better through artistic activity breaks down barriers. Where speech is unavailing and diplomacy is an uncertain aid, music, painting, drama and sport can bring people closer together. The same holds for scientific research: Science, like art, creates and brings together a universal society which gathers all who love truth and beauty, without division. Thus science and art are, each at its own level, an anticipation of the emergence of a universal peaceful society.

Even economic life should bring people closer together, by making them aware of the extent to which they are interdependent and complementary. Undoubtedly, economic relationships often create a field of pitiless confrontation, merciless competition and even sometimes shameless exploitation. But could not these relationships become instead relationships of service and solidarity, and thereby defuse one of the most frequent causes of discord?

Justice and Peace Within Nations

9. While peace should be everyone's concern, the building of peace is a task that falls directly and principally to political leaders. From this point of view the chief setting for the building up of peace is always the nation as a politically organized society. Since the purpose for which a political society is formed is the establishment of justice, the advancement of the common good and participation by all, that society will enjoy peace only to the extent that these three demands are respected. Peace can develop only where the elementary requirements of justice are safeguarded.

Unconditional and effective respect for each one's imprescriptible and inalienable rights is the necessary condition in order that peace may reign in a society. Vis-à-vis these basic rights all others are in a way derivative and secondary. In a society in which these rights are not protected, the very idea of universality is dead, as soon as a small group of individuals set up for their own exclusive advantage a principle of discrimination whereby the rights and even the lives of others are made dependent on the whim of the stronger. Such a society cannot be at peace with itself: It has within it a principle leading to division.

For the same reason, a political society can really collaborate in building international peace only if it is itself peaceful, that is to say if it takes seriously the advancement of human rights at home. To the extent that the rulers of a particular country apply themselves to building a fully just society, they are already contributing decisively to building an authentic, firmly based and lasting peace (cf. *Pacem in Terris*, 11).

Justice and Peace Between Nations

10. While peace within individual nations is a necessary condition for the development of true peace, it is not enough in itself. The building of peace on a world scale cannot be the result of the separate desires of nations, for they are often ambiguous and sometimes contradictory. It was to make up for this lack that states provided themselves with appropriate international organizations, one of the chief aims of which is to harmonize the desires of different nations and cause them to converge for the safeguarding of peace and for an increase of justice between nations.

By the authority that they have gained and by their achievements, the great international organizations have done remarkable work for peace. They have of course had failures; they have not been able to prevent all conflicts or put a speedy end to them. But they have helped to show the world that war, bloodshed and tears are not the way to end tensions. They have provided, so to speak, experimental proof that even on the world level people are able to combine their efforts and seek peace together.

The Peace Dynamism of Christianity

11. At this point in my message I wish to address more especially my brothers and sisters in the church. The church supports and encourages all serious efforts for peace. She unhesitatingly proclaims that the activity of all those who devote the best of their energies to peace forms part of God's plan of salvation in Jesus Christ. But she reminds Christians that they have still greater reasons for being active witnesses of God's gift of peace.

In the first place, Christ's word and example have given rise to new attitudes in favor of peace. Christ has taken the ethics of peace far beyond the ordinary attitudes of justice and understanding. At the beginning of his ministry he proclaimed: "Blessed are the peacemakers, for they shall be called children of God" (Mt. 5:9).

He sent his disciples to bring peace from house to house, from town to town (Mt. 10:11-13). He exhorted them to prefer peace to vengeance of any kind and even to certain legitimate claims on others—so great was his desire to tear from the human heart the roots of aggressiveness (Mt. 5:38-42). He asked them to love those whom barriers of any sort have turned into enemies (Mt. 5:43-48). He set up as examples people who were habitually despised (Lk. 10:33, 17:16). He exhorted people to be always humble and to forgive without any limit (cf. Mt. 18:21-22). The atittude of sharing with those in utter want—on which he made the last judgment hinge (cf. Mt. 25:31-46)—was to make a radical contribution to the establishment of relations of fraternity.

These appeals of Jesus and his example have had a widespread influence on the attitude of his disciples, as two millennia of history testify. But Christ's work belongs to a very deep level, of the order of a mysterious transformation of hearts. He really brought "peace among men with whom God is pleased" in the words of the proclamation made at his birth (cf. Lk. 2:14), and this not only by revealing to them the Father's love but above all by reconciling them with God through his sacrifice. For it was sin and hatred that were an obstacle to peace with God and with others: He destroyed them by the offering of his life on the cross; he reconciled in one body those who were hostile (cf. Eph. 2:16, Rom. 12:5). His first words to his apostles after he rose were: "Peace be with you" (Jn. 20:19).

Those who accept the faith form in the church a prophetic community: With the Holy Spirit communicated by Christ, after the baptism that makes them part of the body of Christ, they experience the peace given by God in the sacrament of reconciliation and in eucharistic communion; they proclaim "the Gospel of peace" (Eph. 6:15); they try to live it from day to day, in actual practice; and they long for the time of reconciliation when, by a new intervention of the living God who raises the dead, we shall be wholly open to God and our brothers and sisters. Such is the vision of faith which supports the activity of Christians on behalf of peace.

Thus, by her very existence the church exists within the world as a society of people who are reconciled and at peace through the grace of Christ, in a communion of love and life with God and with all their brothers and sisters, beyond human barriers of every sort; in herself she is already, and she seeks to become ever more so in practice, a gift and leaven of peace offered by God to the whole human race. Certainly, the members of the church are well aware that they are often still sinners in this sphere too; at least they feel the grave responsibility of putting into practice this gift of peace. For this they must first overcome their own divisions, in order to set out without delay toward the fullness of unity in Christ; thus they collaborate with God in order to offer his peace to the world. They must also of course combine their efforts with the efforts of all men and women of good will working for peace in the different spheres of society and international life.

The church wishes her children to join, through their witness and their initiatives, the first rank of those preparing peace and causing it to reign. At the same time, she is very aware that, on the spot, it is a difficult task, one that calls for much generosity, discernment and hope, as a real challenge.

Peace as a Constant Challenge to Christians

12. Christian optimism based on the glorious cross of Christ and the outpouring of the Holy Spirit is no excuse for self-deception. For Christians, peace on earth is always a challenge because of the presence of sin in man's heart.

Motivated by their faith and hope, Christians therefore apply themselves to promoting a more just society; they fight hunger, deprivation and disease; they are concerned about what happens to migrants, prisoners and outcasts (cf. Mt. 25:35-36). But they know that while all these undertakings express something of the mercy and perfection of God (cf. Lk. 6:36, Mt. 4:48), they are always limited in their range, precarious in their results and ambiguous in their inspiration. Only God the giver of life, when he unites all things in Christ (cf. Eph. 1:10), will fulfill our ardent hope by himself bringing to accomplishment everything that he has undertaken in history according to his Spirit in the matter of justice and peace.

Although Christians put all their best energies into preventing war or stopping it, they do not deceive themselves about their ability to cause peace to triumph, nor about the effect of their efforts to this end. They therefore concern themselves with all human initiatives in favor of peace and very often take part in them. But they regard them with realism and humility. One could almost say that they relativize them in two senses: They relate them both to the self-deception of humanity and to God's saving plan.

In the first place, Christians are aware that plans based on aggression, domination and the manipulation of others lurk in human hearts, and sometimes even secretly nourish human intentions in spite of certain declarations or manifestations of a pacifist nature. For Christians know that in this world a totally and permanently peaceful human society is unfortunately a utopia, and that ideologies that hold up that prospect as easily attainable are based on hopes that cannot be realized, whatever the reason behind them.

It is a question of a mistaken view of the human condition, a lack of application in considering the question as a whole; or it may be a case of evasion in order to calm fear, or in still other cases a matter of calculated self-interest. Christians are convinced, if only because they have learned from personal experience, that these deceptive hopes lead straight to the false peace of totalitarian regimes. But this realistic view in no way prevents Christians from working for peace; instead, it stirs up their ardor, for they also know that Christ's victory over deception, hate and death gives those in love with peace a more decisive motive for action than what the most generous theories about man have to offer; Christ's victory likewise gives a hope more surely based than any hope held out by the most audacious dreams.

This is why Christians, even as they strive to resist and prevent every form of warfare, have no hesitation in recalling that, in the name of an elementary requirement of justice, peoples have a right and even a duty to protect their existence and freedom by proportionate means against an unjust aggressor (cf. *Gaudium et Spes,* 79). However, in view of the difference between classical warfare and nuclear or bacteriological war—a difference so to speak of nature—and in view of the scandal of the arms race seen against the background of the needs of the Third World, this right, which is very real in principle, only underlines the urgency for world society to equip itself with effective means of negotiation.

In this way the nuclear terror that haunts our time can encourage us to enrich our common heritage with a very simple discovery that is within our reach, namely that war is the most barbarous and least effective way of resolving conflicts. More than ever before, human society is forced to provide itself with the means of consultation and dialogue which it needs in order to survive, and therefore with the institutions necessary for building up justice and peace.

May it also realize that this work is something beyond human powers!

Prayer for Peace

13. Throughout this message, I have appealed to the responsibility of people of good will, especially Christians, because God has indeed entrusted peace to men and women.

With the realism and hope that faith makes possible, I have tried to draw the attention of citizens and leaders to a certain number of achievements or attitudes that are already feasible and capable of giving a solid foundation to peace. But, over and above or even in the midst of this necessary activity, which might seem to depend primarily on people, peace is above all a gift of God—something that must never be forgotten—and must always be implored from his mercy.

This conviction is certainly seen to have animated people of all civilizations who have given peace the first place in their prayers. Its expression is found in all religions. How many men, having experienced murderous conflicts and concentration camps, how many women and children, distressed by wars, have in times past turned to the God of peace!

Today, when the perils have taken on a seriousness all their own by reason of their extent and radical nature, and when the difficulties of building peace have taken on a new nature and seem often insoluble, many individuals may spontaneously find themselves resorting to prayer, even though prayer may be something unfamiliar.

Yes, our future is in the hands of God, who alone gives true peace, And when human hearts sincerely think of work for peace it is still God's grace that inspires and strengthens those thoughts. All people are in this sense invited to echo the sentiments of St. Francis of Assisi, the eighth centenary of whose birth we are celebrating: Lord, make us instruments of your peace: where there is hatred, let us sow love; where there is injury, pardon; when discord rages, let us build peace.

Christians love to pray for peace, as they make their own the prayer of so many psalms punctuated by supplications for peace and repeated with the universal love of Jesus. We have here a shared and very profound element for all ecumenical activities. Other believers all over the world are also awaiting from almighty God the gift of peace, and, more or less consciously, many other people of good will are ready to make the same prayer in the secret of their hearts.

May fervent supplications thus raise to God from the four corners of the earth! This will already create a fine unanimity on the road to peace. And who could doubt that God will hear and grant this cry of his children: Lord, grant us peace! Grant us your peace!

[20]   Pope John Paul II, Impact of a Nuclear War. Teams of scientists associated with the Pontifical Academy of Sciences were sent by Pope John Paul II to meet with world leaders in the United States, the Soviet Union, Great Britain, France and the United Nations. The text of their message follows. January, 1982.

Oct. 7-8, 1981, under the chairmanship of Professor Carlos Chagas, president of the Pontifical Academy of Sciences, at the headquarters of the academy (Casina Pius IV, Vatican City), a group of 14 specialized scientists from various parts of the world assembled to examine the problem of the consequences of the use of nuclear weapons on the survival and health of humanity.

Although most of these consequences would appear obvious, it seems that they are not adequately appreciated. The conditions of life following a nuclear attack would be so severe that the only hope for humanity is prevention of any form of nuclear war. Universal dissemination and acceptance of this knowledge would make it apparent that nuclear weapons must not be used at all in warfare and that their number should be progressively reduced in a balanced way.

The above-mentioned group discussed and unanimously approved a number of fundamental points which have been further developed in the following statement.

Recent talk about winning or even surviving a nuclear war must reflect a failure to appreciate a medical reality: Any nuclear war would inevitably cause death, disease and suffering of pandemonic proportions and without the possibility of effective medical intervention. That reality leads to the same conclusion physicians have reached for life-threatening epidemics throughout history: Prevention is essential for control.

In contrast to widespread belief, much is known about the catastrophe that would follow the use of nuclear weapons. Much is known too about the limitations of medical assistance. If this knowledge is presented to people and their leaders everywhere, it might help interrupt the nuclear arms race. This in turn would help prevent what could be the last epidemic our civilization will know.

The devastation wrought by an atomic weapon on Hiroshima and Nagasaki provides direct evidence of the consequences of nuclear warfare, but there are many theoretical appraisals on which we may also draw. Two years ago, an assessment undertaken by a responsible official agency described the effect of nuclear attacks on cities of about 2 million inhabitants. If a 1-million ton nuclear weapon (the Hiroshima bomb approximated 15,000 tons of explosive power) exploded in the central area of such cities, it would result, as calculated, in 180 square kilometers of property destruction, 250,000 fatalities and 500,000 severely injured. These would include blast injuries such as fractures and severe lacerations of soft tissues, thermal injuries such as surface burns, retinal burns and respiratory tract damage and radiation injuries, both acute radiation syndrome and delayed effects.

Even under optimal conditions, care of such casualties would present a medical task of unimaginable magnitude. The study projected that if 18,000 hospital beds were available in and around one of these cities, no more than 5,000 would remain relatively undamaged. These would accommodate only 1 percent of the human beings injured, but it must be stressed that in any case no one could deliver the medical service required by even a few of the severely burned, the crushed and the radiated victims.

The hopelessness of the medical task is readily apparent if we consider what is required for the care of the severely injured patients. We shall cite one case history, that of a severely burned 20-year-old man who was taken to the burn unit of a Boston hospital after an automobile accident in which the gasoline tank had exploded.

During his hospitalization he received 140 liters of fresh-frozen plasma, 147 liters of fresh-frozen red blood cells, 180 milliliters of platelets and 180 milliliters of albumin. He underwent six operative procedures during which wounds involving 85 percent of his body surface were closed, including artificial skin. Throughout his hospitalization, he required mechanical ventilation. Despite these and many other heroic measures which stretched the resources of one of the world's most comprehensive institutions, he died on his 33rd hospital day.

His injuries were likened by the doctor who supervised his care to those described for many of the victims of Hiroshima. Had 20 score of such patients been presented at the same time to all of Boston's hospitals the medical capabilities of the city would have been overwhelmed. Now, consider the situation if, along with the injuries to many thousands of people, most of the medical emergency facilities had been destroyed.

A Japanese physician, Professor M. Ichimaru, published an eyewitness account of the effects of the Nagasaki bomb. He reported:

> I tried to go to my medical school in Urakami which was 500 meters from the hypocenter. I met many people coming back from Urakami. Their clothes were in rags and shreds of skin hung from their bodies. They looked like ghosts with vacant stares.
>
> The next day I was able to enter Urakami on foot and all that I knew had disappeared. Only the concrete and iron skeletons of the buildings remained. On each street corner, we had tubs of water used for putting out fires after air raids. In one of these small tubs, scarcely large enough for one person, was the body of a desperate man who sought cool water. There was foam coming from his mouth, but he was not alive. I cannot get rid of the sounds of the crying women in the destroyed fields.
>
> As I got nearer to the school there were black, charred bodies with the white edge of bones showing in the arms and legs. When I arrived some were still

alive. They were unable to move their bodies. The strongest were so weak that they were slumped over on the ground. I talked with them and they thought that they would be OK but all of them would eventually die within two weeks. I cannot forget the way their eyes looked at me and their voices spoke to me forever.

It should be noted that the bomb dropped on Nagasaki had a power of about 20,000 tons of TNT, not much larger than the so-called "tactical bombs" designed for battefield use.

But even these grim pictures are inadequate to describe the human disaster that would result from an attack on a country by today's stockpiles of nuclear weapons which contain thousands of bombs with the force of 1-million tons of TNT or greater.

The suffering of the surviving population would be without parallel. There would be complete interruption of communications, of food supplies and of water. Help would be given only at the risk of mortal danger from radiation for those venturing outside of buildings in the first days. The social disruption following such an attack would be unimaginable.

The exposure to large doses of radiation would lower immunity to bacteria and viruses and could, therefore, open the way for widespread infection. Radiation would cause irreversible brain damage and mental deficiency in many of the exposed in utero. It would greatly increase the incidence of many forms of cancer in survivors. Genetic damage would be passed on to future generations, should there be any.

In addition, large areas of soil and forests as well as livestock would be contaminated reducing food resources. Many other harmful biological and even geophysical effects would be likely, but we do not have enough knowledge to predict with confidence what they would be.

Even a nuclear attack directed only at military facilities would be devastating to the country as a whole. This is because military facilities are widespread rather than concentrated at only a few points. Thus, many nuclear weapons would be exploded.

Furthermore, the spread of radiation due to the natural winds and atmospheric mixing would kill vast numbers of people and contaminate large areas. The medical facilities of any nation would be inadequate to care for the survivors. An objective examination of the medical situation that would follow a nuclear war leads to but one conclusion: Prevention is our only recourse.

The consequences of nuclear war are not, of course, only medical in nature. But those that are compel us to pay heed to the inescapable lesson of contemporary medicine: Where treatment of a given disease is ineffective or where costs are insupportable, attention must be turned to prevention. Both conditions apply to the effects of nuclear war. Treatment would be virtually impossible and the costs would be staggering. Can any stronger argument be marshalled for a preventive strategy?

Prevention of any disease requires an effective prescription. We recognize that such a prescription must both prevent nuclear war and safeguard security. Our knowledge and credentials as scientists and physicians do not, of course, permit us to discuss security issues with expertise. However, if political and military leaders have based their strategic planning on mistaken assumptions concerning the medical aspects of a nuclear war, we feel that we do have a responsibility.

We must inform them and people everywhere of the full-blown clinical picture that would follow a nuclear attack and of the impotence of the medical community to offer a meaningful response. If we remain silent, we risk betraying ourselves and our civilization.

(Signed: Carlos Chagas, Rio de Janeiro; E. Armaldi, Rome; N. Bochkov, Moscow; L. Caldas, Rio de Janeiro., H. Hiatt, Boston; R. Latarjet, Paris; A. Leaf, Boston; J. Lejeune, Paris; L. Leprince-Ringuet, Paris; G. B. Marini-Bettolo, Rome; C. Pavan, Sao Paulo; A. Rich, Cambridge, Mass.; A. Serra, Rome; V. Weisskopf, Cambridge, Mass.)

PART TWO

NORTH AMERICAN CATHOLIC BISHOPS' STATEMENTS

[1] U.S. Conference of Catholic Bishops, Human Life in Our Day, November 15, 1968

The responsibility of moral leadership is the greater in the local Church of a nation whose arsenals contain the greatest nuclear potential for both the harm that we would wish to inpede or the help it is our obligation to encourage. We are acutely aware that our moral posture and comportment in this hour of supreme crisis will be assessed by the judgment of history and of God.

We renew the affirmation by the Council that "the loftier strivings and aspirations of the human race are in harmony with the message of the Gospel" (n. 77). We speak as witnesses to the Gospel, aware that issues of war and peace test the relevancy of its message for our generation, particularly in terms of the service of life and its dignity. We seek to speak in the spirit of that Gospel message, which is at heart a doctrine of non-violence rather than violence, of peace understood as Jesus proclaimed it. (Jn. 14:27)

We call upon American Catholics to evaluate war with the "entirely new attitude" for which the Council appealed and which may rightly be expected of all who, calling themselves Christians, proclaim their identity with the Prince of Peace. We share with all men of good will the conviction that a more humane society will not come "unless each person devotes himself with renewed determination to the cause of peace" (n. 77). We appeal to policy makers and statesmen to reflect soberly on the Council teaching concerning peace and war, and vigorously to pursue the search for means by which at all times to limit and eventually to outlaw the destructiveness of war....

Of one mind with the Council, we condemn without qualification wars of aggression however their true character may sometimes be veiled. Whatever case there may have seemed to exist in other times for wars fought for the domination of another nation, such a case can no longer be imagined given the circumstances of modern warfare, the heightened sense of international mutuality and the increasingly available humane means to the realization of that mutuality. [pp. 30-31]

The Council did not call for unilateral disarmament; Christian morality is not lacking in realism. But it did call for reciprocal or collective disarmament "proceeding at an equal pace according to agreement and backed up by authentic and workable safeguards" (n. 82)....

Meanwhile, it is greatly to be desired that such prospects not be dashed by irrational resolves to keep ahead in "assured destruction" capability. Rather it is to be hoped that the early ratification by the Senate of the Non-Proliferation Treaty ... will hasten discussion of across the board reduction by the big powers....

The Council's position on the arms race was clear. To recall it: "Therefore, we declare once again: the arms race is an utterly treacherous trap for humanity.... It is much to be feared that if this race persists, it will spawn all the lethal ruin whose path it is now making ready" (n. 81).

Nonetheless, the nuclear race goes on....

We seriously question whether the present policy of maintaining nuclear superiority is meaningful for security. There is no advantage to be gained by nuclear superiority, however it is computed, when each side is admittedly capable of inflicting overwhelming damage on the other, even after being attacked first. Such effective parity has been operative for some years. Any effort to achieve superiority only leads to ever higher levels of armaments as it forces the side with lesser capability to seek to maintain its superiority. In the wake of this action—reaction phenomenon comes a decrease in both stability and security.

The National Conference of Catholic Bishops pledges its united efforts toward forming a climate of public opinion for peace. . . .[*pp. 34-35*]

[2] Archbishop Peter Gerety, Bishop of Newark, Testimony before the U.S. Senate Foreign Relations Committee, January 21, 1976

1. U.S. STRATEGIC AND MILITARY POLICY

Perhaps the oldest and most refined ethical issue in Christian political morality is the morality of the use of force. Living in one of the two strategic superpowers makes this issue of prime importance for the religious communities. I will point toward two examples which manifest the nature of the moral question in U.S. strategic policy.

A. The Possession and Use of Nuclear Weapons

We live in the nuclear age; at the heart of the military question is the fact of nuclear weapons. A representative and authoritative Catholic statement on the morality of nuclear weapons is found in the document *Gaudium et Spes* of Vatican II.

Synthetically stated, the conciliar text lays down three principles regarding nuclear weapons: *first*, use of these weapons against cities and populated areas is prohibited in a special way because of their destructive capacity; *second*, while use is prohibited, the possession of these weapons for deterrence may possibly be legitimated as the lesser of two evils;

third, even deterrence is questionable unless it is conceived as an interim expedient accompanied by extraordinary efforts to negotiate their limitation and reduction.

These three principles direct our attention toward three areas of U.S. strategic policy: the possible use of nuclear weapons; the posture of our deterrent; and the policy of arms limitation. My purpose here is to comment on the state of these questions, not to provide a final moral judgment on them.

First, on the basis of statements of our government officials, it is clear that we are prepared to use nuclear weapons which are presently targeted against cities. This policy has been developed in tandem with a similarly declared policy on the part of the Soviet Union. In technical terms we both rely upon a counter-city strategy. The paradox of this position, as the Vatican Council noted, is that it preserves a "kind of peace" at the cost of threatening to perform mass murder. The rationale of the policy seems to be to make the threat of nuclear war so devastating that it will keep either side from initiating it.

A moral reflection grounded in the Vatican Council's position can acknowledge the utility of the deterrence function of nuclear weapons but cannot legitimate their counter-city use. Indeed the following text of the Council's document seems directed precisely at the intended use of most of our nuclear weapons:

> Any act of war aimed indiscriminately at the destruction of entire cities or extensive areas along with their population is a crime against God and man himself. It merits unequivocal and unhesitating condemnation. *(Gaudium et Spes)*

The Council explicitly condemned the use of weapons of mass destruction, but refrained from condemning the possession of such weapons as a deterrent. The Council did not pass direct judgment on the strategy of nuclear deterrence, but it is clear that its tolerance for deterrent strategies is conditional on the desire to keep the barrier between possession and actual use as high as possible. This raises certain questions about the use of tactical or other nuclear weapons which may, in themselves, or in their intended use, escape the condemnation of the Council as weapons of lesser destructiveness to cities and populations.

In recent years a strategic concept known as "counterforce strategy" has emerged which envisages the use of strategic nuclear weapons primarily on military targets as preferable to targeting them on cities and large populated areas. An objection to this strategy (which has not yet been officially adopted) is that such use of nuclear weapons tends to break down the barrier between possession and use of weapons of mass destructiveness, i.e., makes nuclear war more likely. A similar objection attaches to the use of tactical (battlefield) nuclear weapons in Central Europe or (perhaps in lesser measure in Korea) where the "first use" of such weapons appears to be part of approved strategy.

I do not seek to adjudicate the details, ethically or empirically, of this complex strategic discussion, but I would personally be of the opinion that moves to erode the barrier against use of nuclear weapons, whether of the tactical or strategic variety, are not in the best interests of maintaining peace.

As I have indicated already, the other condition placed upon a deterrence strategy by the Council is that efforts must continually be made to reduce the level of armaments. In hearings such as these our attention should be directed toward the question whether our efforts of arms limitation and reduction are commensurate with the dangers with which we and others are constantly threatened.

The results of our efforts thus far are not strikingly successful. The presently agreed upon levels of nuclear parity are set far above the capabilities now possessed by either of the superpowers. Admittedly, the responsibility here does not rest upon the United States alone or even principally with us; it is shared by both superpowers.

The point to be made, however, is that the treacherous trap of the arms race continues vertically between the superpowers and horizontally through proliferation of nuclear weapons to third countries. Admittedly, arms limitation in either of these categories even with the best of intentions on all sides is not easily achieved. After surveying the evidence of past and present policies, however, one is left with the uneasy feeling that a policy which is designated to protect our survival by correlating survival with nuclear security may unwittingly be risking the survival of ourselves and others.

In the nuclear age there are risks inherent in seeking too much security as well as in possessing too little. Some questions seem legitimate in the debate about what constitutes real security: could our security be as well assured with a lesser deterrent capability? Would it be unreasonably hazardous to experiment with some unilateral reduction in U.S. capabilities? I believe these are real, not rhetorical, questions. I offer them as a contribution from recent Catholic teaching, to the resolution of complex policy issues.

[3] U.S. Bishops' Statement, To Live in Christ Jesus, November 11, 1976

The Church has traditionally recognized that, under stringent conditions, engaging in war can be a form of legitimate defense. But modern warfare, in both its technology and in its execution, is so savage that one must ask whether war as it is actually waged today can be morally justified.

At the very least all nations have a duty to work to curb the savagery of war and seek the peaceful settlement of disputes. The right of legitimate defense is not a moral justification for unleashing every form of destruction. For example, acts of war deliberately directed against innocent noncombatants are gravely wrong, and no one may participate in such an act. In weighing the morality of warfare today, one must also take into consideration not only its immediate impact but also its potential for harm to future generations: for instance, through pollution of the soil or the atmosphere or damage to the human gene pool.

With respect to nuclear weapons, at least those with massive destructive capability, the first imperative is to prevent their use. As possessors of a vast nuclear arsenal, we must also be aware that not only is it wrong to attack civilian populations but it is also wrong to threaten to attack them as part of a strategy of deterrence. We urge the continued development and implementation of policies which seek to bring these weapons more securely under control, progressively reduce their presence in the world, and ultimately remove them entirely.

[4] U.S. Conference of Catholic Bishops, Pastoral Letter on Moral Values, November, 1976

Peace

We are also obligated as Americans and especially as Christians to reflect profoundy upon war and, more importantly, upon peace and the means of building it.

The church has traditionally recognized that, under stringent conditions, engaging in war can be a form of legitimate defense. But modern warfare, in both its technology and in its execution, is so savage that one must ask whether war as it is actually waged today can be morally justified.

At the very least all nations have a duty to work to curb the savagery of war and seek the peaceful settlement of disputes. The right of legitimate defense is not a moral justification for unleashing every form of destruction. For example, acts of war deliberately directed against innocent noncombatants are gravely wrong, and no one may participate in such an act. In weighing the morality of warfare today, one must also take into consideration not only its immediate impact but also its potential for harm to future generations: for instance, through pollution of the soil or the atmosphere or damage to the human gene pool.

A citizen entering the military service is fulfilling a conscientious duty toward his country. He may not casually disregard his nation's conscientious decision to go to war in self-defense. No members of the armed forces, above all no

Christians who bear arms as "agents of security and freedom," can rightfully carry out orders or policies requiring direct force against noncombatants or the violation of some other moral norm. The right to object conscientiously to war in general and the right of selective conscientious objection to a particular war should be acknowledged by government and protected by law.

With respect to nuclear weapons, at least those with massive destructive capability, the first imperative is to prevent their use. As possessors of a vast nuclear arsenal, we must also be aware that not only is it wrong to threaten to attack them as part of a strategy of deterrence. We urge the continued development and implementation of policies which seek to bring these weapons more securely under control, progressively reduce their presence in the world, and ultimately remove them entirely.

[5] U.S. Conference of Catholic Bishops, The Gospel of Peace and the Danger of War, February 15, 1978

In his Day of Peace Message for 1978, Pope Paul VI again called upon the community of the Church and the entire human community to reflect upon the meaning of peace in a world still marked by multiple forms of violence. Among these the spectre of technological warfare is the unique menace of the age. Listen to the Holy Father:

> We would like to be able to dispel this threatening and terrible nightmare by proclaiming at the top of our voice the absurdity of modern war and the absolute necessity of Peace—Peace not founded on the power of arms that today are endowed with an infernal destructive capacity (let us recall the tragedy of Japan), nor founded on the structural violence of some political regimes, but founded on the patient,

rational and loyal method of justice and freedom, such as the great international institutions of today are promoting and defending. We trust that the magisterial teachings of our great predecessors Pius XII and John XXIII will continue to inspire on this fundamental theme the wisdom of modern teachers and contemporary politicians. (Paul VI, *No to Violence, Yes to Peace,* January 1, 1978).

As teachers in the Church these words of Pope Paul speak to us with a special resonance. His annual messages on the Day of Peace constitute a striking fulfillment of the mandate of Vatican Council II: "to undertake an evaluation of war with an entirely new attitude." (*Gaudium et Spes,* para. 80) Such a new attitude was clearly evident in the 1976 intervention of the Holy See at the United Nations when it said that the arms race is "to be condemned unreservedly" as a danger, an injustice and a mistake. ("A Plea for Disarmament," *Osservatore Romano,* June, 1976)

The dangers of the arms race are a concern and a challenge to the whole human family. Moreover, all the members of the universal Church are called to witness to the Gospel of Peace. For the Church in the United States, however, the prophetic words of the Holy Father have a special significance. No nation has a more critical role in determining the delicate balance between the dangers of war and the possibilities of peace. It is an illusion to think the U.S. bears this responsibility alone; but it is a more dangerous deception not to recognize the potential for peace that our position in the world offers to us.

In 1978 two events will highlight the U.S. role and responsibility in the arms race. The first is the forthcoming VIII Special Session of the United Nations on Disarmament. The second is the continuing debate in the U.S. about a SALT II agreement with the Soviet Union designed to place new limits on nuclear weapons. It is not our purpose in this statement to engage in a detailed analysis of either of these topics, but to identify them as two instances of political debate in which the moral issues of the arms race can be articulated along with its technical dimensions.

The primary moral imperative is that the arms race must be stopped and the reduction of armaments must be achieved. ("A Plea for Disarmament") In pursuit of these objectives several specific choices must be made to bring the superpower arms race under control quantitatively and qualitatively, to restrain the proliferation of nuclear weapons, and to place restrictions on the rapid growth of conventional arms sales in the world.

Each of these complex issues requires separate treatment so that the relationship of moral and technical factors can be articulated and weighed. The evaluation must occur within the policy process and in the wider ambit of informed public discussion. Catholic teaching on the morality of war has traditionally been designed to speak to both of these audiences. The teaching seeks to establish a moral framework for policy debate and to provide pastoral guidance for individuals. It is incumbent upon us as bishops and other members of the Church, especially lay Catholics with particular competencies relevant to preserving peace, to fulfill this task today.

The contemporary resources of Catholic teaching on war and peace are rich. The doctrine of *Pacem in Terris* (1963) and *Gaudium et Spes* (1965) supplies new and fresh religious and moral perspectives to support those who in conscience choose the way of nonviolence as a witness to the Gospel. These same documents affirm, as Catholic teaching traditionally has acknowledged, that some uses of force in defense of the common good are legitimate. Both of these moral positions are rooted in the Gospel and provide for Catholics and others a reasonable and sound means of evaluating questions of war and peace in the modern world. In an effort to contribute to the policy and public debate in the months to come, we will draw from both of these moral positions to speak to specific issues in the arms debate.

Beyond this important task of moral analysis, however, the Church has another role. The Church must be a prophetic voice for peace. In the tradition of the last three popes the Church in our land must explain the meaning of peace, call people and governments to pursue peace and stand against those forces and elements which prevent the coming of true peace. To pursue peace in the political process requires courage; at times it means taking risks for peace. The Church in a competent and careful manner must encourage reasonable risks for peace. To risk requires a degree of faith and faith in turn is based on the hope that comes from prayer. As the Church in this nation we seek to be a moral voice placing restraints on war, a prophetic voice calling for peace and a prayerful community which has the courage to work for peace.

[6] Archbishop John Quinn of San Francisco, as President of NCCB, on President Carter's decision to defer production of neutron warheads, April 14, 1978

President Carter has made a most difficult decision to defer production of neutron warheads of NATO. I believe, however, that it is a reasonable, courageous and morally informed decision, and I wish to indicate my reasons for supporting it.

It can be argued that this weapon is less objectionable than existing tactical nuclear weapons. It is essentially a defensive weapon whose use in battle would probably cause less loss of civilian lives and less damage to property adjacent to the target area, than would the tactical nuclear weapons now deployed. In terms of traditional moral theology this characteristic would be judged as a favorable recommendation for this type of weapon.

In making an ethical judgment on the neutron warhead, however, I believe it is necessary to calculate its moral implications in a broadly defined framework. A principal consideration is the impact of this decision on the arms race. I am concerned, in the spirit so often expressed by Pope Paul VI, that we forestall any major decisions which will intensify the nuclear arms spiral. Special sensitivity should be shown to this question as we approach the opening of the UN Special Session on Disarmament in May.

A second argument against development of the neutron warhead is that the introduction of this new and more "manageable" weapon tends to narrow the gap politically and psychologically between conventional war and nuclear war. In other words, it could render more probable the escalation of any war in Europe to the level of nuclear warfare. Moreover, this analytical statement barely suggests the moral and emotional revulsion provoked in Europe by the debate on neutron warheads. This revulsion may express the deepest feelings of people who are asked to envisage a nuclear war in their homelands. President Carter has perhaps sensed this revulsion in a way which has been overlooked in official discussions of NATO strategy.

Obviously this issue involves complex political and strategic questions with regard to which I cannot claim expertise. My intent, rather, is to underline the moral dimensions of the issue. It is my hope and prayer that the president's decision will help to promote significant progress in controlling the arms race.

[7] Archbishop James Casey, Bishop of Denver, Another Holocaust? The Nuclear Arms Race, Issued prior to a protest against nuclear weapons at a nuclear weapons plant in Rocky Flats, Colorado, April 29-30, 1978

Concerned citizens from various parts of our country and the world are planning a peaceful demonstration at Rocky Flats, Colo., April 29-30. Personally, I am not very fond of demonstrations but I do share their concern about the real dangers of nuclear war and radioactive contamination. For this reason, I am asking the Catholic people of Northern Colorado to consider the authentic teachings of their church and to review a few recent statements relevant to our present situation.

In 1962, Pope John XXIII said:

> Justice, right reason and humanity urgently demand that the arms race should cease; that the stockpiles which exist in various countries should be reduced equally and simultaneously by the parties concerned; that nuclear weapons should be banned. (*Pacem in Terris*, 112)

At the Second Vatican Council, the bishops of the world wrote this:

> The horror and perversity of war are immensely magnified by the multiplication of scientific weapons. For acts of war involving these weapons can inflict massive and indiscriminate destruction far exceeding the bounds of legitimate defense ... Any act of war aimed indiscriminately at the destruction of entire cities or of extensive areas along with their population is a crime against God and man himself. It merits unequivocal and unhesitating condemnation. (*Gaudium et Spes*, 80)

In 1976, the bishops of the United States wrote:

> The church has traditionally recognized, under stringent conditions, engaging in war can be a form of legitimate defense. But modern warfare, in both its technology and its execution, is so savage that one must ask whether war as it is actually waged today can be morally justified... The right of legitimate defense is not a moral justification of unleashing every form of destruction... With respect to nuclear weapons, at least those with massive destructive capacity,

the first imperative is to prevent their use. (*To Live in Christ Jesus*)

Pope Paul VI in 1976 wrote a message for World Peace Day, and he said:

Let ill-fated and dishonorable arms, such as atomic weapons, be proscribed. Let the terrible art which can manufacture them and store them to terrorize peoples be outlawed. We pray that the deadly device may not have killed peace while seeking it.

And later, he called the entire armaments race which is draining the resources of the world, ". . . a danger, an injustice, a violation of law, a form of theft, a mistake, a wrong, a folly."

In a recent book, titled *Ethics and Nuclear Strategy?*, Father Francis D. Winters, S.J., states that the traditional rules for a just war do not apply to the nuclear situation. In fact, he feels that the words "weapons" and "war" should be abandoned in speaking of nuclear conflict because the development of military technology in the last 30 years has so transformed the instruments of war that they require new names to represent a new reality.

This author represents a group of respected moralists who are not passivists but they tell us that any use or even threat of use of nuclear weapons is immoral because these weapons are intrinsically uncontrollable and have massive, deadly consequences. Father Winters writes:

We need adequate military strength to defend human, cultural and political values that have been achieved thus far in the process of human development. Yet, we cannot any longer afford the illusion that nuclear "weapons" provide such security.

In asking you to consider these statements, I am deeply sensitive to the fact that some 3,000 people gain their livelihood at Rocky Flats. For them, the goals of the planned demonstration pose a threat to their daily needs and no one can fault them for their fears and concerns. Every person and institution which support this demonstration at Rocky Flats can do no less than fight for a transition of this facility that includes financial security for the workers and their families.

Perhaps the most disturbing aspect of the current situation is the fatalistic trance that has paralyzed large numbers of us. We pretend that we are powerless and so we seem to merely wait for the inevitable. We are living in a state of nuclear emergency that threatens human existence. We need to awaken from our trance and send a message to our leaders: "Start working for a safe and peaceful future."

Why do I ask you to consider the statements which contain the authentic teachings of the church? The Catholic Church is the oldest Christian guide in moral behavior on the face of our earth; and, it clearly teaches that nuclear warfare is immoral because it is a direct contradiction of its founder's teachings who said he came that we might have life and have it to the full. Essential parts of nuclear weapons are being constructed in our community, and we share in the responsibility for the anger it represents to all who live in our global village.

In preparing this statement, I make no pretensions. I am not a mover or a shaker of world opinion. We must rely on our leaders to send our message to Russia and China and other nuclear powers. We have to start somewhere; and, you and I can at least serve as starters. Our voice may be heard as one crying in the wilderness of a people who seem to be silently and stoically resigned to the inevitability of a nuclear holocaust.

Those of you who watched all or a part of the 9 ½ hour TV documentary drama *The Holocaust* last week will remain deeply disturbed by the incredible inhumanity that took place in our generation. If only we could erase this shameful chapter from the record of human history, but we cannot. However, the spectre of another and perhaps more shameful holocaust has appeared on the horizon of the present day. We dare not stand idly by when the possibility of a nuclear massacre threatens our community, our country, and our world.

[8] Cardinal John Krol, Bishop of Philadelphia, Testimony on behalf of USCC before the Senate Foreign Relations Committee, September 6, 1979

I am Cardinal John Krol, archbishop of Philadelphia. I speak on behalf of the U.S. Catholic Conference comprising more than 350 bishops of the United States, serving more than 50 million Catholics.

I express the sincere gratitude of the USCC for the opportunity to present the views of the Catholic bishops of the United States on the moral aspects of the nuclear arms race.

I. PERSPECTIVE OF THE TESTIMONY

The moral principles underlying my testimony, have been enunciated clearly in papal documents and speeches, and in Vatican Council II. Pius XII pleaded on the eve of World War II:

Nothing is lost by peace, everything may be lost by war (Aug. 24, 1939).

Paul VI, speaking to the General Assembly of the United Nations, said:

No more war, war never again. Peace must guide the destinies of all peoples and of all mankind.... Disarmament is the first step toward peace.... As long as man remains that weak, changeable and even wicked being he often shows himself to be, defensive armaments will also be necessary (Oct. 4, 1965).

Vatican Council II, in its Constitution on the Church in the Modern World, declared:

The arms race is one of the most grevious plagues of the human race, and it inflicts an intolerable injury upon the world (n. 81);

The arms race is not a secure way of maintaining true peace, and the resulting balance of power is no sure and genuine path to achieving it (n. 80);

Since peace must be born of mutual trust between peoples, instead of being forced on nations through dread of arms, all must work to put an end to the arms race and make a real beginning of disarmament, not unilaterally indeed, but at an equal rate on all sides, on the basis of agreements and backed up by genuine and effective guarantees (n. 82).

The principles reflect the authentic position of the Catholic Church and of faithful Catholics. The manner and degree to which these principles are reflected in a particular proposal, such as the Strategic Arms Limitation Treaty II, admits a divergence of views. For this reason I recognize, and I want this committee to know, that while the principles to which we subscribe are clear and generally accepted, the position I present here today is the view of the majority of the Administrative Board of the bishops' conference; it is not a unanimous position within the conference of bishops nor is it the unanimous position of all Catholics in the United States. It is however the official policy of the U.S. Catholic Conference, and in expressing it, we bishops seek to fulfill a role of responsible citizenship as well as religious leadership.

This role requires me to speak the truth plainly. The Catholic bishops of this country believe that too long have we Americans been preoccupied with preparations for war; too long have we been guided by the false criterion of equivalence or superiority of armaments; too long have we allowed other nations to virtually dictate how much we should spend on stockpiling weapons of destruction. Is it not time that we concentrate our efforts on peace rather than war? Is it not time we take that first step toward peace: gradual, bilateral, negotiated disarmament?

It is impossible to regard this treaty as a spectacular achievement in the field of arms control. But we support its ratification as a partial and imperfect step in the direction of halting the proliferation of nuclear weapons and as part of an ongoing process, begun in 1972, to negotiate actual reductions in nuclear arms. Our support is, however, heavily qualified precisely because of the moral principles which govern our view of arms control.

No question of foreign affairs surpasses the arms race in terms of moral complexity and moral content. Along with the correlative issue of world poverty, the arms race forms the heart of the moral agenda of foreign policy.

The massive technical complexity of the arms race in its political and strategic dimensions is something that people in our government grapple with daily. We respect that technical complexity and have tried to assimilate it in this testimony. At the same time, for the church the arms race is principally a problem defined in religious and moral categories.

The specter of war in any form raises for Christian ethics the central question of the taking of human life. Since the life of every single human person bears the sacred dignity of the image of God, the question of the religious and moral significance of warfare has received more sustained reflection in Roman Catholic theology than almost any other moral problem. From St. Augustine's masterful treatment of war in Chapter 19 of *The City of God* to Vatican Council II's injunction to the church that it should "undertake a completely fresh appraisal of war," there has been present in Catholic tradition an abiding determination to limit the impact of war on the human family.

In a nuclear age, the moral sanctions against war have taken on a qualitatively new character. From Pius XII to John Paul II, the moral argument is clear: The nuclear arms race is to be unreservedly condemned and the political process of arms control and disarmament is to be supported by the Christian community.

This pursuit of peace is not based on a naive utopian view of the world. The Christian tradition is eloquent about the vision of peace; it is also realistic about the fact of war. Hence, Vatican Council II, recognizing the inadequate nature of the political structure of the international community, stated that governments cannot be denied the right of legitimate self-defense once every means of peaceful settlement has been exhausted. (Pastoral Constitution on the Church in the Modern World, n. 79)

The perspective which shapes this testimony, therefore, recognizes that some forms of war can be morally legitimate, but judges that nuclear war surpasses the boundaries of legitimate self-defense. The application of this basic moral principle to our present situation requires that we distinguish two problems of the nuclear age: the use of nuclear weapons and the strategy of deterrence. Both are pertinent to our assessment of SALT II.

Prohibition of Use

The primary moral imperative of the nuclear age is to prevent any use of strategic nuclear weapons. This prohibition is expressed in the following passage of Vatican Council II:

Any act of war aimed indiscriminately at the destruction of entire cities or of extensive areas along with their population is a crime against God and man himself. It merits unequivocal and unhesitating condemnation. (Church in the Modern World, n. 80)

This was the only formal condemnation of the council and indicates the seriousness with which the bishops of the world viewed the possible use of what they called "modern scientific weapons." Our first purpose in supporting SALT II is to illustrate our support for any reasonable effort which is designed to make nuclear war in any form less likely. I have said that our support of the treaty is qualified; one reason for this is the paradox of nuclear deterrence.

The Moral Dilemma of Deterrence

The moral paradox of deterrence is that its purpose is to prevent the use of nuclear weapons, but it does so by an expressed threat to attack the civilian population of one's adversary. Such a threat runs directly counter to the central moral affirmation of the Christian teaching on war: that innocent lives are not open to direct attack. The complexity of the moral dilemma is reflected in the statement on deterrence of the American bishops in 1976:

> With respect to nuclear weapons, at least those with massive destructive capability, the first imperative is to prevent their use. As possessors of a vast nuclear arsenal, we must also be aware that not only is it wrong to attack civilian populations but it is also wrong to threaten to attack them as part of a strategy of deterrence. We urge the continued development and implementation of policies which seek to bring these weapons more securely under control, progressively reduce their presence in the world, and ultimately remove them entirely. ("To Live in Christ Jesus," 1976)

The moral judgment of this statement is that not only the *use* of strategic nuclear weaspons, but also the *declared intent* to use them involved in our deterrence policy is wrong. This explains the Catholic dissatisfaction with nuclear deterrence and the urgency of the Catholic demand that the nuclear arms race be reversed. It is of the utmost importance that negotiations proceed to meaningful and continuing reductions in nuclear stockpiles, and eventually, to the phasing out altogether of nuclear deterrence and the threat of mutual-assured destruction.

As long as there is hope of this occurring, Catholic moral teaching is willing, while negotiations proceed, to tolerate the possession of nuclear weapons for deterrence as the lesser of two evils. If that hope were to disappear, the moral attitude of the Catholic Church would almost certainly have to shift to one of uncompromising condemnation of both use *and* possession of such weapons.

With this in mind, the Catholic bishops of this country ask

the Senate of the United States to ratify this treaty because the negotiations which produced it, and the further round of negotiations which it permits, offer the promise of escape from the danger of a nuclear holocaust and from the ethical dilemma of nuclear deterrence.

II. SALT II

Nevertheless, we have serious reservations about this treaty. SALT I had created a hope among people that SALT II would require real reductions on both sides. This hope has not been fulfilled and there is no clear indication that SALT II can revive that hope. That is why some of my fellow bishops and many more concerned Catholics refuse to support SALT II.

The U.S. proposals of 1977 had significant reductions in view but these were rejected by the Soviet Union. The present treaty limits strategic nuclear delivery systems to 2,250 (after 1981) on both sides and this will require the dismantling of about 250 Soviet launchers. Such a reduction is not very significant considering the destructive power (3,550 megatons for the United States and 7,868 megatons for the Soviet Union) that will remain and continue to increase on each side.

Second, the treaty does not preclude either side from proceeding to replace its present land-based ICBMs with a new system, or modifying existing systems within limits, it is true, as to size and number of warheads but obviously embodying significant improvements in accuracy. These systems will obviously be more destructive.

On the other hand it cannot be argued, as do some critics, that the treaty does not constrain Soviet strategic weapons expansion. Under the treaty, the Soviet Union will not be permitted to deploy an already-tested mobile missile (SS-16); it must count all SS-18 missiles as having multiple warheads though some may not; it must stop its current program of deploying additional missiles with multiple warheads by about 1982 and may not increase the number of warheads in existing missiles.

SALT II is thus basically a deceleration, not a reversal, of the nuclear arms race. While the weight of this testimony comes to the conclusion that the quantitative and qualitative limits on delivery systems and weapons constitute an arms control achievement worthy of support, that conclusion becomes harder to defend if one assumes SALT II to be the end of the process. Much more remains to be done.

By far the most numerous opponents of ratification are those who reject the treaty as failing to protect U.S. security. In particular, there are those who argue that this treaty will permit the Soviet Union to achieve a first-strike capability against our land-based ICBMs, and that they will use this threat to challenge and change the strategic balance in various parts of the world. Can this really be reliably predicted? With the United States in possession of a large nuclear arsenal and varied means of delivery would not the leaders of the Soviet Union be insane to start, or threaten to start, a nuclear war even in possession of a first-strike capability vis-à-vis our land-based ICBMs? Can we gainsay the tragic reality that deterrence is still based on the posture and policy of mutual-assured destruction? Even if the Soviet Union were to acquire the capability to neutralize the U.S. Minuteman force of ICBMs, is it not clear that the other legs of the TRIAD will continue to deter a Soviet first strike, if indeed that were the Soviet intention?

Some critics of the treaty, however, do not base their opposition mainly on the premise that the Soviet Union would risk a first strike. Rather they argue that the perception in the world of the Soviet Union having first-strike capability will lead to an adverse shift in the global political balance. I do not pose as a political or technical expert, but I must ask whether in the nuclear age it can be argued that an increment of strategic power can so easily be translated into an effective instrument of political influence. This translation from the strategic balance to specific political conflicts seems particularly complex precisely in those situations in the developing world where forces of nationalism and a plethora of ideological positions are vying for control. The cost of using nuclear weapons on the part of those who employ them has deprived them of much of their strategic utility and has made their political usefulness equally problematical. For example, the Soviet Union has not been able to achieve a decisive political advantage vis-à-vis China, despite the former's admitted military superiority.

On balance, we are satisfied that while the treaty does not require a reduction in nuclear weaponry on either side, at the same time it will not substantially endanger U.S. security. Whatever risks may be involved are worth taking for the sake of ensuring that the SALT II negotiations will be followed quickly by a third round aimed at more significant reductions.

III. BEYOND SALT II

By itself SALT II is no more than a beginning. It creates a certain momentum which should make possible more impressive arms-control achievements. If not, our confidence may have been misplaced. What are the prospects?

It is our hope that the U.S. agenda for future negotiations will be bold and imaginative and that the aim of the negotiators should be real, demonstrable reductions in both weapons and delivery systems. Our negotiating posture should not sacrifice long-term possibilities for real disarmament in the name of short-term tactical advantages in the strategic competition.

It can hardly be a source of satisfaction or pride that the ratification of this treaty may be in doubt or that an arms-control agreement can only be purchased in conjunction with substantially increased expenditures for other arms. There is a prevalent belief in this country that our national security can only be preserved by the dynamic of technological development and investment in new and ever more destructive weapon systems. One reads that the decision to deploy the MX missile is a response to such perceptions but perhaps still not sufficient to reconcile opponents of the treaty.

We have already referred to the opportunities which the treaty affords for further escalation of nuclear weaponry by both sides. It has been argued during these hearings that ratification of the treaty should be linked to a new and massive program for expanding and improving U.S. strategic nuclear as well as conventional forces. If the Congress accepts this advice, the hope which I referred to earlier for a reversal of the nuclear arms race will grow even dimmer.

Many of us remember being told by the then Secretary of Defense Robert McNamara in the late '60s that U.S. security depended on U.S. strategic forces being maintained at a level two or three times greater than that of the Soviet Union in terms of deliverable warheads. The United States now has 9,200 strategic nuclear weapons (re-entry vehicles and aerial bombs) compared to 5,000 for the Soviet Union; yet we are told we are no longer superior, in fact, are facing strategic inferiority and must exert ourselves to maintain or recover "equivalence." Where McNamara once was confident that neither side would be able to acquire a first-strike capability, we are now told that the Soviet Union is acquiring a first-strike capability and that the United States must hasten to do likewise. Witness after witness has told this committee that SALT II is acceptable precisely because it does not prevent the United States from meeting this challenge. Strategic "equivalence" is the new name for the nuclear arms race!

At the time of SALT I, Dr. Kissinger was quoted as asking, "What good is strategic superiority at these levels of numbers?" Are we not justified in asking today if strategic equivalence is an absolute necessity? Is this doctrine not an infallible recipe for continuing the strategic arms race? Are we not moving inexorably toward a situation in which each side has a first-strike capability, a posture and a policy, not of deterrence by mutual-assured destruction, but of readiness for and reliance on the capability for fighting a nuclear war?

We, the Catholic bishops, find ourselves under the obligation of questioning fundamentally the logic of the pattern of events implied by determined pursuit of strategic equivalence. Our purpose in coming before this distinguished committee is to speak on moral-religious grounds in support of arms control designed to be a step toward real measures of disarmament. It would radically distort our intention and purpose if our support of SALT II were in any way coupled with plans for new military expenditures. The treaty should be approved as an arms-control measure, not as a maneuver to increase the strategic budget.

These proposed new strategic systems will require a massive outlay of funds at a time of increasing fiscal stringency. The Constitution of the United States calls upon the executive and legislative branches of our government not only to provide for the common defense but also to establish justice, to promote the general welfare of the nation and to secure the blessings of liberty for ourselves and our posterity. Estimates for the MX missile run from $30 billion upward during the next decade; with the existing national debt at $805 billion and pressure being exerted on legislative bodies at all levels to reduce expenditures, the investment of $30 billion in one weapons system inevitably will result in new limits on spending for essential human services here and abroad.

This topic of the competition of arms for scarce resources has been an abiding concern for me. Speaking at the Synod of Bishops in 1971, I argued then and still believe now that:

> The armaments race violates the rights of the world's poor in a way that is fruitless and intolerable. The reason is that it is not the way to protect human life or foster peace, but on the contrary the causes of war are thereby aggravated little by little.

It is our recommendation that systems like the MX, as well as Trident II, should be considered as negotiable in return for equivalent concessions by the Soviet Union in SALT III. We have been told that the aim of SALT III will be "deep cuts" in the strategic arsenals of both superpowers; we fervently hope this will be true.

As we consider the future of U.S. defense policy, it might be well to review one dimension of the SALT I negotiations. At that time the possibility existed of excluding the deployment of MIRVs; we did not take that option. Now we find that one of the major objections of those opposing SALT II is the threat posed by the Soviets to our land-based ICBMs. The Soviet

MIRV capability is a central element of the threat to our ICBMs, a threat which we might have obviated by a different negotiating posture in SALT I. Our hope is that we will carefully consider the MX and related decisions in the light of their impact on the negotiating process of SALT III. Perhaps the most important single strategic arms-control step would be the elimination of MIRVs from the respective ICBM forces. Unrealistic as it may seem to hardheaded defense planners, the question should be raised now whether the United States could try immediately to negotiate a lower MIRV level for ICBMs.

IV. SUMMARY

The foregoing testimony may be summarized in the following propositions:

1. Catholics reject means of waging or even deterring war which could result in destruction beyond control and possibly a final holocaust of humanity.

2. In particular, strategic nuclear weapons of massive destructiveness and poisonous regional or global aftereffects must never be used.

3. Consequently, the reduction through negotiated agreements and, eventually, the elimination of such weapons, must be the overriding aim of policy. Without it, there can be only one alternative: the indefinite continuation and escalation of the strategic competition. The doctrine of strategic equality, by itself, does not ensure against such competition; rather it almost guarantees it. Some risks must be taken in the direction of control, both to avoid nuclear war and to rescue us from the moral dilemma of nuclear deterrence.

4. SALT II, the result of seven years of negotiation, represents a limited but acceptable agreement which constrains the nuclear forces of both the United States and the Soviet Union, does not jeopardize U.S. security, and can be the beginning of a continuing and necessary process for obtaining meaningful and progressive reductions. The treaty should be ratified by the Senate.

5. This process must not be sacrificed to a narrow and technologically oriented insistence upon exploitation of new nuclear options, including counterforce options. In particular, final decisions regarding deployment of the MX and Trident II should be deferred until the utility of those options for negotiation in SALT III can be explored.

6. Failure by the United States to take full advantage of the possibilities for further restraints and reductions will eventually rob U.S. foreign and defense policy of moral legitimacy.

Mr. Chairman, the attention of the whole world has been captured by the new pope, John Paul II. He has already taken note of the significance of SALT II for world peace. The pope's remarks came in his weekly Sunday talk before leading the noon Angelus in St. Peter's Square. The SALT accord, he said,

> is not yet a reduction of weaponry or, as could be hoped, a provision for disarmament. But that does not mean that the foreseen measures are not a sign, which we ought to greet with pleasure, of the desire to pursue a dialogue, without which every hope of working effectively for peace could vanish.
>
> Believers and men of good will who feel themselves so impelled by conscience to pledge themselves as "artisans of peace" cannot ignore the importance of anything that favors a climate of alleviating tensions. This helps to encourage other indispensable progress on the road to limitation and reduction of armaments.

The pope asked for prayers "to bring progress to the great cause of laying down weapons and pursuing honest, stable and effective agreements" of peace and concord. It is with such sentiments that the U.S. Catholic Conference submits this testimony to the Foreign Relations Committee.

[9]   Bishop Maurice Dingman, Bishop of Des Moines, An Alternative to War, August 1980

Am I a pacifist bishop? I don't know. But I do know that I have strong convictions when the subject turns to the arms race, disarmament and the nuclear bomb.

For the past two years I have written pastoral letters on the occasion of the anniversaries of the bombings of Hiroshima and Nagasaki. I am very uncomfortable with the "bad example" that we in the United States have set in warfare. We were the first to build an atomic bomb (1943), and we were the first to use it (1945). I believe that it is up to us as a nation to set a better example.

In this my third pastoral letter on the topic, I am limiting myself to one theme. That one theme is the advice that I quoted from Maryknoll Magazine in last year's pastoral: "We can examine our own conscience."

I invite you, in the course of reading this pastoral, to begin your tortuous conscience formation. I am in no mood to use a heavy-handed, authoritarian approach, but I would like to open up some areas of reflection. I do this fully aware of my duty as a bishop to form the consciences of my people.

Our two most recent popes have used this phrase "to form consciences" more and more frequently. Pope John Paul I used it in his remarks to the diplomats of the world on Aug. 31, 1978. He called it a pastoral task. "Forming consciences" was his way of forming "public opinion." He felt that if we had the correct "fundamental principles" then we would guarantee "authentic civilization and real brotherhood between peoples."

In his recent trip to Brazil, Pope John Paul II told the bishops they should inspire the people's consciences.

Each of us has a personal responsibility in conscience to come to some conviction on the issue of atomic warfare, disarmament, etc. In forming my conscience it is necessary for me to turn to someone in whom I have confidence. I am making a very important and a very vital interior decision. I offer two sources in whom I have confidence: first, through the scriptures; and second, the vicar of Christ who speaks in our day and in our time.

Read with me the first, sixth and seventh chapters of Matthew and the sixth chapter of Luke.

The Sermon on the Mount begins with the Beatitudes and then says:

> You have heard the commandment imposed on your forefathers, "You shall not commit murder; every murderer shall be liable to judgment." What I say to you is: Everyone who grows angry with his brother shall be liable to judgment; any man who uses abusive language toward his brother shall be answerable to the Sanhedrin, and if he holds him in contempt he risks the fires of Gehenna. If you bring your gift to the altar and there recall that your brother has anything against you, leave your gift at the altar, go first to be reconciled with your brother, and then come and offer your gift (Mt. 5:21–24).
>
> In Luke, we read: "To you who hear me, I say: Love your enemies, do good to those who hate you; bless those who curse you and pray for those who maltreat you. When someone slaps you on the cheek, turn and give him the other; when someone takes your coat, let him have your shirt as well. Give to all who beg from you" (Lk. 6:27–30).

These are the words of Jesus. A few months ago a newspaper reporter interviewed me. I quoted from scripture about turning the other cheek and later in the mail received a letter vehemently opposed to this kind of thinking. Should we not begin to think of a non-violent approach? Is there any validity in a Mahatma Gandhi approach? Has the time come for us to be Judeo-Christians? The Gospels have something to say. Are we listening?

There is one in our midst today who is recognized as the greatest moral force in the world. The person is the vicar of Christ who speaks for the mystical body of Christ, the body of

Christ, which is the church. His voice has been raised again and again as he speaks the message of Jesus in our time.

I will not cite numerous quotes from his talks here. I will refer only to his impassioned speech to UNESCO in Paris June 2 of this year. He warned these men and women of science against the "horrible prospect of nuclear war" which the world faces.

He said,

> I speak to your intelligence and to your heart, surpassing all passion, ideals and frontiers . . . to tell you, to cry out to you from the depths of my soul . . . the future of man and mankind is threatened, radically threatened . . . I speak to you in the name of this terrible menace which weighs on humanity.

"Consciences must be mobilized," are his words to the scientists. The same words are spoken to all of us.

A week ago I met a professional friend of mine in Des Moines, and we spoke briefly about the danger of war and the necessity of being fully prepared. He was fully convinced we should increase our armaments. I asked if there were not an alternative, perhaps the Mahatma Gandhi approach.

Which position, I ask you, is more in conformity with the Christ of the scriptures and the mystical Christ of today, the church? I am terribly afraid, as Pope John XXIII expressed it in his encyclical on peace, "that the conflagration may be set off by some unexpected and obscure event."

My professional friend and I respect one another, yet we disagree in our stand on arms acceleration and disarmament. This person brought up Hitler's rise to power and the necessity of war. I am quick to say that I was a priest in the 1940s, and that I accepted the "just-war" theory and I supported the obvious need to overcome the evils of Hitler in Western Europe.

But I am not so certain now. A whole new event has happened. Hiroshima has changed my attitude.

Can there be a just war? Do we fulfill the principle of proportionality? St. Augustine, who gave us the just-war theory, would be hard pressed to say that an atomic bomb like the one at Hiroshima preserved that proportion of good over evil.

It is estimated that if one 20-megaton weapon were detonated in central New York City, 7 million people would die from the blast, fire storm and radiation that would follow.

Remember what the American bishops said in 1968 concerning the conflict in Vietnam: "Have we already reached or passed the point where the principle of proportionality becomes decisive?"

As a bishop I am in the business of forming consciences. Would it not be possible to suggest something better than atomic weapons? I suggest imitating Jesus and following the pattern of the Gospels with an emphasis on the Beatitudes. Mahatma Gandhi in India and Martin Luther King Jr. in the United States used non-violence and achieved much.

Suppose we were to take a small part of our time, our talent and our treasure that we are spending on preparations for war and suppose we were to put these efforts into training for non-violent actions for peace. What would happen? Instead of arming for an offensive tactic, why could we not concentrate on defensive measures? The savings could help the poor.

I conclude by saying that I do not have the answers. But I do plead for "constant and patient dialogue" that will lead to your formation of conscience. There must be an alternative to war. In forming your conscience I ask you to listen to Christ speaking in the scriptures and to the vicar of Christ speaking in our time.

Praying that America may increasingly become "one nation, under God, indivisible, with liberty and justice for all," I am sincerely yours in Christ.

[10]   Bishop P. Francis Murphy, Auxiliary Bishop of Baltimore, War and Peace: Questions and Convictions, September 15, 1980

I am delighted to be with you this evening. I cannot adequately express my joy and my appreciation to each of you, to Fathers Forker and Gerosky, and to Doctor Wickenheiser, for this opportunity to speak and listen to you on the topic of peace and peacemaking. I am very impressed with the overall context of a 24-hour period of prayer, teaching and personal reflection in the college as an appropriate climate in which to inaugurate your draft-counseling center. The members of the Archdiocesan Justice and Peace Commission join me in thanking you for your willingness to establish this center to assist any young men (and women) who may be faced with the moral decision of entering the draft and possible military combat.

It is in light of this context that I have been asked to address the church's new understanding of war and peace and the arms race, both nuclear and conventional.

Here at Mount St. Mary's you are breaking ground by undertaking a counseling program for young men for whom the registration for the armed forces is a present actuality, and a possible draft into the armed forces exists as a distinct possibility. I commend you and I congratulate you for the courage and vision which this undertaking demonstrates, because, as with anything new and different, it raises questions—many questions not asked before and perhaps in many cases not even contemplated. It is to each of you here at Mount St. Mary's that I direct the challenge to break this new ground, to ask these difficult questions.

If I may begin the questioning: What must be the mind-set of the Christian today about what warfare has become? Where does one start in determining what can be characterized as a Christian attitude regarding warfare? In seeking to offer a response, let me follow the accepted procedure of the church in studying any moral question. Let us look first into the Gospels, the church's teaching and practice, and then into our history and our personal experience and knowledge.

The Gospels

First, a look at scripture. Let us not fall victim to the fundamentalist view of the scriptures that the Gospels paint only one picture of Jesus. Jesus is at one time meek and mild and humble of heart. At other times he states that he has come to bring fire on the earth and to set one family member against another. It is not without some reason that many articles bearing on the subject of the historical Jesus begin with the catchy and not at all flippant title: "Will the real Jesus please stand up!"

The Gospels are not political theory. There is no single sentence I can quote about war and peace. There are principles Jesus has given to his disciples to apply to historical situations. There is a mind-set and a vision of how persons should live and treat one another. Most of all there is the example of Christ who was non-violent and forgiving in accepting civil authority's unjust death sentence. Over the centuries, the church has had the responsibility of trying to apply the vision of Jesus.

We can learn from our beginnings—our roots, the Gospels—what is the gift which Jesus, the prince of peace, has given to his followers, to the members of the faithful community. The first message from and about the Messiah, the kernel of the Christian message, is peace, *shalom*. This word means completion, a state of perfection not achieved by human effort but given by God. The first recollection of the earliest community about their risen Lord was the Easter message of "peace." This was his message to those who had abandoned him and let him die virtually alone. But his first reappearance to them was not to scold, not to reprimand, but rather to share with them the message of *shalom*.

Through the many years during which the gospel tradition was passed on orally, there was only one message: the Master brings peace. As time passed, memories and recollections were added to the story of the risen Lord; the Gospel began to be formed and was eventually written down. Only Matthew and Luke take us to the very beginnings of the story of the Messiah, and it is in the Christmas story that the first message about the Messiah bears a striking resemblance to the Easter message of the risen Lord. The angels announced: You have nothing to fear; you are awaiting the prince of peace.

The message is clear and unmistakable. There is nothing new about the attitude that is demanded of Christians who would make their own the gospel imperative about the attainment and maintenance of peace on earth.

Now that we have taken a brief opportunity to reflect on the gospel message about the Messiah, I would like to turn our attention to the way in which the message of Jesus was evidenced in the lives of some of the early Christians.

Christian Pacifism

We have seen that, pressed to express the message of Jesus in one word, the evangelist chose *shalom*. How was this translated into Christian action by some of the followers of Jesus? According to some scholars, in the first century of Christianity, the age of persecution, there was a tradition of pacifism—Christians would not bear arms and participate in warfare. While this belief was not held by all Christians, some of the earliest conscientious objectors include Origen, St. Justin Martyr, Lactantius, Maximilian and St. Martin of Tours. Their reasoning rested on the bedrock of the Gospel of Jesus, particularly the Sermon on the Mount. Its contradictions dramatize the enormous distinction between the natural creature (the "old creature") and the supernatural creature (the "new creature") of the Gospel.

The contradictions are as challenging and dramatic today for each of us as they were long ago for Origen, Martin and Justin. "You have heard it said," Jesus told his hearers, "love your friends and hate your enemies." He went on, of course, to add: "But I say to you, love your enemies and pray for those who persecute and mistreat you, that you will become children of your Father in heaven."

Just-War Theory

In the fourth century, in the time of Constantine and the Roman Empire, St. Augustine developed the "just-war theory." Its basis: "the use of force in defense of the common good." The tradition was subsequently developed by Aquinas and is reflected in 20th-century papal teaching. The just-war doctrine presumes that war is evil. To override the presumption, the following conditions must prevail: a just cause, a right intention and a reasonable expectation of success. If these conditions are met the war is considered morally justifiable. Then, in the course of the war, the moral rules of proportionality and non-combatant immunity need to be observed.

On the question of just cause, several situations were considered sufficient to justify going to war: to protect the innocent from unjust attack, to restore rights wrongfully denied or to re-establish an order necessary for decent human existence. Gradually, in Catholic social teaching, the causes considered sufficiently just to legitimate going to war have been reduced to one: self-defense and defense of others under unjustified attack. As recently as 1963, in *Peace on Earth*, Pope John XXIII noted:

> Men are becoming more and more convinced that disputes which arise between states should not be resolved by recourse to arms, but rather by negotiation.
> It is true that on historical grounds this conviction is based chiefly on the terrible destructive force of modern arms. And it is nourished by the horror aroused in the mind by the very thought of the cruel destruction and the immense suffering which the use of those armaments would bring. And for this reason, it is hardly possible to imagine that in the atomic era war could be used as an instrument of justice.

In 1971, it should be noted that the American bishops applied the just-war theory to the Vietnam war and declared it unjust.

Modern Popes

With the advance of modern technology in the 20th century, nations have developed weaponry exceeding in quality and size the means of war and destruction ever known before. The question is: How do we relate the Lord's teaching on peace to the condition of the arms race today?

It is this topic which the recent popes have addressed on a systematic and consistent basis since the beginning of the nuclear age. Pius XII, John XXIII, Paul VI and John Paul II have all spoken to the moral and religious dimensions of the arms race . . . Paul VI and John Paul II in the United Nations. Without specifying this teaching in detail, I can indicate its general lines.

First, Catholic teaching condemns the dynamic of the arms race in the strongest possible terms. At the Second Vatican Council (1965), the bishops called the arms race "an utterly treacherous trap for humanity, and one which injured the poor to an intolerable degree." This judgment was confirmed in a 1976 statement of the Holy See given at the United Nations in which the arms race was condemned as "a danger, an injustice, a theft from the poor, and a folly."

Second, since Pius XII, Catholic teaching on arms control and disarmament has consistently tied such goals to the need for a new political and legal authority in the international community, one which could effectively impose limits on the arms race and act in the name of the universal common good. John XXIII stated the case most forcefully in his encyclical *Peace on Earth*: "The moral order itself, therefore, demands that such form of public authority be established."

Third, within the context of this long-term political-legal objective, Catholic teaching supports any reasonably hopeful initiative for bringing the arms race under control. John XXIII, in *Peace on Earth*, said:

> Justice, right reason, and humanity urgently demand that the arms race should cease: that the stockpiles which exist in various countries should be reduced equally and simultaneously by the parties concerned;

that nuclear weapons should be banned; and that a general agreement should be reached eventually about progressive disarmament and an effective method of control.

The following text from the Vatican Council is representative of a whole series of statements:

Everyone must labor to put an end at last to the arms race, and to make a true beginning of disarmament, not indeed a unilateral disarmament, but one proceeding at an equal pace according to agreement, and backed up by authentic and workable safeguards.

Fourth, the American Catholic bishops stated in a 1976 pastoral letter titled "To Live in Christ Jesus":

Modern warfare, in both its technology and in its execution, is so savage that one must ask whether war as it is actually waged today can be morally justified.

Acts of war deliberately directed against innocent non-combatants are gravely wrong, and no one may participate in such an act. In weighing the morality of warfare today, one must also take into consideration not only its immediate impact but also its potential for harm to future generations; for instance, through pollution of the soil or the atmosphere or damage to the human gene pool.

As possessors of a vast nuclear arsenal, we must also be aware that not only is it wrong to attack civilian populations but it is also wrong to threaten to attack them as part of a strategy of deterrence.

In other words, church teaching condemns not only the arms race but also the threat of using them.

Fifth, in light of the new conditions of modern warfare, Catholic teaching has grown increasingly sensitive to the need for concrete pastoral guidance for individuals faced with moral choices about warfare. This has led to renewed support from church authorities for individuals who take the position of universal conscientious objectors or conscientious objectors selectively opposed to specific wars or specific forms of warfare.

These five dynamic principles highlight the key dimensions of Catholic moral teaching on warfare. They are intended to provide a contribution to public-policy debate and decision on the arms race, as well as pastoral guidance for individuals who must make personal choices about warfare. This function of acting as moral teacher is an essential role for the church in responding to the moral imperative of halting the arms race.

One final note here: In St. Peter's Basilica Jan. 1 of this year, Pope John Paul gave a homily on peace in which he called the attention of the Catholic world and humanity in general to the "immediate and terrible consequences of a nuclear war." Referring to a scientific report, the pope cited the following:

> Death, by direct or delayed action of the explosion, of a populace that might range from 50 million to 200 million persons . . .
>
> In a city stricken by a nuclear explosion, the destruction of all urban services. The terror provoked by the disaster would prevent the supplying of the slightest aid to the inhabitants, creating an apocalyptic nightmare . . .
>
> Just 200 of the 20,000 bombs already estimated to exist would be sufficient to destroy most of the large cities of the world.

These few reflections are enough to raise the question: Can we continue along this way? The answer is clear.

Archdiocesan Counseling Centers

May I say a few words about the decision of the Justice and Peace Commission to establish counseling centers throughout the archdiocese.

Millions of young men in this country are now confronted with the fact of registration for military service. The decisions that young people have to make with regard to registration and the draft are serious moral issues that will shape the course of their lives and the future of the country. They have a right to expect assistance from the church in this time of decision.

The overall Catholic response must always be: Peace must guide the destinies of peoples and all humankind. This principle is the basis of all our thinking and the direction of all our efforts.

The American bishops, while acknowledging the duty of the state to defend society and its correlative right to use force in certain circumstances, have also affirmed the Catholic teaching that the state's decision to use force should always be morally scrutinized by citizens asked to support the decision or to participate in war. We therefore support the right of conscientious objection as a valid moral position derived from the Gospel and Catholic teaching. We support the right of selective conscientious objection.

The present circumstance regarding registration and possible conscription is complex. The issues are not clear. Therefore various responses are possible. We realize that, motivated by love of God and country, young persons may come to different conclusions. Some may refuse to register. Some may see it as their duty to defend their neighbors by bearing arms, while others may be motivated to resist bearing arms. In our counseling centers the counselors will not impose a point of view.

The main thrust of our outreach, therefore, is to offer assistance to all young people who may be faced with possible conscription which could, in turn, lead to actual military combat.

Personal Convictions

I have spoken to you about the message of Jesus and about the church's teaching, especially as it appears in recent statements from the papacy and the American bishops. I would now like to share with you some of my personal convictions.

I do not come to give you easy answers or simple solutions to the complex problems of world peace, economic development and international tensions. I do come to place before you some deep personal convictions of my own conversion after much study, prayer and reflection.

I was a young boy during World War II. I remember clapping during the war movies when our American planes shot down the Nazi or Japanese planes. I have never served in the military. I have lived in and deeply enjoyed the freedom of this country and the many gifts of being an American citizen.

In the 1960s I was influenced by the anti-war activists whose questions forced me to question the morality of our country's involvement in Vietnam. I have seriously studied and publicly spoken out on questions of war, peace and disarmament, and our Christian duty to be peacemakers. I pray the Lord will have mercy on me for my years of silent dissent and lack of interest in a priority of the church's mission that must be at the top of the list.

These are some of my convictions about war and peace. I make my own the words of Bishop Maurice Dingman of Des Moines:

> I do not have answers, but I do plead for constant and patient dialogue that will lead to your formation of conscience. There must be an alternative to war.

Peace is the work of justice. There is a moral imperative to halt the arms race because of the twofold impact it has on the world community: It poses a continuing threat of devastation on a scale unprecedented in human history; and it distorts the priorities of all nations by diverting massive resources from the policies and programs required to meet the needs of large segments of the human family. For example, if half a million dollars were given daily to the poor for each day of the 2,000 years since the birth of Jesus, the sum would not equal last year's world armament budget. This moral imperative of halting the arms race extends to the vertical arms race of the super-powers and to the horizontal arms race as it engages more and more nations in the acquisition of both nuclear and conventional weapons.

The moral imperative is lucidly clear and direct in its content; it is also enormously difficult to achieve in practice. The fulfillment of the imperative in our day requires the concerted efforts of many sectors of life: governments, non-governmental agencies, religious communities, private and public institutions, men and women of good will. This evening is a symbol of what needs to be happening on a daily basis throughout the world. Religious leaders need to see and to teach that the halting of the arms race is a religiously mandated task, not a purely technical or political concern.

I personally oppose the arms race. I believe any form of nuclear war is morally wrong. I also believe it is morally wrong to threaten to use nuclear weapons as a deterrent.

The real question we must ask is: How can we as Christians bring our understanding of gospel values to the resolution of international conflicts and tensions? If you personally or, for example, as future directors of international corporations pursue those values that run contrary to many current American economic values, you will have tremendous impact on the world. Even at a human level of basic self-interests, we may not live to enjoy the fruits of our labors. With all the blessings we have received from modern technology, we have also created the means to destroy our entire civilization.

I am a person who is often terrified by thoughts of the world's annihilation by nuclear warfare. Lord Mountbatten, one of the leading military officers of the 20th century, argued strongly against the use of nuclear weapons shortly before his sudden and tragic death:

> There are powerful voices around the world who still give credence to the old Roman precept—if you desire peace, prepare for war. This is absolute nuclear nonsense ... A new world war can hardly fail to involve the all-out use of nuclear weapons. Such a war would

not drag on for years. It could all be over in a matter of days.

And when it is all over, what will the world be like? Our fine buildings, our homes will exist no more. The thousands of years it took to develop our civilization will have been in vain. Our works of art will be lost. Radio, television, newspapers will disappear. There will be no means of transport. There will be no hospitals. No help can be expected for the few mutilated survivors in any town to be sent from a neighboring town—there will be no neighboring towns left, no neighbors, there will be no help, there will be no hope.

Yet I am a believer in God's gift of peace to the entire human family. Peace-building is a continuous effort, a constant struggle to find alternatives to war. It takes education and action. I am convinced the church in its hidden treasury of teaching can become a powerful influence in the world to mold public opinion and to assist the one human family in finding the peace that the world cannot give.

Challenge to Mount St. Mary's

Our Catholic academic centers have traditionally dedicated themselves to explore and to question the issues and events of our world in such a way that we might live more enlightened lives in accordance with the values of the Gospel of Jesus and the heritage of the church.

Perhaps no greater challenge faces us in our contemporary world than the realities of the escalating arms race and the growing threat of a nuclear holocaust. Recently some of the scientists who helped to invent the atom bomb gathered in New Mexico to commemorate their role. They lamented the fact that this instrument, originally intended to be a weapon which would bring lasting peace, had become a new device causing a human nightmare, the possible devastation and annihilation of humankind. We are indeed perilously on the edge of nuclear suicide.

As a college which calls itself a confessional school dedicated to the values and teaching of Jesus, may I invite you to consider how each and all of you might be committed to studying and researching alternatives to war?

What would it be like if Mount St. Mary's were known as a "peace college"? How would the attitudes, values, atmosphere of this campus change? What would it look like if there were academic courses and programs which researched the roots of war, studied and developed peaceful and non-violent means to remedy the causes of war and violence? Is it possible to dream about a Mount St. Mary's corporately discussing and promoting something like SALT II, calling for a ban on nuclear proliferation, pointing out the consequences of the MX missile, the Trident submarine, the neutron bomb, and the like?

Can we re-image ourselves as a Roman Catholic, confessional, academic community in search for a new international economic order, responding to the global questions of hunger and malnutrition, the energy crisis, refugees, world mineral resources, environmental pollution, etc.? Can we perceive ourselves as a college dedicated to the critical questions of our times?

Are you educating yourselves to know the meaning of war and peace, the political, social, economic and cultural realities which make for a world of violence and death, and, in contrast, what values and projects lead to a world of peace and life?

The most important question: Are you studying and living a spirituality of peace which comes primarily from the Gospels of Jesus? Are you familiar with the teachings of the three popes of peace? Do you study their reflections starting with *Peace on Earth* of John XXIII to John Paul II's talk to the United Nations last fall?

Are you praying for peace and life in your personal prayer and in your public liturgical prayer? Do you preach homilies on peace?

Have you, as a whole community, ever considered joining Pax Christi? Is there a study group of this kind on this campus today?

These are some of my questions. I am certain each of you, whether you are a member of the administration, faculty or student body, can dream about the tremendous potential you have to contribute to a worldwide movement for justice and peace.

Be a sign of hope in the darkness, in the midst of violence and death, in the madness of the escalating arms race. Say no to war and to the means of war and yes to becoming a community dedicated to researching peaceful alternatives to war and violence.

Our task is to provide for the world a sign and source of hope that we can bring the arms race under control. It is a sign that must be proclaimed in speech and action. In the face of the massive complexity of the nuclear age, people easily become paralyzed by a sense of helplessness. This paralysis can place us at the mercy of the technological dynamic of the arms race. Against this tendency toward paralysis, we must keep alive the hope of peace. The church and all religious communities call persons to recognize that hope for humankind does indeed depend on each person accepting responsiblity for peace. We need to make flesh the words of Paul VI before the United Nations:

> No more war, war never again. Peace! It is peace that must guide the destinies of peoples and all humankind.
>
> May you be happy and blessed for bringing the peace of Christ to fruition, for you shall be numbered among the people of God.

[11]   U.S. Conference of Catholic Bishops, Pastoral Letter on Marxism, November 13, 1980

Pope John XXIII devoted the entire pastoral section of his encyclical *Pacem in Terris* to this issue:

> Today the universal common good poses problems of worldwide dimensions, which cannot be adequately tackled or solved except by the efforts of public authorities endowed with a width of powers, structures and means of the same proportions: that is, of public authorities which are in a position to operate in an effective manner on a worldwide basis. The moral order itself, therefore, demands that such a form of public authority be established (*Pacem in Terris*, 137).

The church recognizes the depth and dimensions of the ideological differences that divide the human race, but the urgent practical need for cooperative efforts in the human interest overrules these differences. Hence Catholic teaching seeks to avoid exacerbating the ideological opposition and to focus upon two problems requiring common efforts across the ideological divide: keeping the peace and empowering the poor. Conscious of the great delicacy and complexity of keeping the peace in the age of nuclear deterrence and proliferation, the supreme pontiffs of the past four decades have, again and again, turned their attention to the question of war and peace. John XXIII insistently appealed:

> Justice, then, right reason and humanity urgently demand that the arms race should cease; that the stockpiles which exist in various countries should be reduced equally and simultaneously by the parties concerned; that nuclear weapons should be banned; and that a general agreement should eventually be reached about progressive disarmament and an effective method of control (*Pacem in Terris*, 112).

The efforts to control the proliferation of arms, however, ought to be a work of true cooperation, aimed at effective control of the nuclear arms race in all its dimensions. Moreover, the Christian's obligation to work for world peace does not require that he cease to recognize the right to autonomy of nations or national groups that have been illegitimately deprived of their freedom.

[12] Bishop Frank J. Harrison, Bishop of Syracuse, Catechetics and the Work of Justice, March 24, 1981

I am writing to you on the occasion of the first anniversary of the death of Archbishop Romero of El Salvador. I am asking a strong, positive response to our mission of promoting justice and peace education throughout our diocese. As you may know, the ministry of justice and peace is among the three highest priorities for diocesan and local planning during the next five years. Education and catechesis for peace and justice is important not only to realize that priority; as the 1971 synod reminds us, justice is a constitutive dimension of catechesis itself. So I have directed the education vicariate to make the dimension of justice and peace stronger in all our forms of educational ministry, and I am asking for your active support of this work.

The teachings of our modern popes, the Second Vatican Council and my fellow American bishops point unmistakably to the centrality which justice and peace concerns occupy in authentic catechesis. We hardly need the reminder that such catechesis and the action that flows from it are urgently, even desperately, needed in our world and in our time. We would be fools to underestimate the problems and challenges facing us as a nation and as a world. Yet we would likewise be false to our faith, our hope and our power in Christ Jesus if we gave the impression that we had nothing to say, nothing to give or did not possess a God-given mandate to act on behalf of justice and peace in the world.

As leaders in this ministry, you are the persons who do and should spell out the ways justice and peace education should proceed in your communities. To assist and support you in your work, the education vicariate has new materials and resource listings that will be available to you in the near future. Education staff persons will soon be meeting to plan various regional, cluster and parish opportunities to share and learn ways in which we can do a more effective job of justice education. My task as your bishop is to proclaim this vital dimension of the teaching ministry and to ask for your best efforts.

* * *

Peace, Violence, Respect for Life
National weapons systems, the arms race and readily available personal weapons are unfortunate facts of life to which we have, alas, become accustomed. Violence to individuals, in families, in communities and between great and small nations betrays the peace to which we are called. In themselves those experiences of violence are sources of injustice and chaos for each of us.

* * *

To all this sinfulness of persons and structures, the Gospel says a clear no. To all these problems, humane, Christ-like remedies can and must be found. And as followers of Christ, we are called to bring both relief and justice to all those suffering injustice in whatever form it occurs. As Catholic Christians we have the resources and the clear command to join with all men and women of good will to teach and live a better way.

[13] Archbishop Raymond Hunthausen, Bishop of Seattle, Address at the Pacific Northwest Synod of the Lutheran Church in America, July 12, 1981

I am grateful for having been invited to speak to you on disarmament because it forces me to a kind of personal disarmament. This is a subject I have thought about and prayed over for many years. I can recall vividly hearing the news of the atomic bombing of Hiroshima in 1945. I was deeply shocked. I could not then put into words the shock I felt from the news that a city of hundreds of thousands of people had been devastated by a single bomb. Hiroshima challenged my faith as a Christian in a way I am only now beginning to understand. That awful event and its successor at Nagasaki sank into my soul, as they have in fact sunk into the souls of all of us, whether we recognize it or not.

I am sorry to say that I did not speak out against the evil of nuclear weapons until many years later. I was especially challenged on the issue by an article I read in 1976 by Jesuit Father Richard McSorley, titled "It's a Sin to Build a Nuclear Weapon." Father McSorley wrote:

> The taproot of violence in our society today is our intention to use nuclear weapons. Once we have agreed to that, all other evil is minor in comparison. Until we squarely face the question of our consent to use nuclear weapons, any hope of large-scale improvement of public morality is doomed to failure.

I agree. Our willingness to destroy life everywhere on this earth for the sake of our security as Americans is at the root of many other terrible events in our country.

I was also challenged to speak out against nuclear armament by the nearby construction of the Trident submarine base and by the first-strike nuclear doctrine which Trident represents. The nuclear warheads fired from one Trident submarine will be able to destroy as many as 408 separate areas, each with a bomb five times more powerful than the one used at Hiroshima. One Trident submarine has the destructive equivalent of 2,040 Hiroshima bombs. Trident and other new weapons systems such as the MX and cruise missiles have such extraordinary accuracy and explosive power that they can only be understood as a buildup to a first-strike capability.

First-strike nuclear weapons are immoral and criminal. They benefit only arms corporations and the insane dreams of those who wish to "win" a nuclear holocaust.

I was moved to speak out against Trident because it is being based here. We must take special responsibility for what is in our own back yard. And when crimes are being prepared in our own name, we must speak plainly. I say with deep consciousness of these words that Trident is the Auschwitz of Puget Sound.

Father McSorley's article and the local basing of the Trident are what awakened me to a new sense of the gospel call to peacemaking in the nuclear age. They brought back the shock of Hiroshima. Since that re-awakening five years ago, I have tried to respond in both a more prayerful and more vocal way than I did in 1945. I feel the need to respond by prayer because our present crisis goes far deeper than politics. I have heard many perceptive political analyses of the nuclear situation, but their common element is despair. It is no wonder. The nuclear arms race can sum up in a few final moments the violence of tens of thousands of years, raised to an almost infinite power—a demonic reversal of the Creator's power of giving life. But politics is itself powerless to overcome the demonic in its midst. It needs another dimension. I am convinced that a way out of this terrible crisis can be discovered by our deepening in faith and prayer so that we learn to rely not on missiles for our security but on the loving care of that One who gives and sustains life. We need to return to the Gospel with open hearts to learn once again what it is to have faith.

We are told there by our Lord:

> Blessed are the peacemakers. They shall be called children of God. The Gospel calls us to be peacemakers, to practice a divine way of reconciliation. But the next beatitude in Matthew's sequence implies that peacemaking may also be blessed because the persecution which it provokes is the further way into the

kingdom: Blessed are those who are persecuted in the
cause of right. Theirs is the kingdom of heaven.

To understand today the gospel call to peacemaking and
its consequence, persecution, I want to refer especially to these
words of our Lord in Mark:

If anyone wants to be a follower of mine, let that person renounce self and take up the cross and follow
me. For anyone who wants to save one's own life will
lose it; but anyone who loses one's life for my sake,
and for the sake of the Gospel, will save it (Mk.
8:34–35).

Scripture scholars tell us that these words lie at the very
heart of Mark's Gospel, in his watershed passage on the meaning of faith in Christ. The point of Jesus' teaching here is inescapable: As his followers, we cannot avoid the cross given to
each one of us. I am sorry to have to remind myself and each
one of you that by "the cross" Jesus was referring to the
means by which the Roman Empire executed those whom it
considered revolutionaries. Jesus' first call in the Gospel is to
love of God and one's neighbor. But when he gives flesh to that
commandment by the more specific call to the cross, I am
afraid that like most of you I prefer to think in abstract terms,
not in the specific context in which our Lord lived and died.
Jesus' call to the cross was a call to love God and one's neighbor in so direct a way that the authorities in power could only
regard it as subversive and revolutionary. "Taking up the
cross," "losing one's life," meant being willing to die at the
hands of political authorities for the truth of the Gospel, for
that love of God in which we are all one.
      As followers of Christ, we need to take up our cross in the
nuclear age. I believe that one obvious meaning of the cross is
unilateral disarmament. Jesus' acceptance of the cross rather
than the sword raised in his defense is the Gospel's statement
of unilateral disarmament. We are called to follow. Our security as people of faith lies not in demonic weapons which

threaten all life on earth. Our security is in a loving, caring God. We must dismantle our weapons of terror and place our reliance on God.

I am told by some that unilateral disarmament in the face of atheistic communism is insane. I find myself observing that nuclear armament by anyone is itself atheistic and anything but sane. I am also told that the choice of unilateral disarmament is a political impossibility in this country. If so, perhaps the reason is that we have forgotten what it would be like to act out of faith. But I speak here of that choice not as a political platform—it might not win elections—but as a moral imperative for followers of Christ. A choice has been put before us: Anyone who wants to save one's own life by nuclear arms will lose it; but anyone who loses one's life by giving up those arms for Jesus' sake, and for the sake of the Gospel of love, will save it.

To ask one's country to relinquish its security in arms is to encourage risk—a more reasonable risk than constant nuclear escalation, but a risk nevertheless. I am struck by how much more terrified we Americans often are by talk of disarmament than by the march to nuclear war. We whose nuclear arms terrify millions around the globe are terrified by the thought of being without them. The thought of our nation without such power feels naked. Propaganda and a particular way of life have clothed us to death. To relinquish our hold on global destruction feels like risking everything, and it is risking everything—but in a direction opposite to the way in which we now risk everything. Nuclear arms protect privilege and exploitation. Giving them up would mean our having to give up economic power over other peoples. Peace and justice go together. On the path we now follow, our economic policies toward other countries require nuclear weapons. Giving up the weapons would mean giving up more than our means of global terror. It would mean giving up the reason for such terror—our privileged place in the world.

How can such a process of taking up the cross of non-violence happen in a country where our government seems paralyzed by arms corporations? In a country where many of the citizens, perhaps most of the citizens, are numbed into passivity by the very magnitude and complexity of the issue while being horrified by the prospect of nuclear holocaust? Clearly some action is demanded—some form of non-violent resistance. Some people may choose to write to their elected representatives at the national and state level, others may choose to take part in marches, demonstrations or similar forms of protest. Obviously there are many ways that action can be taken.

I would like to share a vision of still another action that could be taken: simply this—a sizable number of people in the state of Washington, 5,000, 10,000, 500,000 people, refusing to pay 50 percent of their taxes in non-violent resistance to nuclear murder and suicide. I think that would be a definite step toward disarmament. Our paralyzed political process needs that catalyst of non-violent action based on faith. We have to refuse to give incense—in our day, tax dollars—to our nuclear idol. On April 15 we can vote for unilateral disarmament with our lives. Form 1040 is the place where the Pentagon enters all of our lives and asks our unthinking cooperation with the idol of nuclear destruction. I think the teaching of Jesus tells us to render to a nuclear-armed Caesar what that Caesar deserves—tax resistance. And to begin to render to God alone that complete trust which we now give through our tax dollars to a demonic form of power. Some would call what I am urging "civil disobedience." I prefer to see it as obedience to God.

I must say in all honesty that my vision of a sizable number of tax resisters is not yet one which I have tried to realize in the most obvious way—by becoming one of the number. I have never refused to pay war taxes. And I recognize that there will never be such a number unless there are first a few to give the example. But I share the vision with you as a part of my own struggle to realize the implications of the Gospel of peace given us by our Lord. It is not the way of the cross which is in question in the nuclear age, but our willingness to follow it.

I fully realize that many will disagree with my position on unilateral disarmament and tax resistance. I also realize that one can argue endlessly about specific tactics, but no matter how we differ on specific tactics, one thing at least is certain. We must demand over and over again that our political leaders make peace and disarmament, and not war and increased armaments, their first priority. We must demand that time and effort and money be placed first of all toward efforts to let everyone know that the United States is not primarily interested in being the strongest military nation on earth, but in being the strongest peace advocate. We must challenge every politician who talks endlessly about building up our arms and never about efforts for peace. We must ask our people to question their government when it concentrates its efforts on shipping arms to countries which need food, when it accords the military an open checkbook while claiming that the assistance to the poor must be slashed in the name of balancing the budget, when it devotes most of its time and energy and money to developing war strategy and not peace strategy.

Creativity is always in short supply. This means that it must be used for the most valuable purposes. Yet it seems evident that most of our creative efforts are not going into peace but into war. We have too many people who begin with the premise that little can be done to arrange for a decrease in arms spending since the Soviet Union is bent on bankrupting itself on armaments no matter what we do. We have too few people who are willing to explore every possible path to decreasing armaments.

In our Catholic Archdiocese of Seattle I have recommended to our people that we all turn more intently to the Lord this year in response to the escalation of nuclear arms, and that we do so especially by fasting and prayer on Monday of each week. That is the way, I believe, to depend on a power far greater than the hydrogen bomb. I believe that only by turning our lives around in the most fundamental ways, submitting ourselves to the infinite love of God, will we be given the vision and strength to take up the cross of non-violence.

The nuclear arms race can be stopped. Nuclear weapons can be abolished. That I believe with all my heart and faith, my sisters and brothers. The key to that nuclear-free world is the cross at the center of the Gospel and our response to it.

The terrible responsibility which you and I have in this nuclear age is that we profess a faith whose God has transformed death into life in the person of Jesus Christ. We must make that faith real. Life itself depends on it.

Our faith sees the transformation of death through the cross of suffering love as an ongoing process. That process is our way into hope of a new world. Jesus made it clear that the cross and empty tomb didn't end with him. Thank God they didn't. We are living in a time when new miracles are needed, when a history threatened by overwhelming death needs resurrection by Almighty God. God alone is our salvation, through the acceptance in each of our lives of a non-violent cross of suffering love. Let us call on the Holy Spirit to move us all into that non-violent cross of suffering love. Let us call on the Holy Spirit to move us all into that non-violent action which will take us to our own cross and to the new earth beyond.

[14]   Archbishop Raymond Hunthausen, Bishop of Seattle, Interview from *Our Sunday Visitor* by Bruce Smith, August 9, 1981

Visitor: Why do you think there has been such a tremendous response to your speech on disarmament?

Hunthausen: I am convinced it's because I said something about taxes. Disarmament, on its own, might have created some stir, but both issues together have certainly caused the interest.

V: What type of reaction have you been receiving within the Seattle Archdiocese?

H: We are hearing a whole mixture of things. The response is much more positive than negative by about three or four to one. There have been some strong statements by people who

are opposing my stand but, as I said, they have been more positive than negative.

V: Have you had any response from other members of the hierarchy?

H: I had sent copies of the speech to all of the bishops in Region 12. I saw several of the bishops from Region 12 and they
definitely support the statement. A number of them, though,
say they haven't brought themselves to the position of tax resistance. But I haven't either.

I think the media is zeroing-in on the tax issue to the
point where they are seeing that as the primary issue. I don't
think that is the primary issue at all. The issue in my mind is
the armaments race. It continues to escalate.

I don't feel I am saying anything different than the Holy
Father is saying or the Second Vatican Council said on the armaments race. But nothing has happened through all of those
statements. I feel that if it is an immoral position, if it is an
immoral direction we are moving in, then, as people of God,
we have to continue to say something about it. We have to be
personally responsible to try to effect that.

V: People are focusing in on the statement of tax resistance.
Have you personally come to a decision to resist by this
means?

H: No, I have not, but I wouldn't tell you if I had. I don't want
people to do this because I am doing it. I want people to examine this, come to a personal stance and, before God, decide
what they are going to do.

The country needs a mandate with this. The current administration is moving toward arms escalation because it feels
it has a mandate. I am not of that opinion. I am not leveling
any blame. I'm just simply seeing the evil of the whole issue. If
there is going to be any change in our country, it has to come
from a response by the people.

People don't know how. We are a little confused, frustrat-
ed and overwhelmed by the complexity and the horrendous
nature of the arms race. Yet, we have to take responsibility for
it.

V: You are, then, advocating that people withhold taxes as a
protest of the arms race?

H: No. My comment (on tax resistance) was more in the nature of wonderment. I was wondering what would happen in
this country if many people did (withhold taxes). I wondered
what kind of change this would effect.

I truly feel that somehow we have to register a shift in direction. I make every acknowledgment of the fact that the position and the whole idea of unilateral disarmament is radical.

I see the Americans and the Russians saying, "we'll do
something if they'll do something." I don't feel that is the major issue. If this is wrong and if it is deeply immoral, as I believe this is, then it seems to me that on the very basis of that,
we have got to be willing to take a step and move in another
direction.

In my talk, I made mention that this is idolatry. We are
putting our faith in weapons of destruction, rather than God.
Acknowledging all the while that these weapons of destruction have gone to such an extent that we are capable, in an in-
stant, of annihilating, we are still willing to live with that. I
don't think as people of God we should be willing to accept
that.

V: There has been some criticism of you that an archbishop
shouldn't be making strong statements on issues such as this.
What is your response?

H: I think that an archbishop and the Church have the responsibility to relate what is happening in the world to the people.
And there is nothing affecting the life of our people more dra-
matically than is the arms race.

Some would argue that I should never have mentioned

tactics. I make the recommendation of unilateral disarmament and some would say that I have no right to do so and that maybe I should have stopped by simply pointing out the moral or immoral nature of something that exists in our world. I personally feel that is unrealistic. One has to say, "if it is immoral, what are we going to do about this?"

I simply make some suggestions. I am not telling people what to do. But I am urging them to face up to their personal responsibilities in the matter.

V: What kind of scenario do you see taking place if the United States unilaterally disarmed?

H: There is no way I can tell you that. There's no way I can paint that picture. But if, as a people, we were willing to come to that stance, this would signify to me a deep conversion on our part. We would be seeing ourselves and the world in a totally different way.

We are not likely to unilaterally disarm unless we have a change of heart. That change of heart would bring all sorts of additional changes in the way we spend our money, how we help people, what we do with diseases, hunger and the needs of the world. These are going begging now.

That wouldn't necessarily change the Russians. There again, it seems to me that one has to make a faith response. I emphasize repeatedly that this is a call to faith, not a political statement. It is a call to people to recognize God in their lives. I would hope that there was a move to somehow unilaterally disarm. We would be establishing a trust level that has never been established.

It is not going to be easy and it is not going to be instantaneous. Before that trust level is established, we may even be laughed at. All sorts of scenarios could develop. We could be the brunt of all sorts of unsavory reactions. At the same time, we could hope for a different reaction.

The arms race is a numbers game. We have got the power to overkill I don't know how many times. It makes no sense. It is idiocy. And yet we get caught up in that syndrome and we don't seem to be able to get away from it. People will argue, "Yes, it is a numbers game. It's the only way to keep the peace." My own feeling is that if we continue in the direction we are aimed, it is evident what is going to happen. I am not at all certain what is going to happen if we head in this other direction (unilateral disarmament), but there is certainly more hope there. Particularly when one puts his peace and confidence and trust in God.

V: Does the same basic pacifism you profess about nuclear arms apply to conventional weapons as well?

H: I suppose I would say that is where I am coming to personally. You could put this back into a discussion on the Just War Theory—that the theory goes out the window when you are talking about nuclear arms because the proportionality (the good gained outweighs the violence wrought) is gone.

I think that is fanciful to talk about. To say that it is okay to engage in war with conventional weapons but not with nuclear weapons is playing games . . .

It depends on the circumstances and I think it has been demonstrated over the last number of years here in the United States. It has been stated that we are maintaining a defense posture and not a first strike posture. Our weapons today belie that. We are certainly in a position for a first strike.

V: Basically, your call to a kind of war-tax resistance is a call to civil disobedience. What are your views on civil disobedience?

H: I am not advocating anything in violation of the law. Law is to be honored. But I am saying that this is of such magnitude, that the values are in such conflict, that it takes a violation of the law, a breaking of the law, to gain attention or to satisfy one's conscience.

We continually look back at Nazi Germany and say, "How could they have not said or not done something about the Holocaust?" I am of that mind at the moment. It is the same kind of moral dilemma. An individual has to say, "Am I or am I not a part of it?" and, if so, "How do I register that and what do I do about it?"

V: Is that the reason you compared the local Trident submarine base with Auschwitz?

H: No, not really. Any place where there is a nuclear weapon can be considered an Auschwitz. This is true wherever there is such an installation and we must draw the comparison to the millions that were destroyed in Nazi Germany and the infinitely more people we can now destroy with the weaponry we have available. Admittedly, we haven't done it. But we do possess the willingness . . .

[15] Bishop Anthony M. Pilla, Bishop of Cleveland, World Peace—The Call of the Church, August 6, 1981

In the Sermon on the Mount, Jesus promised his followers that they would be called children of God, but he accompanied the blessing with a condition: "Blessed are the peacemakers . . ." This is a call to action, a call to work for peace and promote harmony among all peoples, a call to build up the Kingdom of God. As with every action which Jesus demands, the call to peacemaking requires a committed response on our part. There is no place for half-heartedness or reserve in pursuit of peace. Jesus expects the total response of mind, heart, body and spirit. He gives us his Spirit to help us make a response appropriate to our particular time in history and the conditions which endanger us.

Never before in the history of humanity has the power for the destruction of so many human lives been so concentrated in the hands of so few persons. Even the overwhelming destruction of human life during the years 1939–1945 cannot compare with the annihilation possible with nuclear weapons. Daily our lives are affected by a preoccupation with the arms race. Therefore, the Spirit of God is leading Christians and other believers alike to re-examine their stands on war and armaments. The Spirit is asking us to question in faith whether we can tolerate even the possibility of nuclear war in the face of the Lord's call to love God and our neighbor, our enemies and those who persecute us. Moved by the Spirit, recent popes have been unrelenting in their condemnation of nuclear arms and war as a solution to political differences. They denounce them in strong terms, calling them "a treacherous trap for humanity," "a terrible mechanism of general destruction."

The Catholic Church throughout history has stood firmly for the protection of human life in all its forms. Murder, violence, and abortion are all condemned as crimes against God and humanity because they deprive persons of life. The questions addressed here deal with the greatest destroyer of human life: war. In light of our capacity to make and use weapons powerful enough to destroy all living things on Earth, those who follow Christ and believe in the sanctity of human life must ask themselves: Can war be justified in our nuclear age? What are the moral implications of thermonuclear technology and the arms race? In what terms should Catholics and Christians think about the questions raised by the awesome power of atomic weapons? What are the modern teachings of the Catholic Church on war and nuclear technology?

Those who build atomic weapons defend them by arguing that they are necessary to maintain peace; that their production creates jobs; that the threat of them is preventing World War III; that the more we have, the safer we are. These arguments rationalize the arms race, but they do not morally justify it. As Christians, we must counter such militaristic logic with a whole new set of moral questions. As Catholics, we look to the teachings of the Church for guidance in answering the questions we raise.

St. Augustine's theory of a "just war," teachings of Vatican II and the popes since John XXIII, the speeches of John Paul II before the United Nations and at Hiroshima, and research of various independent Catholic groups help us formulate our own responses to the questions we raise. It is imperative, given the potential for Earth's destruction in the advent of a nuclear war, that conscientious Christians examine these issues and take serious action to address them. The gift of life is at stake.

Traditionally, the Catholic Church has used St. Augustine's doctrine of a just war to determine whether a nation has moral grounds for becoming involved in a military conflict. This doctrine was developed as an alternative to the more perfect but less practical pacifist approach which condemned all violence without exception. According to St. Augustine, a nation or people would not be denounced for waging war if and only if the following criteria were met:

1. The decision for war must be made by a legitimate authority.
2. The war must be fought for a just cause.
3. War must be taken only as a last resort.
4. There must be a reasonable chance of "success."
5. The good to be achieved by the war must outweigh the evil that will result from it. (Proportionality)
6. The war must be waged with just means (in accordance with natural and international law).

If even one of these conditions were not met in a particular conflict, that conflict would be perceived by the Church as contrary to the fifth commandment, morally reprehensible, and a crime against God. The criteria are so constructed that though they allow some wars to be perceived as just, most fall into the latter category and are condemned.

St. Augustine's standards were applicable to traditional, non-nuclear wars, limited engagements between professional soldiers on defined battlegrounds. However, when the United States dropped the first atomic bomb on Hiroshima in 1945, an entirely new dimension was added to military conflict. Nuclear weapons made possible the total destruction of entire innocent civilian populations in a very short amount of time. Not only was such annihilation against rules 5 and 6 of the just war doctrine, it far overstepped rule 4 by giving the aggressor overwhelming odds for success. Also, the simplicity and power of one atomic warhead made rule 1, assent of a legitimate authority, and rule 2, need for a just cause for aggression, easily bypassable by anyone in control of a bomb. Finally, the presence of nuclear technology led to the "first strike" philosophy and the arms race, thus negating rule 3. So nuclear weapons clearly break all St. Augustine's standards for justice. Even more, they create the potential for mass destruction *even if* they are used in accordance with the just war doctrine.

Should we have nuclear weapons?
Will the stockpiling of weapons continue indefinitely without resulting in war?
Or will their existence tempt those in power to use them?

Pope John XXIII wrote: "Justice, right reason and humanity ... urgently demand that the arms race should cease; that the stockpiles which exist in various countries should be reduced equally and simultaneously by the parties concerned; that nuclear weapons should be banned, and that a general agreement should eventually be reached about progressive disarmament and an effective method of control" (par. 112, *Pacem in Terris*, 1963). The Bishops of Vatican II said, ". . . the arms race is an utterly treacherous trap for humanity ... If this race persists, it will eventually spawn all the lethal ruin whose path it is now making ready" (par. 81, *Constitution on the Church in the Modern World*, 1965). Pope John Paul II told the United Nations General Assembly in 1979: "The continual preparations for war demonstrated by the production of ever more numerous, powerful and sophisticated weapons in various countries show that there is a desire to be ready for war, and being ready means being able to start it; it also means taking the risk that sometime, somewhere, somehow, someone can set in motion the terrible mechanism of general destruction" (par. 10).

Is the tremendous cost of nuclear weapons a justifiable use of world resources in light of widespread poverty and hunger?
Could those resources be better used to ease human suffering?

According to the Vatican II Bishops, "While extravagant sums are being spent for the furnishing of ever new weapons, an adequate remedy cannot be provided for the multiple miseries afflicting the whole modern world ... The arms race ... injures the poor to an intolerable degree" (par. 81, *Constitution on the Church in the Modern World*). Pope Paul VI's encyclical *On the Development of Peoples* says: "When so many people are hungry, when so many families suffer from destitution, when so many remain steeped in ignorance, when so many schools, hospitals and homes worthy of name remain to be built, all public or private squandering of wealth, all expenditure prompted by motives of national or personal ostentation, every exhausting armaments race, becomes an intolerable scandal. We are conscious of our duty to denounce it" (par. 53, 1967). John Paul II's encyclical, *Redemptor Hominis*, is even more specific: "We all know well that the areas of misery and hunger on our globe could have been made fertile in a short time, if the gigantic investments for armaments at the service of war and destruction had been changed into investments for food at the service of life" (par. 110, 1979). The Holy See's 1976 statement to the U.N. General Assembly says, "Even when they are not used, by their cost alone armaments kill the poor by causing them to starve."

Are atomic bombs really deterrents to large-scale war?
Do they promote peace?
Is a peace maintained by their presence really the "Peace of Christ"?

In 1979, Pope John Paul II asked the United Nations: "But can our age still really believe that the breathtaking spiral of armaments is at the service of world peace? In alleging the threat of a potential enemy, is it really not rather the intention to keep for oneself a means of threat, in order to get the upper hand with the aid of one's own arsenal of destruction?" He also said, in his World Day of Peace message: "The very existence of the arms race can even cast a suspicion of falsehood and hypocrisy on certain declarations of the desire for peaceful coexistence. What is worse, it can often even justify the impression that such declarations serve only' as a cloak for opposite intentions" (1980, *Truth: The Power of Peace*). The same sentiment is echoed in the U.S. Bishops' pastoral, *To Live In Christ Jesus*: "Not only is it wrong to attack civilian populations but it is also wrong to threaten to attack them as part of a strategy of deterrence" (1976).

What will be the result if nuclear weapons are used?
Can there be a "limited" nuclear war?

John Paul II told the people of Hiroshima: ". . . nuclear stockpiles have grown in quantity and in destructive power. Nuclear weaponry continues to be built, tested, and deployed. The total consequences of full-scale nuclear war are impossible to predict, but even if a mere fraction of the available weapons were to be used, one has to ask whether the inevitable escalation can be imagined and whether the very destruction of humanity is not a real possibility" (par. 3, *War Is Death*, 1981).

In general, what must the Church do to address
the problems of nuclear weapons and arms escalation?
What alternatives to military conflict can be found to
solve international problems?

Pope Paul VI said: "No more war, war never again! Peace, it is peace which must guide the destinies of peoples" (1965 address before the U.N. General Assembly). The Bishops of Vatican II urged: "New approaches initiated by reformed attitudes must be adopted to remove this trap and to restore genuine peace by emancipating the world from its crushing anxiety" (par. 81, *Constitution on the Church in the Modern World*, 1965). The Synod of the Bishops of the World suggested that

". . . the United Nations (is) the beginning of a system capable of restraining the armaments race, discouraging trade in weapons, securing disarmament and settling conflicts by peaceful methods of legal action, arbitration and international police action. It is absolutely necessary that international conflicts should not be settled by war, but that other methods better fitting human nature should be found. Let a strategy of non-violence be fostered also, and let conscientious objection be recognized and regulated by law in each nation" (par. 65, *Justice in the World*, 1971). The U.S. Bishops' pastoral *To Live In Christ Jesus* recommends ". . . the continued development and implementation of policies which seek to bring these weapons more securely under control, progressively reduce their presence in the world, and ultimately remove them entirely" (1976).

Pope John Paul II has addressed these questions most strongly: "It is therefore necessary to make a continuing and even more energetic effort to do away with the very possibility of provoking war, and to make such catastrophes impossible by influencing the attitudes and convictions, the very intentions and aspirations of governments and peoples" (par. 10, 1979 address to the U.N. General Assembly). "We cannot sincerely condemn recourse to violence unless we engage in a corresponding effort to replace it by courageous political initiatives which aim at eliminating threats to peace by attacking the roots of injustice" (par. 9, *Truth: The Power of Peace*, 1980). "Let us pledge ourselves to peace through justice; let us take a solemn decision, now, that war will never be tolerated or sought as a means of resolving differences; let us promise our fellow human beings that we will work untiringly for disarmament and the banishing of all nuclear weapons; let us replace violence and hate with confidence and caring" (par. 6, *War Is Death*, 1981). "Peace must always be the aim: peace pursued and protected in all circumstances" (par. 5, *War Is Death*, 1981).

What can we do as individuals to begin working toward peace?
How can small religious groups—parishes, schools, clergy and lay communities, diocesan agencies—address these problems of worldwide significance?

In our church community, we can pledge time and energy to pray over, consider, discuss, and implement the following suggestions:

1. Opposing modern war and weaponry as strongly as we oppose abortion, racism and poverty. We can use pulpits, classrooms, parishes, and all church institutions to encourage Catholics to understand and to act on the official Church teachings about war and peace. Some ways to do this are:

  a. Establishing a Peace and Justice Committee in each parish as a functioning part of the Parish Council.
  b. Asking each Deanery, the Deanery Forum, the Commission on Catholic Community Action, and the Social Concerns Commission of the Diocesan Pastoral Council to study the above statement and consider how they can implement it.
  c. Instituting an annual Peace Week to advance peace education in the diocese.
  d. Suggesting ways the new Communications Collection can promote education on peace and modern war through mass media.
  e. Planning Liturgies for national holidays to raise awareness of the difference between patriotism and militarism.
  f. Examining the relationship of Catholic educational institutions to the military and to industry that supports nuclear armaments.
  g. Establishing programs for peace studies and education for the educators (e.g. clergy institutes, teacher training, Lenten series, Alternatives to Violence courses, etc.).

2. Urging Catholics involved in the production of weapons of mass destruction to reconsider the moral implications of their jobs; those who are asked to give or obey orders to use nuclear weapons ought to meditate on the morality of such actions.

3. Helping Catholics form right consciences regarding military service and training; efforts should be made to extend recognition under the law to selective conscientious objection.

4. Encouraging Catholics to support efforts to establish a World Peace Tax Fund as an alternative to "praying for peace and paying for war."

5. Giving serious thought to the implications of maintaining a lifestyle based on unbridled consumerism and energy consumption while a majority of the world's population suffers need and deprivation.

6. Suggesting that the Friday rule of abstinence serve as a personal penitential act commemorating the Crucifixion, as a symbolic sharing in the deprivation of the world's poor (caused in great part by the arms race).

7. Training draft counselors, keeping on file statements for men choosing to be conscientious objectors, and training Catholics to represent the religious voice on draft boards.

8. Supporting and participating in the Nuclear Weapons Freeze Campaign and similar efforts.

How can we be patriotic if we take these positions?

Those who govern us do so by our consent. Patriotism neither presupposes nor requires acquiescence to their every decision. Our nation's democratic traditions support, indeed are hinged upon, the right and responsibility of the governed to question and scrutinize the decisions and policies of public officials. Our country has witnessed much social progress in the last two decades, notably in civil rights, because of the courage of relatively few people who were willing to challenge the policies and practices of the many.

Even more important, our Christian responsibility requires us to bring Gospel values to bear on the actions of our governments. As the prophets criticized the immorality of the societies in which they lived, so we must unite to oppose the evils inherent in our own political system. The emphasis placed on military buildup and weapons proliferation in our country is one such evil.

* * *

Our moral obligation as Christians and Catholics is to support and defend all human life. The presence of nuclear weapons and the readiness of those in power to use them contradict that obligation. Therefore, it is imperative that we take action *now* to end the proliferation of nuclear arms, the reliance on militarism, and the use of war to alleviate international problems. We can no longer delay. The risk to human life is too great. As John Paul II told the people of Hiroshima:

> Some people ... might prefer not to think about the horror of nuclear war and its dire consequences. Among those who have never personally experienced the reality of armed conflict between nations, some might wish to abandon the very possibility of nuclear war. Others might wish to regard nuclear capacity as an unavoidable means of maintaining a balance of power through a balance of terror. *But there is no justification for not raising the question of the responsibility of each nation and each individual in the face of possible wars and of the nuclear threat.* (par. 2, 1981) (emphasis added)

[16]   Archbishop John Roach, Bishop of St. Paul-Minneapolis, On decision of President Reagan to stockpile the neutron bomb, August 12, 1981

Pope John Paul II closed his address to the United Nations in 1979 with a challenge to the logic of the arms race:

> The ancients said: 'If you want peace, prepare for war!' But can our age still really believe that the

breathtaking spiral of armaments is at the service of
world peace? In alleging the threat of a potential enemy, is it really not rather the intention to keep for
oneself a means of threat, in order to get the upper
hand with the aid of one's own arsenal of destruction?

The decision of the Reagan administration to develop and
stockpile the neutron (enhanced radiation) warhead in the
United States should be evaluated in light of the Holy Father's words. It is a grave question whether the decision enhances the fragile and precarious stability of the nuclear
balance of terror or whether, in fact, it simply adds to the
"breathtaking spiral of armaments" which both superpowers
are relentlessly pursuing.

In 1978 my predecessor, Archbishop John R. Quinn,
voiced concerns about the development of the neutron warhead by the Carter administration. On the same grounds, I
share these concerns about its development by the Reagan ad-
minstration. It is useful to recall Archbishop Quinn's position,
since the content of the political-moral problem has not
changed since 1978. He said:

It can be argued that this weapon is less objectionable
than existing tactical nuclear weapons.... In terms
of traditional moral theology this characteristic
would be judged as a favorable recommendation for
this type of weapon.

In making an ethical judgment on the neutron
warhead, however, I believe it is necessary to calculate its moral implications in a broadly defined
framework. A principal consideration is the impact of
this decision on the arms race. I am concerned, in the
spirit so often expressed by Pope Paul VI, that we
forestall any major decisions which will intensify the
nuclear arms spiral.

A second argument against development of the
neutron warhead is that the introduction of this new
and more "manageable" weapon tends to narrow the

gap politically and psychologically between conventional war and nuclear war. In other words, it could render more probable the escalation of any war in Europe to the level of nuclear warfare.

The significant difference between 1978 and 1981 is not the content of the problem posed by the neutron warhead, but the context in which the decision to develop this tactical nuclear device is made. There seems to be renewed interest in policy circles today about the possibility of fighting and containing a nuclear war. That interest has in turn produced proposals for strategies and weapons designed to show our adversaries and allies that we have the capacity and will to undertake "limited" nuclear war if necessary.

The very danger against which Archbishop Quinn warned in 1978 appears closer to realization today: the almost unconscious process of reducing the political, psychological and strategic barriers to the use of nuclear weapons. The decision to develop the neutron warhead may contribute to this process. Before proceeding with this decision, we should ask what is gained by contributing to the conviction that nuclear war under any circumstance could be a rational policy choice or a justifiable moral course.

In his testimony supporting the ratification of the SALT II agreements, Cardinal John Krol said: "The primary moral imperative of the nuclear age is to prevent any use of strategic nuclear weapons." The observance of this imperative requires that it be used to judge any strategic doctrine, weapons systems or strategies which comprise the arms race. We can gravely impair future prospects for reversing the arms race by decisions made on weapons and strategies today. One must seriously ask whether the decision to develop the neutron warhead blurs the distinction between conventional war and the qualitative moral-political leap one makes in moving to nuclear war in any form.

The questions and concerns of the statement are based on the conviction that the political and moral barriers to nuclear war should be made clear and stronger today. I question whether the neutron warhead serves that objective.

[17] Bishop Leroy T. Matthiesen, Bishop of Amarillo, Nuclear Arms Buildup, August 21, 1981

The announcement of the decision to produce and stockpile neutron warheads is the latest in a series of tragic anti-life positions taken by our government.

This latest decision allegedly comes as a response to the possibility of a Soviet tank attack in central Europe.

The current administration says the production and stockpiling of neutron bombs are a logical step in a process begun in 1978 under the previous administration.

Thus both Democratic and Republican administrations seem convinced that in accelerating the arms race they are carrying out the wishes of the American people.

The matter is of immediate concern to us who live next door to Pantex, the nation's final assembly point for nuclear weapons, including the neutron bomb.

It is clear now the military can—perhaps must—think in only one way: Each enemy advance in arms technology and capability must be met with a further advance on our part. No matter that the enemy must then, perforce, respond with a further advance of its own. No matter that we already have the capability of destroying each other many times over and that soon other nations of this imperiled planet will possess the same awesome power.

God's gifts may be used for evil or good, for war or peace. The God of Israel warned the people of ancient times that the military use of the horse is "a vain hope for safety. Despite its power, it cannot save" (Ps. 33:17). Is not the military use of nuclear energy likewise a vain hope for safety? Despite its incredible power it cannot save.

Enough of this greater and greater destructive capability. Let us stop this madness. Let us turn our attention and our energies to the peaceful uses of nuclear energies: for the production of food, fiber, clothing, shelter, transportation.

We beg our administration to stop accelerating the arms race. We beg our military to use common sense and moderation in our defense posture. We urge individuals involved in the production and stockpiling of nuclear bombs to consider what they are doing, to resign from such activities and to seek employment in peaceful pursuits.

Let us educate ourselves on nuclear armament. Let us support those who are calling for an end to the arms race. Let us join men and women everywhere in prayer that peace may reign.

[18]   Archbishop John R. Quinn, Bishop of San Francisco, Pastoral Statement: Instruments of Peace—Weapons of War, October 4, 1981

On October 4, 1981, we celebrate the 800th anniversary of an extraordinary man, the Patron Saint of our City, St. Francis of Assisi.

His simple example of service, Gospel poverty, his spirit of prayer, and joyful love of God's creation gave life to the Church and the world of the Middle Ages. Reflecting on the life of St. Francis may remind us of the value of life in the final few years of the twentieth century—and empower us to confront courageously whatever threatens to dehumanize or destroy God's gift of life and peace today.

Francis is the one saint whom all succeeding generations have agreed to canonize. A clear reflection of Christ, he represents for every age a life-giver and healer. He dedicated his life to visiting the hospitals and prisons, he served the sick and gave to the poor: his money, his clothes, himself. His life, rooted in God, and at peace with God in his own heart—he was a maker of peace.

Francis preached by word and deed. He had a special devotion to Christ crucified and followed Christ's radical example of absolute poverty, purity, obedience to the Father's will, brotherly love and simplicity of life. He felt called to follow Christ without withdrawing from the world, and he continually called the world to holiness. The source of his own holiness was his prayer. Throughout his life Francis repeatedly interrupted his activity to retreat to a solitary hermitage to reflect and pray. A contemplative in the world, his relationship with his Creator was so close that he lucidly saw God in all creation and Christ in every human creature.

For the people of our consumer and nuclear age, Francis is again a prophet of poverty and peace. His Christian example reminds us of our critical need for a clear moral perspective on what is unquestionably one of the greatest life or death issues threatening us today: the weapons of nuclear war and our escalating race to produce them.

The Issue

The continued existence of the human race is seriously endangered today by the threat of nuclear destruction. Pope John Paul II spoke of this crisis in his Address to the United Nations on October 2, 1979:

> The continual preparations for war demonstrated by the production of ever more numerous, powerful and sophisticated weapons in various countries show that there is a desire to be ready for war, and being ready means being able to start it. ... It is therefore necessary to make a continuing and even more energetic effort to do away with the very possibility of provoking war ... (nn. 10–11).

The famous German theologian, Romano Guardini, commented at the end of World War II that the preeminent human question for the last half of the twentieth century would be whether we could develop the moral capacity to control the power we had created. The phrasing here is important: our dilemma arises from the fact that we have created a vast military technology without thinking through its moral implications.

This same dilemma was raised by Albert Einstein who, at the dawn of nuclear age, recognized the enormous and terrible impact of nuclear bombs: "The splitting of the atom has changed everything save our modes of thinking, and thus we drift toward unparalleled catastrophe."

In considering a Christian response to the arms race, we must, as Einstein warns, change our very ways of thinking. Nuclear weapons are not simply conventional weapons on a larger scale. They are qualitatively of a whole different order of destructiveness. Their tremendous explosive force, as well as their enormous and terrible side effects, will irrevocably alter our ecological system, genetic structures for generations to come, and the fundamental fabric of our social systems. The neutron bomb, for example, even though it is being promoted as a "clean" bomb for use only as a "theater" or "tactical" weapon, is a deadly instrument of mass destruction, and its use could easily ignite a global nuclear conflagration. It contributes to the dangerous illusion that a "limited" nuclear war can be fought and won.

At the present time, the United States has a stockpile of nuclear weapons equivalent to 615,000 times the explosive force of the bomb dropped at Hiroshima. With that stockpile we can destroy every major Soviet city 40 times over. The Soviet Union, in its turn, can destroy every major American city 17 times over. The Soviet and U.S. stockpiles together contain the equivalent of 12 tons of TNT for every man, woman and child in the entire world.

At the end of the 1950's, both Russia and America had already amassed enough weapons to absorb a first strike and still destroy the other's society completely. Nevertheless, the U.S. continues to build 3 nuclear warheads every day. This madness has continued year after year, and it accounts for a large portion of the $1.6 *trillion* which has been budgeted for the Pentagon over the next five years. The military research and procurement budget for 1986 is set at just under $1 billion per day.

In human terms, excessive spending on arms production takes lives just as surely as if the weapons produced had actually been put to use. The extreme poverty that is endured by one-third of the human race is in large part a direct byproduct of an arms race out of control. The billions of dollars presently being spent on arms each year throughout the world is surely an appalling form of theft in a world where so many persons die each day of starvation and privation.

The obsessive drive for security through nuclear weaponry has not brought security, either for the 6 nations which now have strategic nuclear capacity, or for the 40 other nations who will possess that capacity by 1985. Rather, by straining the world economy and diverting resources from urgent human needs, the arms race has intensified international instability and has itself become the major threat to security among nations.

The physical and social destruction which would result from a nuclear blast borders on the unthinkable. It is now clear to a growing segment of the medical community that no effective medical response can be conceived to deal with the human suffering and damage that would result. All efforts must therefore be directed toward prevention; healing after the fact will be beyond the physicians' art.

All of these facts constitute the context of Pope John Paul II's moving statement at his recent visit to Hiroshima: "To remember Hiroshima is to abhor nuclear war. To remember Hiroshima is to commit oneself to peace. . . . Let us promise our fellow human beings that we will work untiringly for disarmament and the banishing of all nuclear weapons; let us replace violence and hate with confidence and caring."

The Teaching of the Church

Where does the Church derive its moral teaching on questions of war and peace? The Gospels present the pattern that must be normative in all our reflections: "You shall not kill, and whoever kills shall be liable to judgment" (Mt. 5:21); "Put away your sword. Those who live by the sword will die by the sword" (Mt. 26:52); "Love your enemies, do good to those who treat you badly" (Lk. 27:36).

The Gospel teaching does not rule out the right of nations

to protect themselves against unprincipled and dangerous enemies. Modern Popes have recognized our right to responsible self-protection. For example, Pope Paul VI taught in his address to the United Nations General Assembly: "As long as men and women remain those weak, changeable and wicked beings that they often show themselves to be, defensive arms will, unfortunately, be necessary" (October 4, 1965).

The moral problem arises, however, when the effects of our defensive weapons are no longer fully predictable or within our control. As long ago as 1954, Pope Pius XII raised this problem and clearly taught that when warfare "involves such an extension of . . . evil that it entirely escapes from human control, its use must be rejected as immoral. . . . The pure and simple annihilation of all human life . . . is not permitted for any reason whatsoever" (Address to Delegates of the Eighth Congress of the World Medical Association, in Rome, September 30, 1954).

The teaching of the Church is clear; nuclear weapons and the arms race must be condemned as immoral.

A pivotal statement of this doctrine is found in the Second Vatican Council's *Pastoral Constitution of the Church in the Modern World*. There the Council warns:

> The horror and perversity of war are immensely magnified by the multiplication of scientific weapons. For acts of war involving these weapons can inflict massive and indiscriminate destruction far exceeding the bounds of legitimate defense. . . . With these truths in mind, this most holy Synod makes its own the condemnation of total war already pronounced by recent Popes, and issues the following declaration: **Any act of war aimed indiscriminately at the destruction of entire cities or of extensive areas along with their population is a crime against God and humankind. It merits unequivocal and unhesitating condemnation.** (n. 80)

Such a strong condemnation is inevitable when we judge the realities of nuclear warfare in the light of the Church's traditional "just war" principles. Those classic moral principles clearly teach that for a war to be even reluctantly permitted, all of the following conditions must be met:

1. The decision for war must be made by a legitimate authority.
2. The war can be fought only to defend against unjust agression.
3. War must be waged only as a last resort.
4. There must be a reasonable chance of achieving the objective for which the war is waged.
5. The good to be achieved by the war must outweigh the evil that will result from it. This is called the principle of proportionality. One cannot "destroy a city in order to save it."
6. The war must be waged according to the principles of natural and international law. For instance, indiscriminate mass destruction of civilian populations is never justified, for whatever reason.

If we apply each of these traditional principles to the current international arms race, we must conclude that a "just" nuclear war is a contradiction in terms. Even a brief comment on only the final two of these principles will serve to support that conclusion.

Strategic nuclear weapons are designed precisely and exclusively to destroy entire cities and their populations. It is hard to imagine a more lethal instrument of indiscriminate mass destruction of civilian non-combatant populations.

Furthermore, physicians, physicists and even military planners have described all too graphically the biological, environmental and genetic damage that will result for generations from the explosive and radioactive power of a single thermonuclear weapon. What good could possibly be proportionate to such uncontrollable destruction and suffering? Is it

likely that survivors of such a holocaust could describe themselves in any sense as victors?

Our Response

My brothers and sisters, not only the peace of the world
but the very survival of the human experiment is at stake. If
we accept the inescapable conclusion that, as the Church
clearly teaches, nuclear weapons and the arms race are essentially evil, what kind of response are we called upon to make?

None of us can answer that question for another; we must
each answer for ourselves. Some may be called, like Francis
800 years ago, to a radically prophetic response. Open to the
voice of the Spirit within us, we must find our own response to
the deadly nuclear challenge as individuals, as families, and
as a community of faith and hope. I would suggest three areas
in which we might support one another in this common affirmation of life.

First, I invite all Catholics of the Archdiocese to join with
me in setting aside one day every month as a day of prayer
and fasting for an end to the arms race. This personal and
communal penitential act will both witness to our total dependence on God and affirm our faith that it is ultimately only
God's grace which can change our hearts in this critical time
of need. I would suggest the First Friday, or, in honor of St.
Francis, the fourth day of each month.

Further, I recommend that broad-based educational programs on the teaching of the Church regarding nuclear weapons and the arms race be created in parishes, schools, colleges
and universities of the Archdiocese, and that peace and justice
committees be established in every parish. The Archdiocesan
Commission of Social Justice stands ready to be of every possible assistance in these efforts.

And finally, I urge you to find practical expression for
your Christian concern in the political and social arenas.
Three particular possibilities for action come immediately to
mind.

First, there is a growing national campaign calling for a
"Nuclear Arms Freeze," i.e., a halt right now to any further

development or deployment of nuclear weapons by the United States or the Soviet Union. As a first realistic step toward a process of bilateral disarmament, I urge your active cooperation with other religious and community groups in this campaign.

Second, since many in the medical community are now convinced that it is dangerously deceptive to pretend there can be any effective medical response in the case of a thermonuclear attack, I urge the administrators and staff of Catholic Health Facilities to join all those who are vigorously opposing the intentions of the Department of Defense to establish a "Civilian-Military Contingency Hospital System" if this System is based on the illusion that there can be an effective medical response in the case of nuclear war.

Third, much greater support is needed for developing creative proposals for converting military weapons technology to civilian production uses. Such a restructuring of national priorities must begin at the local level and in a variety of industries. I urge you to become aware of the alternatives which are being explored in this important area, and to express your active interest and concern to legislative representatives at every level.

Conclusion

I call upon all the Catholic people of the Archdiocese of San Francisco, as well as all people who find in Saint Francis a prophet of peace and non-violence, to work for bilateral disarmament and the elimination of nuclear weapons. Let us replace violence and mistrust and hate with confidence and caring. Let us make our own the prayer of St. Francis of Assisi:

> Lord, make me an instrument of Your peace.
> Where there is hatred, let me sow love;
> Where there is injury, pardon;
> Where there is doubt, faith;
> Where there is despair, hope;
> Where there is darkness, light;

Where there is sadness, joy.
O Divine Master, grant that I may seek not so much
    to be consoled
As to console;
To be understood as to understand;
To be loved as to love;
For it is in giving that we receive;
It is in pardoning that we are pardoned; and
It is in dying that we are born to Eternal Life.

[19] The Canadian Conference of Catholic Bishops, Neutron Bomb, October 26, 1981

Humanity seems to be rushing at breakneck speed to nuclear self-destruction. There is a growing sense among people today that the arms race is out of control. A global holocaust within this generation looms as a distinct possibility. The superpowers appear insensitive to the stakes involved, namely the annihilation of life on this planet which the Lord of Creation called "GOOD" (Gen. 1:5).

Into this world, already overshadowed by nuclear overkill, comes the neutron bomb. It is the latest and the most devastating weapon to appear on the assembly line of death. In a tragic twist of irony, the United States government announced its decision to proceed with the development of the neutron bomb on August 9 of this year, the thirty-sixth anniversary of the atomic bomb attack on the people of Nagasaki.

The teachings of the Church have steadfastly resisted the arms race. "Any act of war," declared the Fathers of the Second Vatican Council, "aimed indiscriminately at the destruction of whole cities . . . and their inhabitants is a crime against God and humanity itself." The Church has repeatedly declared that "the arms race is to be condemned unreservedly," "it is an injustice," "it is a form of theft," "it is completely incompatible with the spirit of humanity and still more with the spirit of Christianity."

In Hiroshima this year, Pope John Paul II spoke of "a new world-wide consciousness against war and a fresh determination to work for peace." The Holy Father went on to say that "there is no justification for not raising the question of the responsibility of each nation and each individual in the face of the nuclear threat." The development of the neutron bomb compels us to deal with some profound issues facing the future of our common humanity on this planet.

The American decision pushes the United States and the Soviet Union into a perilous cold war climate. Rather than making us more secure, it creates conditions that heighten international insecurities which could lead to the first nuclear strike. Indeed, "limited nuclear war" is a dangerous game which threatens to turn our planet into a giant crematorium.

The neutron bomb, with its "enhanced radiation warhead," particularly offends the deepest sensibilities of humanity. To describe a bomb as "clean" because it preserves *property* and destroys only *people* simply demonstrates how morally bankrupt our civilization has become. To exult in the destruction of humanity while saving inanimate property violates our most cherished ideals: namely that people are made in the image of God and that human life has a sacred value. Indeed, nothing else illustrates quite so clearly the perversion of values in our time.

We therefore join our fellow bishops in the United States and the growing number of American citizens in condemning the decision of their government on the neutron bomb. We also ask members of the Catholic community and the people of Canada to oppose vigorously the build-up of nuclear arms by all nations and especially the United States and the Soviet Union. At some point we must say: STOP. That time is now.

We believe, for the sake of its own citizens and the rest of the world, the Canadian government must take its responsibility to do everything possible to challenge the United States' initiatives on the neutron bomb. The proliferation of nuclear weapons, especially by one of the superpowers, is a critical problem of global proportions. As a member of NATO and a partner with the Americans in a military alliance, the time has come for Canada to insist that all governments face the moral and political responsibilities of nuclear armament.

In days of old, the prophet Isaiah warned: "Woe to others ... who build their hopes on cavalry, who rely on the number of chariots and on the strength of mounted men but never look to the Holy One of Israel." (Isaiah 31:1) Moreover, Jesus taught us not only to be good citizens but also to remember our creaturehood and let God be God. "Give back to Caesar what belongs to Caesar and to God what belongs to God." (Luke 22:21)

Today we urge members of the Catholic community and all citizens to join in the struggle against nuclear arms. We call on you to make your opposition known to all government decision makers. We pledge ourselves to support creative initiatives seeking the conversion of warlike mentalities and social change for justice and peace. In this regard, we particularly emphasize the work of Development and Peace.

Finally, we invite all families and Christian communities to pray to the Lord for guidance along the path of authentic peace based on "justice and social love."

[20]   Archbishop John R. Roach, Bishop of St. Paul–Minneapolis, Address on the State of the Church, November 19, 1981

RELIGION'S RIGHTS

After a year of serving as your President I am even more grateful to you for this privilege than I was when I accepted a year ago. In honesty, however, I must tell you that if you think that Archbishop John Quinn was radiant a year ago when he completed his term, wait until you see me two years from now. I am so grateful to Bishop Kelly and his staff and to all of you for the cooperation and support which I have felt each day during this past year.

As a rule of thumb for keeping friends, "never discuss re-

ligion or politics" has a long history in our culture. It has received the status of the secular commandment. At times it is
even taken as a corollary of the constitutional principle of separation of church and state.

I agree fully with the principle of separation of church
and state. I do not agree that absence of dialogue about and
between religion and politics serves either the church or the
state. Three complementary considerations support the propo-
sition that we should reverse cultural custom and initiate an
explicit, public, systematic dialogue about the relationship of
religious communities and the political process in the United
States.

Moral Choice

The first case can be drawn from the content of existing
public policy discussion in the land. Whether we like it or not,
a whole range of policy choices are permeated by moral and
religious themes today: from the debate on abortion to decision making about Poland, from care of the terminally ill to
the fairness of budget cuts, the direction our society takes
must include an assessment of how moral and religious convictions relate to the technical dimensions of policy.

The second case is based on the content of the religious
traditions as they are understood and expressed today. Our
own faith community is an example but not an isolated instance of how the social vision of faith increasingly calls the
Church to a public theology and public witness on political
questions.

The third case is drawn from existing social atittudes in
our country. Recently the Connecticut Mutual Life Insurance
Company sponsored a survey on "American Values in the
1980's." The report concludes:

> Our findings suggest that the increasing impact of re-
> ligion on our social and political institutions may be
> only the beginning of a trend that could change the
> face of America.

This conclusion is based on data showing that people with strong religious convictions influence the political process out of proportion to their numerical strength. This fact can be evaluated in different ways. History teaches vividly that the expression of religious conviction through the political process is not necessarily a blessing to a society. The key question is how religious belief is related to political practice. This is the question which requires that a systematic discussion of religion and politics take place within our religious organizations and in the public arena where people of all faiths and no religious faith are called as citizens to set the direction of our society. A systematic discussion from a Catholic perspective involves two themes: The Church's own understanding of her role in society; and the expression of that role in regard to specific public issues.

I. RELIGION IN POLITICS: THE INSTITUTIONAL QUESTIONS

There are two questions which shape our role in society: The theological question and the constitutional question. The theological question is the way the Church has articulated the content of its social ministry. When the United States Catholic Conference addresses El Salvador or the impact of budget cuts on the poor, when bishops speak on the arms race, when Catholics individually or collectively oppose abortion and capital punishment in defending the sanctity of life, then it must be made clear that these actions are rooted in, directed by, in fulfillment of a theologically grounded conception of the Church's ministry.

That ministry in the socio-political order is shaped by two themes. The first is the religious conviction about the dignity of the human person and the spectrum of obligations and rights through which human dignity is preserved and promoted in the political process. These concepts have been key ideas in the Catholic tradition from the first social encyclical, Leo XIII "On the Condition of Labor," to John Paul II's "On Human Work." In the intervening years of the 20th Century, each of the social encyclicals has defended the dignity of the person in the face of diverse and changing threats to human dignity and human rights.

The moral vision of the social ministry was qualitatively strengthened by a second theme: the ecclesiology of Vatican II in "The Pastoral Constitution on the Church in the Modern World." The decisive contribution of the Pastoral Constitution is the way it defined the protection of human dignity and the promotion of human rights as properly ecclesial tasks, an integral part of the Church's ministry. This marriage of the moral vision and the ecclesial vision provides the basis of the social ministry. In the language of the Council, the task of the Church in the political order is to stand as the sign and safeguard of the dignity of the person.

Political Context

To fulfill this role in a political context requires that the Church not only teach the moral truths about the person, it must also join the public debate where policies are shaped, programs developed and decisions taken which directly touch the rights of the person, locally, nationally and internationally. This is precisely what John Paul II was talking about in speaking to American Catholics in his homily at Yankee Stadium:

> Within the framework of your national institutions and in cooperation with all your compatriots, you will also want to seek out the structural reasons which foster or cause the different forms of poverty in the world and in your own country, so that you can apply the proper remedies.

When the Church responds to this theological imperative, the constitutional question arises: how should it fulfill its social role in the context of the American and political tradition? Specifically, can the Church play an active role without violating separation of church and state?

In answering that question it is essential to recognize the

distinction between state and society. The Western Constitutional tradition embodies the judgment that the state is a part of society, and not to be identified with all of society. Beyond the state is a realm of free political activity where individuals and groups act to give content to the fabric of social life.

On the basis of this distinction between state and society, a twofold affirmation can be made about the Church's role in society. On the one hand, Catholic theology can and should support and defend the separation of church and state, the principle that religious organizations should expect neither favoritism nor discrimination because they are religious. On the other hand, we should not accept or allow the separation of church and state to be used to separate the church from society. To accept this would be to reduce the Church, or any religious organization to a purely private role. This, in turn, would prevent the Church from fulfilling an essential dimension of its ministry: preaching the Gospel truth about every dimension of existence, personal and social, public and private, individual and institutional moral questions. At the constitutional level, there is no conflict between the theological vision which calls the Church to active engagement in the social arena and the American political tradition which provides for religious organizations to participate in shaping society as voluntary associations imbued with the needed moral and religious vision. The concept of religious divisiveness is not only ill-founded in relation to our constitutional tradition: it is noxious when it is used to inhibit this participation.

The theological and constitutional questions shape our understanding of the Church's role in society. They set the foundation for engaging the issues which are the heart of social ministry.

H. RELIGION AND POLITICS: THE ISSUES AND THE INSTITUTIONS

Before examining specific issues it is appropriate to deal with a current, highly visible instance of these general principles. A focal point in the debate about religion and politics has been the role played by the Moral Majority. In my judgment two points should be made.

First, some have argued that the Moral Majority's role is an example of why religion and politics should be kept absolutely separate, and religious organizations should be silent on political questions. I reject this contention while defending the right, in the terms defined above, of the Moral Majority or any religious organization to address the public issues of the day.

The right of religious organizations, of varying views, to speak must be defended by all who understand the meaning of religious liberty and the social role of religion. But religious organizations should be subjected to the same standards of rational, rigorous presentation of their views as any other participant in the public debate. Moreover, religious organizations, which address the moral dimensions of public issues, are to be judged by the standards of competent moral analysis. Particularly relevant are the issues of "how one defines a moral issue" and the consistency with which moral principles are defended across a range of moral issues.

These same standards of discourse are the ones by which our position should be tested. Neither the rigor of reasonable argument nor the controversy which surrounds the role of religion and politics should make us timid about stating and defending public positions and key issues. Allow me to indicate the direction of a consistent moral vision rooted in Catholic social thought.

On a global scale, the most dangerous moral issue in the public order today is the nuclear arms race. The Church in the United States has a special responsibility to address this question, a responsibility underscored by Pope John Paul in his remarks at the White House in 1979. The United States Catholic Conference has addressed the issue often, most notably in Cardinal Krol's testimony in the Salt II agreements.

It is an unhappy fact that strategic arms control discussions are presently stalemated, even as the technological and strategic dynamics of the arms race proceeds. It is perhaps the convergence of these two themes which has moved a number of American bishops to address the arms race recently in terms that are both prophetic and profoundly important.

Moral Urgency

Certainly the sense of moral urgency about the arms race is what stands behind the establishment of our Committee on War and Peace about which Archbishop Bernardin, its chairman, will speak at this meeting. Without prejudging the complex work of that committee as it sets our future direction on the arms race, it is useful to say clearly what we already know from Catholic teaching. The Church needs to say "no" clearly and decisively to the use of nuclear weapons. This is surely the direction of Vatican II teachings on the arms race and its condemnation of attacks on civilian centers. The "no" we utter should shape our policy advice and our pastoral guidance of Catholics.

It is not useful to blur the line of moral argument about the use of nuclear weapons at a time when the secular debate is openly discussing the use of limited nuclear weapons and winnable nuclear wars.

Second, the abortion issue: the horrors of nuclear war, though hardly fantasies, are possibilities at present. But the horror of legalized permissive abortion is tragically real. The destruction of unborn life now occurs in the nation at the staggering rate of one and one-half million abortions annually.

Nearly nine years after the Supreme Court decision of 1973 initiated this carnage, who can doubt that it is time to say, enough! Human dignity and human rights are mocked by this scandal. The concept of just law is mocked by the evasions used to create and continue it.

There is, thank God, some reason for encouragement at present. Our elected representatives increasingly recognize the need to correct the situation. As you know, Senate Hearings are now taking place on proposals for this purpose. Our Conference has recently given its support to one of these, a realistic constitutional remedy which holds out hope for undoing the damage done by the abortion decision. I call upon all pro-life people to unite at this crucial moment.

Law, of course, is not the total solution to the evil of abortion. We remain committed to the proclamation of the Gospel message concerning sanctity of human life, and to the practical steps and programs required to eradicate the conditions which cause some to turn to abortion as a solution to personal or social problems. But we also recognize the need for a remedy in law, in order to undo the harm done under the guise of law. Without this, "the sanctity of human life" can only be a hollow phrase.

The Poor

Third, the poor among us. Papal statements on the arms race have consistently condemned it because of the misallocation of scarce resources it entails. These statements have typically referred to the global level of the issue, but at a time of scarce resources here they take on meaning in a domestic debate on social policy. The proposed expenditure of 1.5 trillion dollars for defense over the next five years stands in stark constrast to budget cuts which threaten the food, the health care and the education of the poor. In the past it was presumed in the United States that we could spend whatever we decided for defense and still be a compassionate society. That assumption is today denied in fact; what is spent for guns directly reduces what is available for the quality of care and life for the least among us.

In the past few years we have often heard from the Church in Latin America the pastoral principle of "the option for the poor". Implementing that principle in our more complex economy faces different challenges. But the principle also has meaning for us. It means that while we are concerned about the larger "macro" questions of the economy, we will give specific weight to how any overall solution touches the poor.

We are called to this role of advocacy for the poor not only by our social teachings but also by our experience in the Campaign for Human Development and Catholic Charities across the country. This ministry with and for the poor confirms the moral vision of our teaching. The Old Testament prophets were right: the quality of our faith is tested by the character of justice among us.

We know from experience the impossible choices the poor face in our society, not between guns and butter, but between bread and rent, between money for heating oil and the need to pay for health care for children. We know also that private agencies of the nation cannot fill the gap created by recent cuts. We have neither the resources nor, I suppose, even the mandate to do this. We will do our part, but our own social teaching calls upon the state to do its part.

Religion and politics always come back to the person, to the way society respects or fails to respect a person. The Church must raise its voice clearly about justice, because choices now before us as a nation can erode the conditions which support human dignity. Today those of us who visibly represent a religous vision must be clear about our task. We must carry forward the debate about religion and politics because both have a central contribution to make to preserving all that is valuable in the life of each person and the lives of all the people who constitute this society. To serve the person is to honor the Creator. We are called to reverence both in our ministry.

[21] **Archbishop Joseph Bernardin, Bishop of Cincinnati, Report on War and Peace, U.S. Bishops' Annual Meeting, Washington, D.C., November 16-19, 1981**

WAR AND PEACE

There is abroad in the Church today an intense concern about the nuclear arms race and the danger it poses for ourselves and others. In response to that concern, the leadership of the NCCB judged it necessary to set aside time for an oral report on the work of the NCCB ad hoc Committee on War and Peace. As chairman of that Committee, I wish to share with you some perspectives on its work, and to receive your counsel and your views on this most urgent moral question.

In these remarks I will review the Committee's origin, indicate the framework of Catholic teaching within which we will function and examine some of the questions and issues we face.

The Committee's Origin and Composition

The Committee had its origin in a resolution of 1980 General Meeting of the NCCB. After an extended exchange among the bishops on a variety of questions regarding the moral and pastoral challenge posed by modern warfare, we voted to pursue a study which would review the NCCB position thus far and would set a direction for the Episcopal Conference in the future. In light of this resolution Archbishop Roach asked me to chair the Committee; Bishops George Fulcher, Thomas Gumbleton, John O'Connor and Daniel Reilly have agreed to serve with me. I wish to express my appreciation to each of them, since it is clear that we have undertaken an extremely delicate and difficult task. The Committee will be staffed and assisted by Mr. Edward Doherty and Father Bryan Hehir from the USSC. They in turn will be assisted by Professor Bruce Russett of Yale University. Professor Russett is a professor of political science. He is presently the editor of *The Journal of Conflict Resolution,* one of the leading peace research journals in the United States. He brings exceptional qualifications to this task. The Committee is also privileged to have Sister Juliana Casey, I.H.M. and Father Richard Warner, C.S.C., from the LCWR and CMSM, assisting it in its work.

Our Committee did not become operative until late spring. We have had two meetings, and have drawn up a roster of consultants spanning the fields of biblical studies, moral theology, foreign and defense policy and strategic experts, as well as interested Catholic voices in local movements on war and peace. We will receive the views of these various witnesses in our deliberations. Our report to the bishops, which we will propose for consideration as a pastoral letter of the NCCB, will be ready for the 1982 November meeting.

The Framework of Catholic Teaching

As bishops doing a moral-religious analysis of contemporary warfare within the tradition of Catholic moral teaching, we do not start from scratch. As religious leaders in a nation which possesses an awesome arsenal of destructive power, we are also heirs of a body of moral teaching from the universal Church, and we have ourselves contributed to that teaching by our previous statements on war and peace. In addition, there is available to us a significant corpus of theological commentary, as well as several contributions from individual bishops in our conference over the past several years. Within the past few months, a substantial number of Bishops have spoken strongly and explicitly on a number of issues, particularly the escalating arms race.

A thorough review of Catholic teaching on war and peace would require an assessment of biblical and patristic literature as well as significant contributions from every major era of Catholic theology. Particularly revelant for our work, however, is the papal and conciliar teaching of the nuclear age, reaching from Pope Pius XII through Pope John Paul II.

The *Pastoral Constitution on the Church in the Modern World* (P.C.) of Vatican II has a unique status among recent statements, since it has set the theological framework for Catholic thinking about contemporary warfare. The conciliar text called the Church to undertake an evaluation of warfare with an entirely new attitude, and it provided an example of what that attitude should be. The P.C. made four principal contributions to the moral debate about war and peace.

First, in its assessment of scientific weapons of mass destruction, of which nuclear weapons are the principal example, it uttered a clear condemnation. It condemned attacks on civilian centers or large populated areas as a crime against God and humanity (par. 80). Second, it supported the right of conscientious objection, a pacifist position, in the clearest statement we have yet in Catholic teaching. Third, it reasserted the right of nations to acts of legitimate defense, an acknowledgement that some uses of force, under restricted conditions, could be justified. Fourth, it raised but did not resolve the moral issues posed by the doctrine of nuclear deterrence.

I have said that the P.C. has set the framework of Catholic thinking on war in the last fifteen years. This is not due to an absence of other statements since 1965, but because these other statements reflect the elements of the conciliar teaching. Primary among them have been the Day of Peace messages of Paul VI and John Paul II, the powerful statement of the Holy See to the United Nations in 1976 and the Address of John Paul II at the United Nations in 1979.

The theological and pastoral consequences of the P.C. have not produced one single viewpoint in the Church but have resulted in a series of related positions. We have seen the emergence of a significant school of Catholic pacifism, now supported by an authentic statement of Catholic teaching. We have seen others use the traditional moral categories of noncombatant immunity, just cause, and proportionality to enter the Vietnam debate as well as the debate on U.S. nuclear policy. Most recently, the unfinished agenda of the conciliar text, a judgment on the possession of nuclear weapons for deterrence purposes, has become a central issue for many groups in the Church both in the United States and Europe.

While these developments have been generating in the wider ecclesial community, our episcopal conference has taken a series of positions from 1968 to 1980. The principal texts have been the pastoral letters, *Human Life in Our Day* (1968) and *To Live in Christ Jesus* (1976), along with Cardinal Krol's testimony on SALT II before the Senate Foreign Relations Committee (1979) and the Administrative Board's *Statement on Registration and the Draft* (1980). Our statements have reflected the wider debate in the Church, but they have also contributed to it on key issues. We have spoken to some issues with more specificity than any other episcopal conference.

In *Human Life in Our Day* and then in subsequent statements in 1972 and 1980, we acknowledged the continuing legitimacy of service in the military as a service to society, but we also endorse the right of conscientious objection, a pacifist position, and selective conscientious objection, a conclusion which can be drawn from traditional just war theory. These three categories have particular pastoral relevance, since they are designed to aid an individual faced with either voluntary or compulsory military service. In *To Live in Christ Jesus,* we made our first explicit judgment on the possession of nuclear weapons, arguing that not only the use but the threat to use them against civilian centers is wrong.

Cardinal Krol's 1979 testimony rendered a more extended evaluation of the nuclear question. It made three interrelated moral judgments. First, the primary moral imperative is to prevent any use of nuclear weapons under any conditions. Second, the testimony judged that the possession of nuclear weapons in our policy of deterrence cannot be justified in principle, but can be tolerated only if the deterrent framework is used to make progress on arms limitation and reductions. The third principle, a corollary of the second, is the imperative for the superpowers to pursue disarmament. Indeed, as Cardinal Krol stated, the phasing out altogether of nuclear deterrence and the threat of mutual assured destruction must always be the goal of our efforts.

This body of moral teaching, along with the theological commentary it has stimulated, provides us with some firm principles and it leaves us with some open questions. The Vatican Council's teaching on the responsibility of personal conscience on the issue of warfare has already had an effect in the life of the Church, and calls us to provide for effective methods of conscience formation on issues of war and peace. The Council opened the deterrence question and left it for precisely the kind of debate we now see in the Church. Cardinal Krol's testimony has led many to ask if the failure to move toward meaningful arms limitation in the last two years will yield a new judgment on deterrence policy from the bishops. Our statement on the draft in 1980 calls for further elaboration if the possibility of a draft moves closer.

It is precisely these questions, and others too numerous to

mention which face the Committee. The escalating pace of the arms race intensified the moral urgency to address such issues. Let me share with you now some thoughts on major areas of concern which surely will be the subject of our deliberations.

The Questions and the Issues

My purpose in this concluding section is to provide some issues which illustrate but are not meant to exhaust the scope of the Committee's concerns.

The first question is the need for a positive theology of peace. Much of the traditional moral literature has been aimed at limiting the destructiveness of war; such moral teaching has been and will continue to be needed. The thrust of the P.C. and the major papal texts of the last twenty years, however, call for a more comprehensive and constructive approach to the question of war and peace. We are summoned to a positive theology of peace. This is surely implied in Vatican II's mandate to evaluate war with an entirely new attitude. We must find ways to call the Christian community to be a sign and source of peace in our society.

In developing a theology of peace we will need to draw upon many resources. The contribution of pacifist thought has not been a central theme in Catholic theology for many centuries. One should not simply equate a theology of peace with a pacifist position, but we will need to probe the nonviolent philosophy and position in our deliberations.

Secondly, the stringent limits placed on the use of force in the modern age by the popes from Pius XII to John Paul II need to be affirmed and their implications examined today. In evaluating which, if any, reasons can justify the use of force in the modern age, we will be shadowed by the nuclear threat at every step. But our experience with the moral turmoil provoked by Vietnam highlights the need for an assessment on non-nuclear uses of force. Periodically in the last decade the threat of an oil boycott has produced proposals that the United States be prepared to fight a conventional war over oil. Some of these proposals seem to take it for granted that the justification to do this for oil or other resources is self-evident. In an age of interdependence, when access to resources is ever before us, and when developing countries have a new determination to exercise their sovereign rights over resources in their territory, the traditional categories of just cause, right intention, and proper authority to initiate the use of force may take on renewed importance as tools to assess policy proposals and intentions in our society. Sharpening the just cause questions may give us a valuable instrument to evaluate a self-proclaimed right to access to resources even at the price of war.

While both a theology of peace and an examination of conventional war are difficult issues, it probably will be the moral problem of nuclear war which will present the Committee its most challenging task. This is so for a number of reasons.

First, the United States first developed atomic and hydrogen weapons and used atomic weapons with consequences so frightful that Paul VI and John Paul II have both said it can never be allowed to happen again. Both as Catholics and Americans we hold a special responsibility to see that this first nuclear use is also the last.

Second, the United States is among the countries which have concentrated on the development of nuclear weapons of greater accuracy. Increasingly we have built our national security around these weapons.

Third, in recent years the nuclear strategy of the United States has supplemented our reliance on deterrence with a greater declaratory willingness to fight "limited" nuclear wars, although much expert opinion seriously doubts the limits can be maintained.

Fourth, as I have indicated, the position taken by the American bishops raises challenging questions about U.S. policy. The failure, after so many years, of effective arms limitation, the growing official readiness to contemplate the use of nuclear weapons, and the introduction of highly integrated command and control systems, which may heighten the thrust toward automatic use of our weapons if deterrence fails, all make the need to evaluate existing policy more evident. How we make that evaluation, competently and credibly, is perhaps the most difficult assignment before the Committee.

It is important to note that the hierarchies of Holland, Germany, and England, in response to many in their care, are conducting inquiries into these issues of nuclear policy. It will be highly desirable that we maintain contact with them throughout our study.

It is also important to note that, in undertaking this project, we are fully aware that current tensions are by no means attributable to U.S. policy alone. Clearly, the enormous build-up of nuclear and conventional arms pursued by the Soviet Union in recent years has done more than its share to heighten the peril of the present moment. The duty of responsible moral action falls equally on both superpowers. But if we direct our attention particularly to the United States, it is for the simple reason that we are American citizens and have a right and duty to address our government.

The purpose of all our effort in this study is to fulfill our role as teachers regarding a question which has enormous significance for human life in our time. It will be our objective to speak first to the Church. In this regard, our goal must be not only to state the teaching of the Church on nuclear warfare clearly but to find ways and means to bring this teaching to our parishes, pulpits and schools.

As teachers we must also be concerned about the quality of the public debate. The Church should bring to this debate the best arguments which reason can muster. But beyond this we should bring convictions that help us keep perspective in the face of such an awesome question as nuclear war. We need to be convinced that some actions can never be taken, even for survival; that there are limits to the argument that, because our adversaries are considering something, we must be prepared to do it also. We need to recall that as Americans and as people of faith we are expected to have our own principles, to be prepared to live by them and, in faith, to accept the consequences of doing so.

In the end our study, though political and moral in content, is an expression of an ecclesial responsibility. By living in one of the nuclear superpowers we are called to a specific form of witness. The very created order is threatened by nuclear war. We who believe that we are stewards of life and creation, not its masters, must use all the religious and moral vision we have to prevent a threat to what God has created, what we could destroy but never re-create. The significance of our task must be judged by our awareness of this responsibility. We must learn how to evaluate war with an entirely new attitude.

[22]   29 Bishops' Statement That Possession of Nuclear Weapons Is Immoral, October 1981

As members of the Catholic community in the United States of America we are impelled by our faith vision and our mounting concern over the increased probability of nuclear war to speak our conscience.

1. To place our faith in nuclear weapons will lead to our destruction as a nation.

2. The continuation of the present policy of arms escalation will lead to global disaster by accident, miscalculation, design or madness.

3. The concept of limited 'nuclear war' is folly. The possession of nuclear weapons is immoral.

4. The arms race robs the poor. The arms race wastes the talents of engineers and other highly skilled persons.

5. Continued excessive expenditures for arms has not deterred nor will it deter other nations from acquiring or increasing their nuclear capabilities.

Therefore we call for immediate action on the part of our civil leaders to initiate efforts to stop the arms race by:

1. Supporting an arms freeze

2. Cutting the military budget

3. Taking seriously the UN report on General and Complete Disarmament (Sept. 12th, 1980)

4. Investigating ways to convert our economy to peace time uses.

The Intercommunity Center for Peace and Justice released the names of the following bishops who have endorsed the statement: Bishop Paul F. Anderson, Duluth; Archbishop James V. Casey, Denver; Bishop Thomas J. Costello, Aux., Syracuse; Bishop Elden F. Curtiss, Helena; Bishop Nicholas D'Antonio, Vicar General, New Orleans; Bishop George R. Evans, Aux., Denver; Bishop Joseph A. Ferrario, Aux., Honolulu; Bishop Francisco Garmendia, Aux., New York; Bishop Robert F. Garner, Aux., Newark; Bishop Thomas J. Gumbleton, Aux., Detroit; Bishop Joseph L. Hogan, Ret. Bp., Rochester; Bishop Michael H. Kenny, Juneau; Bishop Thomas Larkin, St. Petersburg; Bishop Steven A. Leven, Ret. Bp., San Angelo; Bishop Raymond A. Lucker, New Ulm; Bishop James P. Lyke, Aux., Cleveland; Bishop Joseph J. Madera, Fresno; Bishop Dominic A. Marconi, Aux., Newark; Bishop Leroy T. Matthiesen, Amarillo; Bishop Joseph L. Imesch, Joliet; Bishop Francis Murphy, Aux., Baltimore; Bishop Francis A. Quinn, Sacramento; Bishop Peter A. Rosazza, Aux., Hartford; Bishop Alphonse J. Schladweiler, ret. Bp., New Ulm; Bishop Walter J. Schoenherr, Aux., Detroit; Bishop Richard J. Sklba, Aux., Milwaukee; Bishop Joseph M. Sullivan, Aux., Brooklyn; Bishop Edward E. Swanstrom, Ret. Aux., New York; Bishop Loras J. Watters, Winona.

[23] Terence Cardinal Cooke, Bishop of New York, Letter to Military Vicariate, December 7, 1981

As we prepare to celebrate the birth of the Prince of Peace, you and the people you serve in the United States Military Vicariate are very much in my thoughts and my prayers.

I am writing to you for two purposes. The first is to respond to inquiries I have received from a number of you; the other is to tell you of a new and important project I am undertaking.

First, the inquiries. These have generally sought further guidance for our Catholic men and women in uniform concerning issues that have been raised here and abroad involving the broad areas of war and peace, with special emphasis on nuclear weapons. I want you to know that I share the widespread concern over these issues. There is a pressing need to pursue peace with justice and to work for the elimination of war. Clearly, the upward spiral in armaments and what it implies must be ended. All reasonable people know that the alternative could be the complete collapse of society, economic disaster, and even, conceivably, the destruction of civilization as we know it. It is encouraging that there are government officials, church leaders and men and women of every walk of life who share a growing sense of urgency and common concern over these matters.

Bishops have a special obligation to present the moral teaching of the Church and to help form the consciences of those people whom they serve. This is always a demanding challenge, and can be, at times, an agonizing task. As Military Vicar, of course, I have a special responsibility for the pastoral care of all Catholics in military service. As you know, Archbishop Joseph T. Ryan, our Coadjutor, and Bishop John J. O'Connor, our Vicar General, are directly associated with me in carrying out that responsibility. They join with me in this letter.

Obviously, at this time, this letter can address only very briefly, and in very simple terms, the main questions that are raised. A much fuller treatment is found in Bishop O'Connor's book, *In Defense of Life,* which I recommend for the guidance of our people.

The key questions we are most frequently asked can be summarized in these two: (1) Has the Church changed its position on military service? (2) Must a Catholic refuse to have anything at all to do with nuclear weapons?

(1) The Church and Military Service.

This can be answered very directly: The Popes, the Second Vatican Council and the Bishops of the United States speaking as a body, have all been very clear on this matter. The position is perhaps best summarized in the words of Vatican

Council II: "All those who enter the military service in loyalty to their country should look upon themselves as the custodians of the security and freedom of their fellow countrymen: and when they carry out their duty properly, they are contributing to the maintenance of peace." *(The Church in the Modern World.)* I do not feel that anything need be added to this. The Church has not changed its position. I am personally proud of the dedication of our military men and women and consider them to be true guardians of peace. They and their families deserve the gratitude of our own nation and the world at large for the sacrifices they make to try to preserve peace with justice under very demanding circumstances.

(2) Catholics and Nuclear Weapons.

To answer this question is more complicated. It requires understanding of several fundamental principles and continuing study.

The Church has traditionally taught and continues to teach that a government has both the right and the duty to protect its people against unjust aggression. This means that it is legitimate to develop and maintain weapons systems to try to prevent war by "deterring" another nation from attacking. Very simply put, police carry guns for the same reason. Under no circumstances may a nation *start* a war, any more than police could decide to go out and shoot people to keep them from committing crimes! Popes have also pointed out that a nation may have the obligation to protect other nations, just as we have the obligation to go to the defense of a neighbor, even though a stranger, being attacked.

Although the Church urges nations to design better ways—ideally, non-violent ways—of maintaining peace, it recognizes that as long as we have good reason to believe that another nation would be tempted to attack us if we could not retaliate, we have the right to *deter* attack by making it clear that we *could* retaliate. In very simple terms, this is the "strategy of deterrence" we hear so much about. It is not a desirable strategy. It can be terribly dangerous. Government leaders and peoples of all nations have a grave moral obligation to come up with alternatives. But as long as our nation is sincerely trying to work with other nations to find a better way, the Church considers the strategy of nuclear deterrence morally *tolerable;* not satisfactory, but tolerable. As a matter of fact, millions of people may be alive in the world today precisely because government leaders in various nations know that if they attacked other nations, at least on a large scale, they, themselves, could suffer tremendous losses of human life or even be destroyed.

It follows clearly that if a strategy of nuclear deterrence can be morally tolerated while a nation is sincerely trying to come up with a rational alternative, those who produce or are assigned to handle the weapons that make the strategy possible and workable can do so in good conscience. The Church *does* condemn the use of any weapons, nuclear or conventional, that would indiscriminately destroy huge numbers of innocent people, such as an entire city, or weapons that would "blow up the world". Every nation has a grave moral obligation to reduce and finally to get rid of such weapons altogether, but the Church points out that this must be done gradually, with all nations cooperating, and with prudence. The Church does *not* require, nor have the Popes of the nuclear age or the Second Vatican Council recommended, *unilateral* disarmament.

In its *Pastoral on the Church in the Modern World,* the Second Vatican Council expressed the Church's position on these matters very clearly, and I believe it would be useful for you to have the following quotations from that Pastoral available.

> War has not ceased to be part of the human scene. As long as danger of war persists and there is no international authority with the necessary competence and power, governments cannot be denied the right of lawful self-defense, once all peace efforts have failed. State leaders and all who share the burdens of public administration have the duty to defend the interests

of their people and to conduct such grave matters with a deep sense of responsibility. However, it is one thing to wage a war of self-defense; it is quite another to seek to impose domination on another nation. The possession of war potential does not justify the use of force for political or military objectives. Nor does the mere fact that war has unfortunately broken out mean that all is fair between the warring parties ...

The development of armaments by modern science has immeasurably magnified the horrors and wickedness of war. Warfare conducted with these weapons can inflict immense and indiscriminate havoc which goes far beyond the bounds of legitimate defense. Indeed if the kind of weapons now stocked in the arsenals of the great powers were to be employed to the fullest, the result would only be the almost complete reciprocal slaughter of one side by the other, not to speak of the widespread devastation that would follow in the world and the deadly after-effects resulting from the use of such arms. ...

Since peace must be born of mutual trust between peoples instead of being forced on nations through dread of arms, all must work to put an end to the arms race and make a real beginning of disarmament, not unilaterally indeed but at an equal rate on all sides, on the basis of agreements and backed up by genuine and effective guarantees.

A nation must ask itself every day: "How much defense is enough? How much is too much?" It is a matter of balance. All life must be considered precious, because every human being is made in God's image. A nation must use resources to protect the unborn, the weak, the old, the helpless, the sick, the imprisoned, the homeless, the poor—those who most need the nation's protection and support. The question of how much the United States spends on military defense involves a number of technical issues about which I have no special expertise. The people at large and their elected representatives have the right and duty to question all aspects of the national budget, including allocations for defense. This is one of the great values and obligations of living in a democracy. We must be gravely concerned at all times about the needs of the poor and assure that appropriate provision is made for those needs. At the same time, we must be very careful about assuming that reductions in defense spending would automatically or completely solve such problems as poverty, hunger and disease in our nation or the world. These issues are tremendously complex and require many other changes in society before they can be adequately resolved. We must do everything we can to effect such changes and to resolve such problems, but even while engaged in efforts to do so, a nation must simultaneously defend *all* its people, the poor as well as the rich, against unjust aggression. There would be little point in a nation's spending all its resources on feeding, clothing, housing and educating the poor, and on other needs, only to leave all its people defenseless if attacked. We must remember, also, that these concerns are not the responsibilities of senior government officials alone. Every individual in uniform and every civilian directly involved in national defense, and particularly in defense industry, must be conscious of the many needs of the nation, especially the needs of the poor, and use the nation's resources responsibly, with meticulous honesty and care.

I know that you and our people may be faced with difficult decisions in the future, and I will try to keep you appraised of the Church's position in each problem situation. I am well aware that a wide variety of opinions have been expressed by some people concerning the directions in which they think the Church should be moving. My responsibility as I see it, as your bishop, is to advise you of the official teaching of the Catholic Church.

Archbishop Ryan, Bishop O'Connor and I sincerely hope that these comments will provide at least modest assistance to all those in uniform trying to serve honorably in the cause of peace with justice for all. Should specific questions or problems arise which you feel require further comment, please do not hesitate to advise us.

Now to the second part of this letter and to the new and important venture on which we are embarking, and for which we need the support of your prayers and moral encouragement.

Almost 10 years ago I issued a "Pastoral Message for Peace" in which I urged that all of us together face the problem of war and begin to develop an instrumentality to prevent future wars. In that Pastoral I asserted what I believe just as strongly today, "that if we do not, with deliberate speed, develop the means of war-prevention and make impossible the waging of war by any nation on this earth, we run the risk of witnessing, in our own time, the very end of human history".

Therefore, as Military Vicar for Catholics and their families in the Armed Forces of the United States and Veterans Administration I am preparing to establish a *House of Prayer and Study for Peace.* It is absolutely imperative that we beg God's help in continuing prayer, if we are to solve problems beyond our mere human powers and mitigate or end the sufferings of war. At the same time, it is essential that we utilize our finest human resources of spirit and intellect, bringing together scientists, scholars and others to study and plan and pray to help the world achieve peace with justice.

It is anticipated that The House of Prayer and Study for Peace will open early in the New Year under the immediate supervision of the Vicar General of the Military Vicariate, Bishop John J. O'Connor who will also serve as Chairman of the Board. The Board of Advisors will include men and women representing a broad spectrum of occupations and disciplines. The daily activities of prayer and study will be supported and carried out by a small staff of religious and lay persons in residence in the House itself. Staff members will communicate with individuals and agencies in the United States and abroad, in an effort to pool resources and share findings, and will simultaneously try to encourage individuals and institutions everywhere to join in prayer that peace with justice will become a reality for all humanity in our lifetime. With our Holy Father, Pope John Paul II, we believe that peace *is* possible. This belief must guide and permeate all our efforts.

As Military Vicar, I must emphasize that the activities of The House of Prayer and Study for Peace will be carried out with respect for all who are dedicated to the same objective, whatever be the approach they follow in accord with their own convictions in conscience, including the maintenance of sufficient armed force to deter aggression and the exploration of strategies of non-violence.

Finally, the hallmark of The House of Prayer and Study for Peace will be the maxim of Pope Paul VI: *If You Wish Peace, Defend Life.* I am convinced that if we are to expect God's help in ending war and achieving peace with justice, we must root our efforts in a recognition of the worth and dignity of all human life, the unborn, the aged, the poverty stricken, the oppressed, the sick, the diseased, the imprisoned, the helpless of both sexes, of all ages, races, creeds and ethnic origins.

[24] Bishop Roger Mahony, Bishop of Stockton, The Call of Christ, Prince of Peace: Becoming a Church of Peace Advocacy, December 30, 1981

During this season of grace, we once again share in the marvelous mystery of the Incarnation—the Son of God becoming one of us in order "to make all things new."

We welcome again Jesus Christ, the Prince of Peace, into our lives and into our world. We recount the wonders of Christ's Birth, announced in proclamations of peace; we raise our voices in joyful song, rejoicing in refrains of peace; and we extend warm gestures of peace to family and friends.

We celebrate on January First the World Day of Peace, gathering together the hopes, longings, and dreams of all peoples in the world that this New Year might draw all of us closer to the reality of genuine and lasting peace.

It is in this context of hope and fervent prayer for worldwide peace that I wish to address all of you during these days given over to reflecting upon Christ, our Prince of Peace.[1]

Introduction

The Secretary of State in Woodrow Wilson's Cabinet resigned his office in 1915 in order to avoid a conflict of conscience connected with taking steps that might lead to war. William Jennings Bryan tendered his resignation, he explained, not because he was an absolute pacifist—he was not—but because involvement in preparation for war was in conflict with his personal vocation to be a "peace advocate."

The Roman Catholic Church, as is well known, has never held a position of absolute pacifism. It accepts the premise that one can legitimately resist evil by force in justified self-defense. It has espoused a complex moral reasoning about the right to declare and engage in warfare known as "the just-war theory." Nevertheless, in recent years, more and more Catholics—our Popes, Bishops in this country and elsewhere, theologians and other scholars, and conscientious priests, religious and lay Catholics throughout the world—have increasingly asked: *how can we become, truly, advocates of peace?*

Today I add my voice to the growing chorus of Catholic protests against the arms race because I believe the current arms policy of our nation, as well as of the Soviet Union, has long since exceeded the bounds of justice and moral legitimacy. Moreover, the arms race makes it impossible effectively to

---

1. This Pastoral Letter is the result of the efforts of many outstanding Catholic scholars, and I wish to both acknowledge and thank them for their love for the Church and the Church's vital voice in the affairs of our times. Our Catholic theologians and scholars are a great treasure for the Church, and I am indebted to them for their thinking, their concern, and their active role in shaping the message of Christ to speak to today's world concerns. In a most special way, I am grateful to Father John A. Coleman and Father Robert Egan for their primary contributions; and to Mr. Ken Butigan, Fathers Richard Bollman, Jack Haughey, Richard Howard and Richard McCormick, and Professor Robert Lieber of the Department of Political Science, Georgetown University, for their special and important roles in shaping this Pastoral Letter.

end the urgent crisis of world hunger. It can no longer be tolerated.

Each day we permit it to continue without protest it perpetuates itself by becoming embedded in our everyday habits and attitudes. What is needed, instead, is a radical change of our hearts and our attitudes—a new awareness of our calling to be a people dedicated to peace.

Varieties of Pacifism

I have said that the Roman Catholic Church is not a pacifist Church, but this needs some qualification. The Bishops of the world at the Second Vatican Council asserted their strong support for those individual Catholics who adopt a position of absolute pacifism. Their words bear repeating here: " ... we cannot fail to praise those who renounce the use of violence in the vindication of their rights and who resort to methods of defense which are otherwise available to weaker parties too, provided that this can be done without injury to the rights and duties of others or of the community itself."[2]

The same Vatican Council document also states: "It seems right that laws make humane provisions for the case of those who for reasons of conscience refuse to bear arms, provided however, that they accept some other form of service to the human community."[3]

We American Bishops extended the range of this principle by supporting the right to "conscientious objection" of Catholics who conclude in conscience, following the reasoning of the just-war theory, that some particular war of their nation is unjust, even if they are not opposed to all wars in principle. We advocated that American law recognizes the right to selective conscientious objection as the legitimate extension of

2. *The Church in the Modern World*, #78 in David O'Brien and Thomas Shannon, eds., *Renewing the Earth: Catholic Documents on Peace, Justice and Liberation*, N.Y.: Doubleday, 1977.

3. *The Church in the Modern World*, #79.

our First Amendment rights to free exercise of religious conscience.[4]

It is even more important to recall that the moral reasoning involved in classic just-war theory led the Bishops at the Second Vatican Council to declare that a form of *nuclear pacifism* is a weighty and unexceptional obligation of Christians. This means that *any use of nuclear weapons, and by implication, any intention to use them, is always morally—and gravely—a serious evil.* No Catholic can ever support or cooperate with the planning or executing of policies to use, or which by implication intend to use nuclear weapons, even in a defensive posture, let alone in a "first strike" against another nation.

This Catholic version of nuclear pacifism follows directly from just-war premises. According to this tradition of moral reasoning, aggressive or "first strike" wars are always immoral. The legitimacy of a defensive use of force depends on certain conditions. One such condition is that there be specific, limited objectives in going to war. Others include: the immunity of non-combatants from direct attack, and the proportionality of specific tactics and weapons to the purpose of the war. Since nuclear weapons involve indiscriminate and massive violence committed against civilian populations, their employment or contemplated use can never be morally permitted. Indeed, the closest thing to an anathema in all of the Second Vatican Council documents are the plain words of *The Church in the Modern World* which enjoin a form of nuclear pacifism on the Catholic conscience: "Any act of war aimed indiscriminately at the destruction of entire cities or of extensive areas along with their population is a crime against God and man himself. It merits unequivocal and unhesitating condemnation."[5]

The Bishops were not inventing a new position in this re-

---

4. cf. The United States Catholic Conference, Declaration on Conscientious Objection and Selective Conscientious Objection, October 21, 1971.

5. *The Church in the Modern World*, #80.

gard, but following the consistent and repeated teaching of the Church since the beginning the the "Atomic Age." On the basis of the just-war theory, during World War II leading Catholic moral theologians in our own country condemned the use of atomic weapons in Hiroshima and Nagasaki, as well as the obliteration bombings of Dresden and Tokyo.

The majority of American Catholic journals, too, in dissent from the wider American public but decidedly in continuity with Catholic moral thinking, condemned the use of atomic weapons in Japan.[6] The prominent Catholic layman, Thomas E. Murray, a member of the Atomic Energy Commission, pronounced three practices of the Allies during World War II immoral and barbaric by the standards of Catholic moral teaching: obliteration bombing, the demand for unconditional surrender, and the atomic bombing of Hiroshima and Nagasaki.[7] This Catholic position on nuclear pacifism has been repeated over and over by Popes John XXIII, Paul VI, and John Paul II. It was affirmed again by the 1974 World Synod of Bishops. In 1976, we American Bishops confirmed it once again in our collective Pastoral Letter, *To Live in Christ Jesus*.[8]

Nor is this nuclear pacifism—this conviction that any use of nuclear weapons or, by implication, intention to actually use them is morally indefensible—a uniquely Catholic position. The World Council of Churches at its New Delhi Assembly in 1961 uttered words similar to those of the Second Vatican Council: "Christians must also maintain that the use of nuclear weapons, or other forms of major violence, against

---

6. cf. John C. Ford, S. J., "The Morality of Obliteration Bombing," *Theological Studies* 5 (1944): 261–309 and "The Hydrogen Bombing of Cities," in William Nagle, ed., *Morality and Modern Warfare: The State of the Question*, Baltimore, 1960 pp. 98–103.

7. Thomas E. Murray, "Morality and Security: the Forgotten Equation," in Nagle, ed., *Morality and Modern Warfare* pp. 58–68.

8. *To Live in Christ Jesus*, National Conference of Catholic Bishops, November 11, 1976.

centers of population is in no circumstances reconcilable with the demands of the Christian gospel."[9]

Indeed, the great physicists, Enrico Fermi and I.I. Rabi, wrote in the addendum to the report by the General Advisory Committee of the Atomic Energy Commission in 1949: "It is clear that the use of such a weapon cannot be justified on any ethical ground which gives a human being a certain individuality and dignity, even if he happens to be a resident of an enemy country. The fact that no limits exist to the destructiveness of this weapon makes its very existence and the knowledge of its construction a danger to humanity as a whole. It is necessarily an evil thing considered in any light."

Now, thirty-two years and fifty-thousand nuclear weapons later, the question of whether the use of nuclear weapons can be justified on any ethical grounds is rarely heard in our national debates and almost never in formal arms negotiations. All attention is riveted on questions such as how to put a ceiling on the further growth in numbers of weapons, for example, by limiting the number of warheads to no more than ten per ICBM or fourteen per sea-launched ballistic missile.

It is the absence of this moral dimension in our public policy discussions and a growing moral callousness which permits some government officials to speak publicly and rashly of "limited" and "winnable" nuclear wars. This has impelled me to add my voice to the growing number of American Bishops who are calling for a fundamental about-face in the arms race.

The Question of Deterrence

For some time many Christian moralists have held that the *possession* of nuclear weapons as a deterrent—but never their use or the intention to actually use them—is morally permissible.

---

9. cf. *The New Delhi Report 1961*, London, 1962, par. 64, p. 108. cf. also the collective Pastoral Letter of the House of Bishops of the Protestant Episcopal Church, U.S.A., against nuclear proliferation, "Apocalypse and Hope," October 9, 1981.

They have reasoned that the *threat* of nuclear retaliation may in fact be preventing the *use* of nuclear weapons. Moreover, they have argued that condemning the possession of nuclear weapons as a deterrent without suggesting practical political and military alternatives is, at best, politically inadequate, and at worst, dangerously naive.

Just as the right to legitimate defense is not a justification for unleashing any and every form of destruction, so moral arguments for the possession of nuclear weapons for deterrence do not constitute support for every national arms policy that is advanced *in the name of deterrence.*

The only possible Catholic support for a national nuclear deterrence policy depends on three related moral judgments: first, that the primary moral imperative is to prevent any use of nuclear weapons under any circumstances; secondly, that the possession of nuclear weapons is always an evil which could, at best, be tolerated, but only if the deterrence strategy is used in order to make progress on arms limitation and reductions; and thirdly, that the ultimate goal of what remains, at best, *an interim* deterrence policy is the eventual elimination of nuclear arms and of the threat of mutual assured destruction.[10]

We need to look, then, at *the facts* of the arms race (1) to see whether: ours is truly an interim deterrence policy aimed at reducing the risks of any use of nuclear weapons; (2) to see whether the framework of deterrence is actually used to reduce arms; and (3) to see whether our goal is really a world free of nuclear threats and terror. It is my judgment that the present United States and Soviet arms policy does not meet the demands of any of these three premises.

Since the first use of an atomic bomb in 1945, the risk of actually using nuclear weapons has escalated in a staggering

---

10. This statement of the moral premises for deterrence is available in Archbishop Joseph Bernardin's Report of the Ad Hoc Committee on War and Peace to the National Conference of Catholic Bishops, November, 1981. It is also the argument contained in the Vatican Declaration on Disarmament to the United Nations, May 7, 1976.

way. Today we can explode the equivalent of *one and a half million* Hiroshima bombs. In the past three years alone, we have increased the destructive power of our nuclear arsenal by fifty percent. Now we are about to embark on the largest single arms build-up in our national history. Having spent over one trillion dollars on defense in the past ten years, we now plan to spend a trillion dollars more in the coming four years and another trillion dollars in the three years after that.[11] Long ago, it would seem, we have ceased looking at deterrence as an interim policy aimed at genuine arms reduction.

Secretary of Defense Robert McNamara estimated that a force of 100 nuclear weapons, with explosive yields of no more than fifty kilotons each would suffice as a "deterrent," because it would be capable of destroying twenty-five percent of the Soviet population, some sixty-five million people, as well as fifty percent of all Soviet industrial capacity. A more cautious estimate assumes that 400 "warheads would constitute a more than adequate deterrence capability."[12] Merely two of our thirty-one Poseidon submarines would, on this basis, be sufficient to guarantee this capability—if deterrence were our real goal.

Instead of 400 warheads, we presently have a total of 11,893 and we plan to build another 18,500 by 1990.[13]

Furthermore, the deterrence envisioned by the tenuous Catholic moral toleration of possession of nuclear weapons as a permissible evil is aimed at deterring the use of *other nuclear weapons* against us. It is not morally permissible to use nuclear weapons to deter mere conventional warfare. Yet, the United States possesses 22,000 tactical nuclear weapons designed for the purpose of use in conventional wars. The Neutron Bomb, for example, is designed mainly to deter Soviet tanks, not other nuclear bombs. In fact, our nation has either threatened to use or actually planned to use nuclear weapons

---

11. cf. Tom Gervasi, *Arsenal of Democracy II,* N.Y.: 1981: p. 2
12. Robert Aldridge, an Aeronautical Engineer, cited in Gervasi, p. 24.
13. cf. Ruth Leger Sivard, *World Military and Social Expenditures, 1981*

against conventional forces on at least nine occasions.[14] Richard Ellis, of the U.S. Strategic Air Command, testified recently that "deterrence can no longer be neatly divided into subgroups such as nuclear and conventional. It must be viewed as an inter-related single entity."[15]

Clearly, we have moved beyond true deterrence to the production and use of nuclear weapons as an assertion of our national superiority. We are being urged to use our nuclear arsenal as "bargaining chips" for diplomatic and political adventures far beyond questions of deterrence. "Bargaining chips" is the language used by the defense establishment, which also speaks of "a *menu* of flexible nuclear options." As Richard Barnet has recently asserted: "Once the nuclear force is regarded as a 'flexible' instrument for achieving purposes beyond the crude one of deterring a nuclear attack with the threat of an all-out counter attack on Soviet society, the arms race becomes a never-ending, infinitely escalating contest."[16]

The moral justification for an interim deterrence policy flows from the right of a nation and its people to security. But no nation or people has any *right* to total supremacy, or superiority in "bargaining chips," or any of the other goals of the new "flexible" nuclear policy. By seeking for something other than a legitimate right to security through limited deterrence capability, we have actually been escalating the risks of nuclear war and undermining the real security of our own nation and the rest of the world.

Though deterrence does not require it, we continue to improve the complex computerized accuracy of our weapons, with the concomitant risks of a computer error triggering a nuclear assault, or of decisions to "launch under attack" being made by people far removed from the President and Joint Chiefs of Staff.

---

14. Gervasi, p. 29, cf. also for this assertion and the evidence, *A Matter of Faith: A Study for Churches on the Nuclear Arms Race*, Washington, D.C.: Sojourners, 1981 pp. 6–13.

15. cited in Gervasi, p. 28.

16. Richard Barnet, *Real Security: Restoring American Power in a Dangerous Decade*, N.Y.: 1981, p. 26.

Since President Carter's Presidential Directive 59 announced in August of 1980, we have also shifted away from a policy of deterrence to a "counter-force" first-strike strategy which does not and cannot make us or anyone else more secure. Now we are constructing weapons such as the Cruise Missile which would elude any verification. These new weapons, in principle, impede any possible arms-limitation agreements between the U.S.A. and the U.S.S.R. We are designing weapons, unneeded for deterrence, which will make it more difficult to achieve genuine bilateral reductions in arms.

The very use of the term, "deterrence," in moral argument has become very dangerous because of its ambiguities. We now need to distinguish between legitimate deterrence strategies and the rhetoric of a spurious "deterrence" within which hawks on each side of the East/West Divide compete to increase arms and provocations, envision fictitious gaps and windows of vulnerability, enter unending inconclusive negotiations which do not really stop the arms race and accelerate our drift toward nuclear collision.

Recently we have heard public officials speak foolishly and imprudently of "limited" and "winnable" nuclear wars, as if to prepare us to accept and accustom ourselves to such moral monstrosity. We have all become so numbed, so used to the nuclear umbrella, that we forget that less than a decade ago no responsible statesman, on either side, ever spoke of actually *using* nuclear weapons. With the present escalation in the arms race, there has also been an escalation in the rhetoric of threats and expectations and conceivable risks. The attitude that it is possible to "win" a nuclear war assumes that there is no longer any such thing as an unacceptable level of population loss. Any level of loss is apparently acceptable so long as our side "wins." In the face of such arrogance, such arridity of feeling and moral bankruptcy, we must not remain silent. This has never been and is not now a position that Catholics can, in any way, endorse or even merely tolerate or leave unchallenged.

With the one exception of the Nuclear Test Ban Treaty, which outlawed all above-ground nuclear detonations, *there has not really been any reduction in the arms race.* Even the Salt I agreement, in 1972, which placed some limits on the quantity of American and Soviet ICBMs and sea-launched ballistic missiles, in no way placed limits on new improvements in the precision, reliability, or explosive yield of those weapons already permitted. Neither did it prevent other qualitative "improvements" such as the development of the Cruise Missile and the Neutron Bomb. The arms race, in fact, continued to escalate after Salt I. As is well known, the U.S. did not ratify the Salt II agreement.

On a number of occasions, since the end of World War II, the American public has been systematically misled into believing in a fictitious strategic bomber "gap" (1948), a strategic "gap" (1956), and missile "gap" (1960). Subsequent evidence showed that no such "gaps" ever existed.[17] In the meantime the arms race continued to escalate. With each new American acquisition, the Soviets rushed to catch up, and vice versa. Now we are making an unprecedented leap in arms expenditure a pre-condition for any arms-limitation talks with the Soviets.

This is not deterrence, nor is it aimed at a genuine reduction of existing arms. At best it envisions a higher plateau of "deputed" security from which alone we might enter guarded and highly limited arms negotiations. Although the language of deterrence is still used, it is curious how each new "gap" allows the introduction of weapons that were, in any case, designed and executed for production before anyone had noticed the "gap"! This is not the kind of deterrence which can be morally permitted. It escalates rather than reduces the arms race.

Many of those who are now urging American arms increases are looking to an American "military superiority" beyond mere deterrence capability—one which will give us a psychological advantage and somehow impress the Soviet

---

17. Robert Aldridge, "The Deadly Race," in *A Matter of Faith*, p. 13. Significantly, all the alleged "gaps" took place in presidential election years. Nuclear policy is allowed to become a political ploy.

leadership with our willingness to risk catastrophe. It looks to a show of superior power and the will to use it, the aim of which is not genuine security, but extended space for diplomatic and political adventures in the world. These people, of course, call themselves "realists." They speak of a "flexible" nuclear policy and "limited" nuclear wars, but in doing so, they both ignore the dangers of escalation—with its terrible risk of the actual use of nuclear weapons—and contribute significantly to this very danger. It is more *realistic,* in my judgment, to devote ourselves to creating the conditions of possibility for peace and disarmament. Those who minimize this danger and believe that the escalation of violence can be controlled in warfare are the ones who have lost touch with reality.

Since I believe the American arms policy has exceeded the moral limits of deterrence and has eroded our real security, and since there has been up until now no serious connection between American arms policy and a serious attempt to reduce arms world-wide, it is my conviction that Catholics no longer have a secure moral basis to support actively or cooperate passively in the current U.S. arms policy and escalating arms race.

I have used the language of Catholic moral tradition, of the classic just-war theory, and the nuanced but tenuous Catholic argument for a limited and interim nuclear deterrence policy. I have used this language because of our Catholic commitment to give compelling and accessible *reasons* for our positions in policy debates with our fellow citizens. As Catholics, we remain committed to a belief in the role of reason in helping us determine, with other men and women of good will, what constitutes the common good and what fulfills the requirements of justice. We believe that the relationship of religious faith to political debate and social action should be mediated by carefully reasoned moral considerations based on shared philosophical and cultural values. It is on this basis, and in reference to these principles, that the present arms policy of the United States can no longer be accepted by us, but must be effectively challenged and changed.

Our Relationship to the Poor

As Christians, however, we understand our deepest identity in another kind of language, in terms of faith and discipleship—as followers of that Jesus who taught us to love our enemies, to hunger and thirst for justice, to be willing to suffer for the cause of peace, to embody the compassion of God in human history. The Gospel urges us, furthermore, to take a special care for the poor and the suffering, both in our own midst and in the whole world. Like Jesus we have set our hearts on a message which is "good news for the poor," news of a God who fills the hungry with good things and sends the rich empty away. (Luke 1: 53)

Because as a nation we have learned that we cannot afford both "guns and butter," we are presently cutting back, swiftly and drastically, on social programs for the poor, the needy, and the handicapped, in order to finance more "bargaining chips," superfluous weapons that we morally dare not ever use. We are caught up in a maddening and grotesque contest of spending and posturing that eats up our wealth and our talent. Such behavior is a contradiction of the Gospel. Meanwhile, more and more people experience the pain and frustration of poverty. Nor is it only the poor in our own country who suffer. Because of a perverse desire for superiority and invulnerability, we seem willing to risk the destruction of the planet itself, and to ignore the desperate need and hunger of millions of people in other nations of the world.

In sheer tonnage, there is more explosive material on earth today than there is food.[18] The world is presently spending $550 billion dollars a year on arms, an amount equal to the *annual income* of those four billion people who make up the poorer *half of the world's population.*[19] We are spending money to prepare for wars which morally could never be fought at the rate of one million dollars every minute. Four hours of such spending could eradicate malaria from the earth. Less than ten hours of such spending would solve the

18. Estimate of Ruth Leger Sivard, cited in Gervasi, p. 1.
19. in Sivard, *World Military and Social Expenditures 1981.*

entire world's hunger problem. The Catholic view of human rights, so strongly urged by recent Popes, includes the right of the hungry *to eat*.

In 1976 the Holy See's delegation to the United Nation's Conference on Disarmament stated: "The arms race is to be condemned unreservedly. By virtue of the nature of modern weapons and the situation prevailing on our planet, *even when motivated by a concern for legitimate defense, the armaments race is, in fact, a danger, an injustice, a mistake, a sin and a folly*." (emphasis added)

The Vatican made explicit the connection between the arms race and world hunger: "The obvious contradiction between the waste involved in the over-production of military devices and the extent of unsatisfied vital needs is in itself an act of aggression against those who are its victims (both in developing countries and in the marginal and poor elements in rich societies). It is an act of aggression which amounts to a crime, *for even when they are not used, by their cost alone, armaments kill the poor by causing them to starve*."[20] (emphasis added)

The arms race continues to divert our moral and intellectual resources, and our practical economies, into the waste and peril of the business of war. It continues to divert our wealth and our resources away from aid, agricultural improvements, the means within our reach to end world hunger. Our deadly "bargaining chips" leave the hungry of the world without hope or means to bargain for survival. Can anyone doubt where the Gospel must lead us here? Can anyone be so cynical as to claim that a desire to feed the hungry, in these circumstances, is "mixing politics and religion"?

As Catholics we belong to a world-wide Church and a community of humankind beyond our national boundaries. This can be a source of blessing for us, an opportunity to represent, in many different, concrete, and practical ways, the profound interdependence of peoples and nations in today's world. As

---

20. The Vatican Declaration on Disarmament to the United Nations, May 7, 1976.

all the recent Popes have reminded us, the question of social justice is now a global question.[21] We must judge the common good, the meaning of justice, and the conditions for the possibility of peace, by criteria wider than "national supremacy." We American Catholics must refuse to judge our national policies by mere nationalistic norms and slogans.

In fact, one major defect in the normal presentations of the classic just-war theory has been its tendency to view reality in bi-polar terms, and to base deterrence on "balances of power" instead of on achieving new institutions that could further delimit the possibilities of war. If we are to become, more and more, a Church of Peace Advocacy, we must correct these defects. Just-war thinking tended to neglect the global implications of war. It taught that the evil of war could be justified only by a comparable good it alone could achieve; but this proportionality was calculated without adequate attention to the complex and long-term effect of arms expenditures on the developing nations. Once we are able to see these ramifications of continued arms race in relation to world hunger and global justice, a new factor enters into our moral arguments, which must now incline the Catholic conscience toward more determined public peace-advocacy.[22]

Whose Interests Are Being Served?

Not only does our present arms policy force us to neglect our own poor, and the disparate poverty and hunger of other nations, but there is good reason to believe that it will destroy our own economy. In a recent contribution to *The Bulletin of Atomic Scientists*, one noted economist argues that our military expenditures have directly contributed to our industrial decline. He concludes that "the arms race has a deeply damag-

---

21. cf., inter-alia, Pope Paul VI, *Populorum Progressio*, #3.

22. For the connections between the arms race, war and the near inability to solve the world problem of hunger without reducing the arms race, cf. *The Global 2000 Report to the President*, a Report prepared by the Council on Environmental Quality and the Department of State, U.S. Government Printing Office, 1980.

ing effect on the free-enterprise economy," and also asserts that "the arms race as it now proceeds does not strengthen free institutions or free enterprise."[23] Another policy analyst asserts that "the war economy has brought us inflation, technological backwardness, maldistribution of wealth, a sinking dollar and unemployment."[24] Still another economic historian refers to "the baroque arsenal" which helps erode our national economy by erecting a perverse hierarchy of values.

In whose interest could our present "war economy" possibly be? It is *not* in the interest of all the millions of ordinary men, women and children, in this country and in the Soviet Union, at whose homes and cities these insane weapons are now aimed. We should not forget the warning of President Dwight D. Eisenhower when he urged us Americans to be wary of "the acquisition of unwarranted influence, whether sought or unsought, by the military-industrial complex. The potential for the disastrous rise of misplaced power exists and will persist. We should take nothing for granted."

The evidence for this "unwarranted influence" of an industrial/military complex is even more obvious today than it was twenty years ago when he made that statement. Of the fifty largest U.S. industrial companies, thirty-two make or export arms. Half of the nation's engineers and scientists work directly or indirectly for the Pentagon. As John Kenneth Galbraith has noted: "There is a certain reluctance in this polite and cautious age to speak of the financial interest in the arms race. Can anything so dangerous, so catastrophic, be motivated by financial interest or personal gain? But the financial analysts and like scholars are not so inhibited: they are currently and eagerly telling their customers and clients of the corporate prospects from the coming increase in the arms budget."[25]

---

23. John Kenneth Galbraith, "The Economics of the Arms Race—and After," in *The Bulletin of Atomic Scientists,* June/July, 1981, pp. 13–16.

24. Barnet, *Real Security,* p. 97.

25. Galbraith, "The Economics of the Arms Race—and After," p. 13.

Many of the technical experts on arms, in fact, constitute the very group whose interest is served by arms-escalation. We must be suspicious of the "expertise" of those who sell and manufacture weapons. Because self-serving interests so often lie behind the claims of this military/industrial complex, we must not allow the larger questions of public policy, especially the inescapable moral questions, to be decided by these so-called experts.

We are all aware, of course, that the United States is not a single actor in this nuclear terror. The Soviet Union does represent a real threat to our national interests and security. Clearly we have a right to genuine security. An industrial/military complex similar to our own exists also in the Soviet Union.

I am not, therefore, advocating *unilateral* disarmament or an unqualified pacifism. But unilateral disarmament is something quite different from serious, persistent, even unilateral, initiatives toward *bi-lateral disarmament*. The goal must be disarmament, arms reduction, not merely a ceiling on new, even more monstrous weapons.

The arms race also cripples the Soviet economy and places severe strains on Soviet institutions. It is in their interest, as well as ours, to withdraw resources from these sterile contests of arms production to other and urgent social issues. The Soviets, including their leaders, like us have children and grandchildren, cities and landscapes which they love, desires and hopes for a better future. We must not evade the real danger posed by Soviet policy, but we must refuse to "demonize" them and caricature their views and aspirations. As Christians called to love even our enemies, we must at least concede their essential humanity and search tirelessly, and with all our energy, for grounds of mutual understanding and accord with them.

What Can We Do?

I am proposing that we search together for the ways to become a peace-advocate Church. We American Catholics will need to become aware of all the true facts and issues concerning the arms race. We will need to make new efforts to continue to educate ourselves about all the relevant factors.

But, first of all, we must pray for a conversion of heart to become the kind of peacemakers spoken of in the Gospel. As peace advocates, Catholics will collaborate with the various existing groups and movements already active in the cause of peace.

We must use every political resource, including support for peace lobbies and pressure on our Congressional Representatives, to ensure that the United States returns to a minimal deterrence policy and initiate serious, comprehensive proposals for arms limitation and reduction based on parity. Successful collective bargaining initiatives always respect parity; arms limitation should attempt to guarantee security on both sides, include clear economic benefits for both sides, and be as comprehensive as possible. Real parity must be the goal in step-by-step reduction of arms.

A reduction of current armaments *by one half* on both sides would still guarantee a mutual capability of totally destroying the other country several times over. It would, furthermore, entail a significant program of industrial/technological conversion to peace time uses. Such a reduction would require the leaders of both nations to confront powerful interests that have a bureaucratic and ideological commitment to the arms race. Their ability to do this successfully would represent the best test of their sincerity in moving toward deterrence as an interim strategy.

Short of an actual reduction, many are now urging a three year *bilateral freeze* by the U.S.A. and the U.S.S.R. on all research, construction, or testing of new nuclear weapons systems. In my judgment, nothing short of these two proposals—of reduction in half or a freeze—will be adequate strategies for the present situation. We Catholics must bear witness to the conviction voiced by Pope John Paul II in his stirring appeal at the memorial to the dead in Hiroshima last year: "Our future on this planet, exposed as it is to nuclear annihilation, depends on one single factor. Humanity must make a moral about-face."

As an American Bishop, I deeply respect our nation's tradition of the separation of Church and State. I would deplore, however, any attempt to turn this legitimate separation into a separation of Church from society or into a privatization of religion that would divorce our faith and hope from public concerns and crucial moral questions that face us all as citizens. I would deplore any attempt to discuss the arms race merely as a "technical" issue—for example, of comparative nuclear engineering—devoid of ethical considerations or religious significance. We must *all* decide what constitutes the true relationship between religious faith and social justice, and I would deplore any attempt by politicians and government officials to claim for themselves some special competence to define this relationship.

As your Bishop, I depend on your freedom of conscience and your Christian imaginations in becoming more effective advocates of peace. I want to avoid, at this time, making more specific recommendations about the steps we must now take. I have reminded you, as I have reminded myself, of what the Catholic teaching is and has been concerning nuclear weapons. I ask you to help one another and to help me to find new approaches for combatting this great evil. The survival with dignity of the whole human race is at stake, and the terrible urgency of threatened starvation for millions of people. Can anyone really believe these are not profoundly religious concerns? Now we must find the way to allow these passionate concerns to become effective action.

During this New Year I shall suggest during those special times of the Church year, such as Lent, the Resurrection of the Lord, Pentecost, and others, ideas which will bring us all together in prayer and action to work for lasting peace.

On the occasion of a national congress of lay Catholics, called by the American Bishops and held in Chicago in 1893, the delegates passed a peace memorial, which they sent in twenty-five languages to the rulers of nations. In this memorial they strongly protested the arms race and they urged a deeper realization that "wars do not settle disputes between nations on principles of right and justice but upon the barbaric principle of the triumph of the strongest."[26] It is the spirit we need to rekindle in American Catholicism so that we may become a Church of Peace Advocacy. It must be possible for us to take the words of Isaiah to heart. Swords must be turned into ploughshares. Nations must stop preparing for war.

With you, in the coming months, I will be trying to understand the consequences of this decision for our Diocese in practical and concrete ways. I end today with the words of the saintly American monk, Thomas Merton. His words do not deny the complexity of the issues of war and peace, but they testify in a powerful way to the new urgency that the Church devote itself to peace-making as its major public responsibility and first priority:

> There are activities which, in view of their possible consequences, are so dangerous and absurd as to be morally intolerable. If we cooperate in these activities we share in the guilt they incur before God. It is no longer reasonable or right to leave decisions to a largely anonymous power elite that is driving us all, in our passivity, towards ruin. We have to make ourselves heard. Christians have a grave responsibility to protect clearly and forcibly against trends that lead inevitably to crimes which the Church condemns and deplores. Ambiguity, hesitation, or compromise are (sic) no longer permissible. War must be abolished.[27]

[25] Bishop James Malone, Bishop of Youngstown, Pastoral Message on Peace, Christmas, 1981

"Peace on earth to those of good will."
How easily this phrase from the midnight Mass Gospel

---

26. cited in James Hennessy, *American Catholics*, N.Y.: 1981, p. 183.
27. Thomas Merton, "Nuclear War and Christian Responsibilty," *Commonweal* 75 (February 9, 1962): 509.

falls from our lips. How much more difficult it is to achieve is screamed at us daily in news headlines of war and rumors of war.

As Christians we are called to be peacemakers. As citizens of a free nation we have the opportunity, the responsibility to make our voices heard in the cause of peace. Paramount among our concerns for peace this Christmas is the crucial question of the unbridled nuclear arms race.

Two years ago when Pope John Paul visited the United Nations he appealed to the world powers to reduce their stockpile of nuclear arms. He urged them to totally eliminate their capacity to destroy each other. The pope said:

> The continual preparation for war, demonstrated by production of ever more numerous, powerful and sophisticated weapons . . . shows that there is a desire to be ready for war, and being ready means being able to start it: It also means taking the risk that sometime, somewhere, somehow, someone can set in motion the terrible mechanism of general destruction.

As Christians we cannot justify into the indefinite future, the world community's capability to trigger a nuclear holocaust. Those who advocate the stockpiling of nuclear arms say that it is a deterrent to all-out war. It is described as "mutually assured destruction." The resulting acronym is appropriate—MAD.

The theory upon which MAD is based is that if a nation has the nuclear capability to destroy its enemies, even in the event of a like attack, this will deter nuclear war.

However, today we hear arguments for "limited nuclear warfare" which suppose that something less than all-out war is possible. That somehow nuclear powers might enter into conflict without unleashing the total destructive force at their fingertips goes against all our past experience as a world community. When Pope John Paul visited Hiroshima he challenged each of us to confront this issue:

In the past it was possible to destroy a village, a town, a region, even a country. Now it is the whole planet that has come under threat. This fact should finally compel everyone to face a basic moral consideration: From now on it is only through a conscious choice and through a deliberate policy that humanity can survive.

It is clear that we can neither as church nor as individual Christians place the responsibility of nuclear arms limitation solely in the hands of the civilian and military experts. We must each examine the issues, come to a decision in conscience of how best these issues be resolved and then work individually and as church to achieve a just resolution.

We cannot individually defuse the world's nuclear stockpile. Indeed our own country is only one party to such negotiations. However as responsible Christians and as citizens of a free country, we have the obligation to inform ourselves and to let our elected and appointed officials know our convictions on the issues.

It is disheartening to note that a recent survey indicated that only 51 percent of U.S. citizens are aware that our nation and the Soviet Union had successfully negotiated an initial Strategic Arms Limitation Treaty. If we are to be able to act as informed Christians and citizens, we must keep abreast of the issues and encourage our leaders to move steadily foward on the path to peace.

Currently the arms limitation talks seem bogged down in the dangerous labyrinth of international political rhetoric and saber rattling. As our nation and the Soviet Union haggle over the placement of nuclear missiles in Europe, we cannot afford the luxury of sitting on the sidelines.

We must urge in the strongest terms possible the serious resumption of SALT talks without delay, without political procrastination.

It would be naive of us to think that the Soviet Union is subject to the same public opinion pressures as our own freely elected officials or that they will readily respond to appeals of Christian conscience. However we do know that even a closed society like the Soviet's must live in the world community. We must encourage both our political and our universal church leaders to continue to exert their influence on the shapers of Soviet policy.

Most of us are not disposed to follow the path of total Christian pacifism, though we respect those who make such commitment. We are not required to advocate unilateral disarmament—indeed to do so might well hasten, rather than impede, our introduction to nuclear conflict. However given the total destructive capacity of nuclear weapons, we cannot indefinitely justify the possession of such arms in the name of peace.

In addition to the complicated question of nuclear disarmament is the persistent problem that the more of our resources that we devote to manufacture weapons for war, the less of our resources we have for human development. There is no guarantee that what we save on guns will be spent on butter; however our long debate over cuts in our national budget indicates that human services are threatened when our arms costs are increased.

This inevitable trade-off between these two concerns—defense of our country and the total well-being of our people—provided the basis for Pope Paul VI's terming the arms race as "an injustice, a theft from the poor, a folly."

As Christians we have an obligation to prayerfully reflect on such gospel passages as deal with peace and justice. (Cf. e.g. Mt. 5-7 and Lk. 6).

As Catholics we have a complementary obligation to keep abreast of church teaching. Resources are available in our diocesan media library, from the Catholic Charities Social Action Department and in our weekly newspaper, The Catholic Exponent.

As citizens of a free country, we have the obligation to keep informed on the issues and to make our convictions known to those in elected and in other decision making roles.

We are reminded during this Christmas season that the peace which Jesus promised is a peace which the world cannot give. It is a peace which goes beyond the issues of nuclear disarmament. It is our life in and with our creator. Let us make the prayer of the late Pope John XXIII our own:

> May Christ inflame the desires of all to strengthen the bonds of mutual love. . . . May all people welcome each other . . . May peace reign!

[26] Bishop William E. McManus, Bishop of Fort Wayne, Indiana, Thinking Morally About Nuclear Weapons, New Year's Day, 1982

Happy New Year! This traditional greeting is a wish, a hope and a prayer, but it is not a prediction.

This year may not be a happy year. It could be the most unhappy year of all time. It could be the year of a nuclear war—a global war, a limited war, a long war, a short war, but nuclear weapons could be used to kill thousands or millions, to injure thousands and millions more, to inflict permanent damage on the whole human race.

Nuclear war is not a fiction writer's fantasy. It is not so utterly horrible that it can't happen. It is not a mere "big stick" deterrent to a hostile nation's aggression. It is not a theory. It's real.

Nuclear war is a real and immediate danger to the very survival of the human race. It is a real and immediate threat to our lives. It can destroy everybody and everything in this 14 Indiana-county diocese.

If a "baby bomb," a 10-megaton nuclear warhead, were to explode over the spot where you now are reading this pamphlet, everyone within a three-mile radius would die and everything would be leveled. Within the next six-mile radius, one of two persons would die, and nine of ten would be severely burned by radiation. Air raid shelters would turn into crematoriums. The injured would be crushed by falling buildings and flying debris in 200-mile-an-hour winds. The victims' lungs would collapse; many would be blinded; shattered ear drums would leave many deaf; infection would spread like a plague because doctors and nurses were killed and hospitals were demolished. Rats would flee damaged sewer systems to spread disease. Clean, uncontaminated water would be scarce, no more than what has been stored safe from the "baby bomb's" radiation.

Will It Happen?

All right, you say, it can happen. It is true that our nation now has enough nuclear weapons to destroy every Soviet city several times over, and the Soviets have a stockpile sufficient to wipe out every U.S. city. But you feel it won't happen—it's too insane, too mad, and nobody but a crazy person would start a nuclear war. It won't happen, you say. Twisting Pope Paul VI's UN statement out of context, you say: "No more war—no more war!" as though wishing for peace would achieve it.

In his novel, *Night,* about the Nazi holocaust of Europe's Jews, Elie Wiesel tells the story of Moshe, an early inmate of a concentration camp, from which he miraculously escaped and returned to the Hungarian village where he had been captured. Quickly he told the small village's remaining inhabitants of Hasidic Jews about the torture and killing in the concentration camp, and he urged them to flee from the village for their lives. Nobody in the village believed Moshe. The more detailed he made his report about the camp, the more convinced the villagers became that he had gone mad. "Crazy talk," they said, and soon after they were carted off to torture and death in a concentration camp they wouldn't believe could be.

Frightening scenarios which scientists write about the destructive force of nuclear weapons, aimed and ready to be fired in moments, may make us wonder whether they're nothing but wild tales far removed from reality. It is difficult to believe that human genius would put together weapons so massively destructive that the amount of their killing and ruin can't be controlled. Thoughtful people, however, have to ask: Has our world gone mad?

We would do well to recall that some of the most bitter opponents of Jesus' Gospel of peace with justice accused him of being a madman. Jesus was denounced as a radical, what some people today would call a "bleeding-heart type." I say, however, that Christians today ought to embrace his Gospel teaching for sanity in a world on the verge of madness.

Moral Questions

The inherent insanity of firing nuclear weapons, supposedly to settle an international dispute, is reason in itself to raise some soul-searching moral questions. These questions are about the morality of nuclear war under any circumstances and about the nuclear arms race, which appears to be getting more intense while the contestants vie for nuclear weapon supremacy.

Merely predicting how many people would die in a nuclear war or describing the terror of this dread calamity will not shed much light on the moral issue whether use of nuclear weapons in warfare is moral or immoral. Extensive use of conventional weapons might cause even more destruction. Technological changes in weaponry have made them increasingly lethal. What's right and wrong with a weapon can't be determined solely by its capacity for destruction.

You and I, therefore, have to search our souls for a personal moral answer to the question whether we can conceive of any circumstances in which our U.S. government would be morally justified to set off its nuclear weapons.

This is a question you and I should try to answer conscientiously in light of our faith, our Church's guidance and our enlightened judgment.

Our answer should not be totally self-centered, a morality only for our own survival, but should, in the spirit of the Gospel, consider all God's people and their right to live in peace.

Our faith recalls God's command not to kill; Jesus' many admonitions to his followers to be peacemakers; the Holy Spirit's peaceful influence in God's kingdom on earth.

Our faith insists that we consider Jesus' Gospel ideals: "You have heard how it was said: Eye for eye and tooth for tooth. But I say to you: Offer the wicked man no resistance. . . . You have learned how it was said: You must love your neighbor and hate your enemy. But I say this to you: Love your enemies and pray for those who persecute you. . . . For if you love only those who love you, what right have you to claim any credit?"

Christian Pacificism

At the time St. Matthew preached these words spoken by Jesus, he was no less a radical peacemaker than is a contemporary Christian pacifist advocating a total abolition of weapons of war and particularly nuclear weapons.

The pacifist position has been officially commended by the Church, as has the right of conscientious objection to military service. "We cannot fail to praise those who renounce the use of violence in vindication of their rights," Vatican Council II said.

One need not be a pacifist, opposed to war of any kind even in defense against aggression, to disapprove of any use whatsoever of nuclear weapons. Many who continue to believe in the morality of a "just war," notably a war of national self-defense, nonetheless hold firm to the moral view that use of any nuclear weapons would be absolutely wrong. Their reasoning is sanctioned by Vatican II's declaration that "any act of war aimed at the destruction of entire cities or of extensive areas along with their population is a crime against God and against humanity. It merits unequivocal and unhesitating condemnation."

The prime reason for the Church's stand is a nuclear weapon's almost uncontrollable capacity for widespread and wanton killing and destruction. There is little probability that in a nuclear war only one nuclear warhead would be exploded with few casualties. The probability is rather that in a major war thousands of non-combatant citizens would be slaughtered and vast areas of God's beautiful earth would be ruined forever.

The Hardest Question

The hardest ethical question of all, I think, is what our moral position ought to be if the United States is the victim of any enemy nation's nuclear attack. The question is hard because it's horrible, and calmly answering it is not easy.

If the Soviets were to explode a nuclear bomb over Washington, D.C., would our nation be morally justified to fire a bomb over Moscow? Would the Soviet's killing of a half million Washingtonians morally justify our nation's killing half a million Moscovites? Would we be justified in immediate retaliation even if we were virtually certain the next Soviet bomb would destroy Chicago and our bomb would destroy Leningrad?

What would our government do in retaliation for a hostile nation's first nuclear strike at the United States or at one of its allies? Ordinary citizens don't know and, in fact, most probably don't have a clear, firm, moral position on what the government should do. Understandably, of course, our government, in the interest of national security, can't divulge its military strategies and secrets and in effect give them away to our enemies. There is, however, little evidence that our nation's government and military leaders have alternative defense strategies to retaliation with nuclear weapons. Our defense apparently would be a strategy to fire off nuclear weapons that would destroy the enemy a few minutes before the hostile bombs destroyed us.

You and I, praying for the Holy Spirit's light, should ask ourselves whether we will join the majority of Catholic moralists who are beginning to see the nuclear bomb as a totally evil thing, something that never should have been put together, a weapon so vile and vicious that it ought to be banned from the face of the earth.

You and I need to pray over this moral matter and beg God's grace for light and for the courage of our moral convictions. Beyond that, we need to arouse our feelings. Nuclear warfare is no good; we should detest and hate it passionately. Loose irresponsible talk about it should anger us. A desire for everything possible to head off the danger of nuclear war should be not only a moral conviction but a profound feeling.

Disarmament

Though nuclear weapons themselves probably are morally evil and their use in warfare is even more evil, it would be extreme to call upon our government immediately to disassemble all our nuclear bombs and systems and to destroy their components. It is, however, perfectly reasonable to question the production of a still larger stockpile of these weapons when those on hand, reliable experts say, are sufficient to destroy any hostile nation, including the Soviets, several times over. An immediate moral imperative for our government is to set a limit on its nuclear arsenal, and, once that limit is reached, if it already has not been met in all phases of nuclear weaponry, to stay with it and thereafter to reduce the stockpile in accord with multinational agreements on disarmament. This policy is the minimum that the reasonable, morally-minded peace-loving citizens have a right to expect of their government.

The minimum policy does not necessarily include an immediate unilateral freeze on all U.S. production of nuclear weapons nor does it outlaw development of more advanced kinds of both defensive and offensive nuclear ballistic systems. There are, however, good reasonable people who are conscientiously convinced that Christian ideals of peace dictate our nation's taking the lead in nuclear weapon disarmament by calling a halt to all further production of nuclear weapons of any kind. This, of course, would involve some risks, e.g., our loss of "nuclear superiority" (the awful idea that we can kill more people than any other nation) and a resultant danger that an enemy nation might take advantage of our alleged "weakness." Perhaps, too, it can be argued reasonably that our nuclear superiority will persuade other nations to "give up the race" and join us in disarmament to support this reasoning.

With a fervent kind of patriotism I believe our nation, of all nations, has the greatest power for peace. It therefore is distressing to see how little progress our nation has made in taking the lead to reduce the world's arsenal of nuclear weapons. Over and over again the headlines read: "Peace talks stalled," and even the pace of talking, not to say anything about international agreements, drags on much slower than the production of new and more devastating nuclear weapons.

Humbly, I think, our nation should try to realize that other nations, both friendly and hostile, must have difficulty in understanding our intentions on disarmament when we are talking among ourselves about our "first-strike capability," "limited nuclear warfare" (presumably waged someplace other than on U.S. territory) and a neutron bomb that would kill people but not wreck their real estate. We don't have the kind of credibility that a predominantly peaceful people deserves.

On the other hand, we have our problems in talking about disarmament and peace to hostile nations with disdain and contempt for our ideals and values. These talks are terribly difficult in an atmosphere of their deep distrust and hostility.

It has been our nation's painful experience to have our peace efforts foiled by our enemy nations' military invasion of defenseless neighbors and by dictatorships' flagrant violations of basic human rights. Our feelings rebel against talking peace and disarmament with the Soviets at this very time when their puppet government in Poland is stamping out a courageous people's quest for freedom and self-determination in their own land. But Poland will be no better off if we refuse to go through with disarmament talks already scheduled with the Soviets.

Deterrence

Our nation's position on nuclear weapons is, I believe, that we never will use them for acts of aggression, will enter into any reasonable agreement to control nuclear weapons, will reduce our stockpile in accord with an enforceable multinational agreement, but we will, for now, hold on to all the weapons we have, increase the stockpile and develop our weapons as a deterrent to the use of nuclear weapons in a war against the United States and/or its allies.

Is it moral?

Some think that the nuclear arms race is destined for an "everybody loses" finish and that our nation's increased production of nuclear weapons will force other nations, including those with expansionist objectives, into a race that can only end in total disaster. These moralists argue that our nation should make the supreme effort for peace even at the risk of losing nuclear weapons superiority.

Other moralists reason that a nation firmly committed to peace and against any aggressive warfare has a moral right to a nuclear weapon strategy of self-defense premised on the persuasive force of deterring aggressive nations from nuclear warfare because of our technical superiority. There is support for this position in traditional Church teaching.

How literally will we take Jesus' words: "You have learned how it was said: You must love your neighbor and hate your enemy. But I say this to you: Love your enemies and pray for those who persecute you"?

This is a question you and I should ponder prayerfully when we address the moral matter of nuclear weapons for deterrence. Jesus' words do not lay down a hard-and-fast rule, but their idealism is not to be discounted as unrealistic piety.

Our prayerful reflection on Jesus' words will remind us that nuclear war would not be a military battle in traditional fashion, but a computer-controlled massacre of millions caught up in an international conflict for which they are in no way guilty. Soviet children, teen-agers, women, and senior citizens whom our nuclear bombs would kill, are people like ourselves with the same fundamental desires for a decent wholesome life. "Love them," the Lord says, but do we when we acquiesce in our nation's aiming at them more and more nuclear bombs? Are we allowed to say, "When the Soviets quit aiming their weapons at our shores and our innocent people, we will ask the president to cut back on our defense"?

A moral judgment about disarmament should not ignore the vast amount of productive good that could be accomplished by spending for peaceful purposes much of the money invested in armaments.

A great military leader elected U.S. President, Dwight D. Eisenhower, said in 1953: "Every gun that is made, every warship launched, every rocket fired signify, in the final sense, a theft from those who hunger and are not fed, those who are cold and are not clothed."

Our Church spoke forcefully in a 1976 Vatican statement: "The armaments race is to be condemned unreservedly. It is an act of aggression which amounts to a crime, for, even when they are not used, by their cost alone armaments kill the poor by causing them to starve."

It may be that a threat even greater to world peace than our nuclear weapons is the pathetic fact that in God's world, for all of whose people he has provided ample resources for decent human living, one-third of the people, living mainly in nations possessing huge armaments, are rich, overfed, overindulged, while two-thirds, living in unarmed nations, eke out a mere subsistence often short of necessary food, clothing, housing, education and medical aid. This is an explosive condition, and even if it were not, a rudimentary kind of Christian charity should compel us to ask how our nation can justify its largest peace-time expenditure for weapons and a reduction in our domestic and foreign aid for the poor. This is a moral matter that calls for a moral response.

Much of this letter has been focused on the moral dimensions of nuclear weapons and disarmament. It has not, however, laid down hard-and-fast moral rules of a kind many Catholics are accustomed to expect whenever the word "morality" is mentioned.

On this topic it must be understood that morally-minded individuals may come to different conclusions on the issues themselves and on what their moral responsibilities are. This letter's purpose, therefore, was to generate some moral reasoning about war and peace and about the nuclear arms race, not to set forth final conclusions and rules and regulations. For the next ten months I will be working with my brother bishops of the United States on a more definitive proclamation of moral guidelines on war and peace. I beg your prayers that it will be a document worthy of the Church's leadership for peace.

Reasonable Catholics, however, have no right to indulge in slaphappy oversimplifications, e.g., "Better to be dead than Red"; "Everything is all right if it's for defense"; "The politicians and generals will call the shots—why should I be concerned"; "The Church ought to keep its nose out of this"; "If the bombs get going, you're dead, so why worry?"

Not to think morally about the morality of nuclear weapons is immoral.

[27] New Jersey Catholic Bishops, Statement on Nuclear Disarmament, March 23, 1982

The destruction of Hiroshima on August 6, 1945 by an atomic bomb released on the face of the earth a new and terrifying force the like of which had never been known in human history. The horror of war was magnified beyond belief because we had finally fashioned for ourselves weapons capable of unimaginable destruction. Nations could now destroy not only each other's armies but also each other's civilizations, and, indeed, life itself. The possibility of such massive and indiscriminate slaughter forces us as disciples of Jesus Christ, called by him to be peacemakers, to re-evaluate our response to the serious questions raised in discussions of nuclear war.

As immense and pervasive as the danger of annihilation is for all the peoples of the world, the great powers seek self-preservation by continuing to build more and more sophisticated weapons so that today they possess a nuclear arsenal one million times as powerful as the bomb which leveled Hiroshima. This quest for false security actually makes massive destruction more probable. The vicious circle which the arms race creates compounds the danger and intensifies the fear.

While spending billions on nuclear weapons, the great powers are failing to assist adequately in enabling, feeding, clothing and sheltering the two-thirds of the human race who are poor. Their own people are burdened by the incredible cost of destructive weapons while undeveloped countries are "deprived of that collaboration they need in order to make social and economic progress." (*Pacem in Terris,* 110)

Even if the nuclear arms buildup were not a way of robbing the poor, as it is, it would have to be condemned as a moral evil because it heightens the probability of a war that would destroy populations indiscriminately. That, the fathers of Vatican II said, is "a crime against God and man himself." Even the threat of such an attack, the American bishops declared in 1976, is immoral.

The questions before us, though complex, must be addressed. They are no longer questions of war or peace but of annihilation or survival.

As followers of Jesus Christ, we are called to be instruments of his peace. Through prayerful reflection and cooperation with our brothers and sisters of all nations, we can achieve peace! We must begin now by speaking out for a mutual reduction of nuclear arms, thus reversing the arms race. Our goal should be nothing less than ridding the world of the evil specter of nuclear holocaust which today threatens to destroy civilization and life itself.

Today, thirty-seven years after Hiroshima, scientists and military men alike are almost unanimous in calling nuclear war "unthinkable." Yet, the military establishment and the arms industry keep preparing for it. So it is that people all over the world are protesting with increasing intensity that we take seriously this threat that hangs over us.

One of the strongest voices raising the alarm is that of Pope John Paul II. He has called with great urgency for the nations to act on mutual disarmament before it is too late. Recently he deplored what he called the scandal of the arms race. During his visit to the United Nations on October 2, 1979, the Holy Father said:

> The continual *preparations for war* demonstrated by the production of ever more numerous, powerful and sophisticated weapons in various countries show that there is a desire to be ready for war, and *being ready* means *being able to start it;* it also means taking the risk that sometime, somewhere, somehow, someone can set in motion the terrible mechanism of general destruction.
>
> It is therefore necessary to make a continuing and even more energetic effort to do away with the very possibility of provoking war, and to make such catastrophes impossible by influencing the attitudes and convictions, the very intentions and aspirations of governments and peoples.

We, the Catholic bishops of New Jersey, urge our fellow citizens to press our government to take deliberate steps toward mutual disarmament with a sense of its great urgency for the future not only of our country but of the entire human family.

[28] Humberto Cardinal Medeiros, Bishop of Boston, *Choose Life*, Easter, 1982

My dear brothers and sisters in Christ:

This Easter Sunday I want to speak to you about a question which is of the highest importance for each of us, for our country and for the whole world. I wish to raise your consciousness to the question of how we should think, pray, and act in a world that lives in increasing fear of nuclear war.

Easter, the feast of the resurrection of Jesus Christ, the Savior and Redeemer of the human race, is God's promise that our destiny is life and not death. Easter is God's call to each of us to love life and promote all that enhances life. Easter calls us all to work among all peoples for peace, for peace protects and fosters life. When the risen Christ came to his assembled disciples in Jerusalem on the first Easter Sunday, his greeting conveyed the gift of peace, "Peace be with you" (John 20:19, 21; Luke 24:36). These words were spoken to people who were deeply afraid. The evangelists tell us that on the morning of the first day of the week, before the risen Lord appeared to them, the disciples had gathered fearfully behind locked doors (cf. Mark 16:10, John 20:19).

They had good reason for their grief and fear. Just three days earlier death on the cross had taken from them the one from whom they had expected fullness of life and freedom (cf. Luke 24:20-21). The resurrection of Christ transformed their grief into joy and their fear into hope. The event we celebrate at Easter led the first believers in Christ to proclaim, "It is he who is our peace" (Ephesians 2:14). We join them in this proclamation of faith and joyfully announce to all that he is also our life.

The Hopes and Fears of Humanity

As I listen to the hopes and fears of the people of the Archdiocese of Boston, I sense that, like them, the hearts of men and women throughout the world today are caught in a state very much like that of Jesus' followers in the time between Good Friday and the first Easter. The disciples looked back on three short days and saw death seemingly destroy the one who had become the source and foundation of all their hopes.

In 1982 when we look back on scarcely more than three short decades, we remember an event which I believe to be the most portentous symbol of death's power that the human race has ever witnessed: the atomic attack on the cities of Hiroshima and Nagasaki. When we remember this horrendous destruction of over 100,000 human lives in a few short hours, we, like Jesus' first followers, are afraid, and our fear leads us to seek protection against the awesome power of death that nuclear weapons have placed in human hands. But unlike the disciples as they remembered Good Friday, we have not gathered in doubt, fear, and shock behind locked doors to grieve and weep. Rather, the fear of nuclear obliteration has led some nations of our world into an increasingly feverish production of more and more of the very weapons of which we are so deathly afraid.

Our choices and our policies seem to be based increasingly on distrust, fear, anxiety, and insecurity. As a consequence, we appear to be led into military postures which increase the human cost of the arms race. Are we convinced that if we want to avoid catastrophe, this escalation of destructive fear must be reversed?

The feast of Easter calls us to a way of living in which hope overcomes anxiety and in which our commitment to building a civilization of life and love upon this earth becomes stronger than our drive to manufacture instruments for the destruction of our planet. Belief in the resurrection of Jesus Christ our Savior not only calls us to life and love, it makes such a way of living possible. Easter is the "Day of the Lord" longed for by the prophets. It is the day on which they foresaw that "kindness and truth shall meet, justice and peace shall kiss" (Psalm 85:11). The resurrection of Christ is the fulfillment of the words of Zechariah, "The day shall dawn upon us from on high, to give light to those who sit in darkness and in the shadow of death, to guide our feet in the way of peace" (Luke 1:78–79).

From the Shadow of Death into the Light of Peace

I want to speak to you with the hope that this Easter can be the beginning of the movement of our nation and of our world out of the shadows of the threat of nuclear death into the light which shows us the way to peace. In the words of Pope John Paul II, I wish to exhort all of us, "to make a continuing and even more energetic effort to do away with the very possibility of provoking war, and to make such catastrophes impossible by influencing the attitudes and convictions, the very intentions and aspirations of governments and peoples."[1]

I wish to search with you for a pathway we can follow that will enable us to survive the knowledge of how to construct nuclear weapons, and I wish to announce some initiatives of the Archdiocesan Justice and Peace Commission to help in that search.

Faith in the resurrection of Christ does not blind us to the real animosity, antagonism and aggression which threaten the peoples of this world today, but I want to profess openly with you that this faith gives us hope which is deeper than all these forces of destruction. Jesus Christ, risen from the dead, is the source of this hope. He can break the iron grip of fear which today seems to drive us ever closer to nuclear catastrophe. I want, above all, to talk to you in the spirit of hope he gives us for our common future.

I wish to speak to you according to the mind of the Holy Father Pope John Paul II. Please listen to his 1982 World Day of Peace Message as he points out how it is God alone who can fulfill our hopes for lasting peace—for peace is a gift of God:

"Christian optimism, based on the glorious cross of Christ and the outpouring of the Holy Spirit, is no excuse for self-deception. For Christians, peace on earth is always a challenge, because of the presence of sin in man's heart. Motivated by their faith and hope, Christians therefore apply themselves to promoting a more just society; they fight hunger, deprivation and disease; they are concerned about what happens to migrants, prisoners and outcasts (Mt. 25:35-36). But they know that while all these undertakings express something of the mercy and perfection of God (Lk. 6:36; Mt. 4:48), they are always limited in their range, precarious in their results and

1. Pope John Paul II. "Address to the General Assembly of the United Nations," October 2, 1979, no. 11 in *Pilgrim of Peace: The Homilies and Addresses of His Holiness Pope John Paul II on the Occasion of His Visit to the United States of America* (Washington, DC: United States Catholic Conference, 1980).

ambiguous in their inspiration. Only God the giver of life, when he unites all things in Christ (Eph. 1:10), will fulfill our ardent hope by himself bringing to accomplishment everything that he has undertaken in history according to his Spirit in the matter of justice and peace.

"Although Christians put all their best energies into preventing war or stopping it, they do not deceive themselves about their ability to cause peace to triumph, nor about the effect of their efforts to this end. They therefore concern themselves with all human initiatives in favour of peace and very often take part in them; but they regard them with realism and humility. One could almost say that they 'relativize' them in two senses; they relate them both to the sinful condition of humanity and to God's saving plan. In the first place, Christians are aware that plans based on aggression, domination and the manipulation of others lurk in human hearts, and sometimes even secretly nourish human intentions, in spite of certain declarations or manifestations of a pacifist nature. For Christians know that in this world a totally and permanently peaceful human society is unfortunately a utopia, and that ideologies that hold up that prospect as easily attainable are based on hopes that cannot be realized, whatever the reason behind them. It is a question of a mistaken view of the human condition, a lack of application in considering the question as a whole; or it may be a case of evasion in order to calm fear, or in still other cases a matter of calculated self-interest. Christians are convinced, if only because they have learned from personal experience, that these deceptive hopes lead straight to the false peace of totalitarian regimes."

Individually and collectively we must work unceasingly for peace, for peace is a constant challenge to Christians. Our Holy Father makes it clear that even a realistic view of all the tensions and conflicts in modern society does not render ineffective our striving for peace. He says:

"This realistic view in no way prevents Christians from working for peace; instead, it stirs up their ardour for they also know that Christ's victory over deception, hate and death gives those in love with peace a more decisive motive for action than what the most generous theories about man have to offer. Christ's victory likewise gives a hope more surely based than any hope held out by the most audacious dreams" (1982 World Day of Peace Message).

For Pope John Paul II genuine peace does not consist in aggressive pacification. Hence he writes:

"This is why Christians, even as they strive to resist and prevent every form of warfare, have no hesitation recalling that, in the name of an elementary requirement of justice, peoples have the right and even the duty to protect their existence and freedom by proportionate means against an unjust aggressor" (Gaudium et Spes, 79).

Without infringing upon this principle we can see how, in a world that is threatened by total nuclear destruction, the need for patient and persistent negotiation is ever more urgent. Our Holy Father expresses the thought in this way:

"However, in view of the difference between classical warfare and nuclear or bacteriological war—a difference so to speak of nature—and in view of the scandal of the arms race seen against the background of the needs of the third world, this right, which is very real in principle, only underlines the urgency for world society to equip itself with effective means of negotiation. In this way the nuclear terror that haunts our time can encourage us to enrich our common heritage with a very simple discovery that is within our reach, namely that war is the most barbarous and least effective way of resolving conflicts. More than ever before human society is forced to provide itself with the means of consultation and dialogue which it needs in order to survive, and therefore with the institutions necessary for building up justice and peace.

"May it also realize that this work is something beyond human powers!"[2]

---

2. Message of His Holiness Pope John Paul II. For the Celebration of the Day of Peace, 1 January, 1982. From the Vatican 8 December 1981 number 12, pp. 17-18.

As we proceed in our consideration of nuclear armament and nuclear war, let us keep in mind this teaching of the Holy Father. It is central to our thinking and meditation.

The Horrors of Hiroshima

At the outset we realize the terrifying fact that the spiral of nuclear arms production has led the human race into a situation of the gravest peril. On August 6, 1945 the news that the first atomic bomb had been dropped on Hiroshima had a profound effect on me when I was still in the seminary. The awareness that an awesome and utterly dangerous power had been discoverd by humanity has been with me ever since that day. For over 36 years I have seen this awareness hover like a storm cloud on the horizons of the minds of all of us. I have had discussions with many of our young people who fear they have no future because they expect a nuclear war to occur before their future arrives.

Recent developments in the quantity and kind of weapons which are being produced now prompt me to repeat the warnings and the plea of Vatican Council II (Gaudium et Spes, 80) and to note that the danger of nuclear destruction is constantly being intensified. With this in mind, I have engaged in dialogue and consultation with many individuals, including experts in the scientific and medical aspects of the nuclear arms race.

As a result of this effort, I have prepared this pastoral letter to help us understand the dangers of nuclear war, to urge all to pray fervently with me that these dangers never become realities, and to encourage educational programs throughout the Archdiocese that will help us to make morally responsible decisions. I can offer the teachings of the Church and raise questions to call your attention to this most serious issue. My responsibility as Archbishop will allow me to do no less for the sake of peace, justice, and human life. I therefore address these words to the members of the Catholic community in the Archdiocese of Boston and to all who hope in God and the human future.

The Magnitude of Nuclear Destructiveness

The overriding urgency of the nuclear arms question is most clearly evident from the sheer magnitude of destruction these weapons are capable of inflicting upon the human race. It is difficult to consider, without becoming numb with fear and even despair, the scope of human suffering and death these weapons can cause. Yet I am convinced that our hope in the risen Christ and our reverence for human life compel us to face, with full awareness, the dangers which confront humanity.

My brothers and sisters in Christ, it is quite clear to me that the potential effects of nuclear war lead us to this somber conclusion: the decision makers in the governments of nations which possess nuclear weapons today hold in their hands the power to cause or to prevent the greatest disaster ever to occur in human history. Moreover, the decisions which will either prevent or bring about nuclear catastrophe are not like those made by governments and generals in previous wars. A full-scale nuclear war could be conducted in a few hours. In such an exchange decisions would have to be made almost instantaneously; the margin of time for deliberation could be minutes not hours, days, or months, as is the case in conventional wars. Thus the policies which are being programmed into the computers of the nations will almost completely determine the split-second choices that will have to be made should a nuclear exchange begin.

For this reason, I am convinced that the time for us as citizens to consider our responsibilities in helping to shape nuclear policies is the present. I regard it as both my right and my responsibility to make what contribution I can to help raise and form public awareness of the moral and human stakes in the nuclear arms race. I make no claim to special competence in the military, scientific or political spheres, but as a human being, a citizen, a Christian, and because of my special responsibilities as Archbishop. I cannot relinquish the task of inquiring into, reflecting upon, and giving expression to the moral implications of the military, scientific and political questions which touch the rights of God and the sacredness of human persons as deeply as do the questions of nuclear armament and nuclear warfare.

In speaking with you on these topics, I am fully aware of the practical separation of Church and state in our country. I ask only that both my fellow Catholics and my fellow citizens consider prayerfully and deeply our moral responsibility as human beings in a world armed with these deadly weapons. In a democracy, citizens bear a responsibility which comes with freedom: the responsibility of helping to shape the direction of their nation's policies. As Pope John Paul II put it in his 1982 World Day of Peace Message, "Peace cannot be built by the power of rulers alone. Peace can be firmly constructed only if it corresponds to the resolute determination of all people of good will. Rulers must be supported and enlightened by a public opinion that encourages them or, where necessary, expresses disapproval."[3] To be responsible together, reflection on criteria for the moral evaluation of the use of military force, which have been developed in the Christian and humanistic traditions of our civilization, can be of great assistance.

Catholic Moral Teaching on War

My brothers and sisters in Christ, I ask you to consider prayerfully with me the theological framework for the moral evaluation of the resort to military force which has been developed through the centuries by the Catholic tradition. To begin with, this framework is based ultimately on the teaching and example of Christ our Lord, who is for us the Way, the Truth, and the Life (cf. John 14:6). It is simultaneously rooted in a fundamental conviction about the dignity and sacredness of every human life, a dignity made all the greater by the life, death and resurrection of Christ our Lord who has called all of us to love our neighbor, even when this neighbor is an enemy (cf. Matthew 5:44). He has stated that all who are peacemakers shall be called children of God (cf. Matthew 5:9).

---

3. Pope John Paul II, *1982 World Day of Peace Message,* number 6, p. 10.

This love of neighbor and vocation to peace leads Christians to profound aversion to war and violence in all its forms. Indeed from the time of Christ the use of non-violent means for redressing injustice has been a goal set forth by Christian teaching. In recent years the Second Vatican Council has reiterated this deep conviction of the Christian tradition: "We cannot fail to praise those who renounce the use of violence in the vindication of their rights and who resort to methods of defense which are otherwise available to weaker parties too, provided this can be done without injury to the rights and duties of others or of the community itself."[4]

The Council went on to acknowledge the legitimacy of conscientious objection to participation in all war and called for nations to acknowledge this legitimacy in laws that "make humane provisions for the case of those who for reasons of conscience refuse to bear arms, provided, however, that they accept some form of service to the human community."[5] While respecting the right of individuals to refuse to shoot or fire at someone, the Council has words of praise for members of the armed forces: "All those who enter the military service in loyalty to their country should look upon themselves as the custodians of the security and freedom of their fellow countrymen: and when they carry out their duty properly, they are contributing to the maintenance of peace."[6]

A more complex moral framework has been generally characteristic of Catholic thought through much of its history—the form of moral reasoning known as the just war theory.

This approach to the morality of the use of force continues to be viewed by the Catholic Church today as a significant help both in guiding individual consciences and in evaluating public policy in accordance with the gospel of Christ and the sacredness of human life. It is a stance which rests on the central obligation to love one's neighbor and to respect the digni-

---

4. *Gaudium et Spes, no. 78.*

5. *Gaudium et Spes, no. 79.*

6. *Gaudium et Spes, no. 79.*

ty of every human person. The just war theory acknowledges that this love and respect can, in some circumstances, call for the defense of human life and dignity by the limited use of force. Its overriding goals are the protection of human persons and the preservation of peace. This teaching recognizes that the demands of justice and the complete avoidance of violence are not in all cases simultaneously realizable in a world touched by human arrogance and sin. Thus the Second Vatican Council has stated that "as long as the danger of war remains, and there is no competent and sufficiently powerful authority at the international level, governments cannot be denied the right to legitimate defense once every means of peaceful settlement has been exhausted."[7] Therefore, "governmental authority and others who share public responsibility have the duty to protect the welfare of the people entrusted to their care, and to conduct such grave matters soberly."[8]

The Council presupposed the traditional Catholic teaching on conditions that must be fulfilled before resort to war can be considered as justified. The conditions are the following:

1) The action must be for the purpose of defending persons who are being unjustly attacked.

2) The use of force must be a last resort.

3) There must be a reasonable hope that the use of force will succeed in righting the wrong it resists.

4) The human cost of the force used must be proportionate to the evil it seeks to overcome.

5) Finally, in the actual course of hostilities the means used must be such that non-combatants are immune from direct attack.[9]

---

7. *Gaudium et Spes, no. 79.* See Pope John Paul II, *1982 World Day of Peace Message,* no. 12.

8. *Gaudium et Spes, no. 79.*

9. For a full discussion of the just war theory as understood on contemporary Roman Catholic moral teaching see J. Bryan Hehir, "The Just War Ethic and Catholic Theology: Dynamics of Change in Continuity," in Thomas A. Shannon. ed., *War or Peace? The Search for New Answers* (Maryknoll, NY: Orbis Books, 1980), pp. 15–39.

Actions which fall outside the limits of these conditions are judged incompatible with the demands of justice and Christian love. The criteria of the just war theory are held in common by the Catholic moral tradition and the humanistic tradition of the West, for they are the criteria which safeguard the dignity of the human person under the circumstances of conflict.[10]

In light of the possible consequences of nuclear war, and the moral criteria just outlined, I ask you to consider carefully the following most urgent questions, and I ask you to search your own consciences for answers.

First: Can there be a justification for the "first use" of nuclear weapons? Is such a "first use" to be judged good or bad, fair or unfair, moral or immoral, just or unjust, compatible or incompatible with the teachings of the Church, with the fundamental respect for human dignity, and with the demand that force never be used aggressively?

Second: Is there a reasonable hope of success in righting the wrong which a nation resists by launching a full-scale attack on another nation, even in retaliation for a nuclear attack which has already been launched against one's own country? Is there such a hope in launching a lesser attack under the same conditions? What would be the moral goodness or the moral evil of such actions?

Third: Is there a proportion between the use of even a small fraction of nuclear forces stockpiled on the earth today and the good to be achieved?

Fourth: Is it possible to use nuclear weapons against an adversary without violating the principle of non-combatant immunity?

Fifth: What is the morality of the use of strategic weapons against military targets on land if such use causes "collateral damage" in the form of deaths, injuries and radiation of vast numbers of innocent persons? What is the morality of the use

10. This humanist tradition is admirably exemplified in Michael Walzer, *Just and Unjust Wars: A Moral Argument with Historical Illustrations* (New York: Basic Books, 1977).

of strategic weapons if such use does not cause such extensive "collateral damage"?

Sixth: What is the moral goodness or evil of the use of nuclear weapons, strategic or tactical, against any target, civilian or military, if such use is likely to lead to escalation to a full-scale strategic exchange? What is the moral goodness or evil, if such a use is not likely to lead to such a catastrophe?

My dear brothers and sisters in Christ, we are indeed reflecting on a most fundamental issue of our day. It is as fundamental as life and death. As Christians we must give it our prayerful attention. After all, we choose life. That is why the Christian community is called to help in the formation of an international consensus to reject ultimately the use of all nuclear arms. I cannot adequately stress this important truth. Let me repeat it from the bottom of my heart and with all the vigor at my command: the Christian community is called to help in the formation of an international consensus to reject ultimately the use of all nuclear arms.

The Responsibility of Catholics
for Peace in the World

Christians are citizens of all the nations of the world. As citizens, American Catholics are rightly concerned with the preservation of freedom and justice in the land which is our home. The call of Christ, however, is not limited by national borders. The community to which Christians owe their ultimate loyalty is the whole family of God's children, the entire human race. The Church is "a kind of sacrament or sign of intimate union with God, and of the unity of all humankind. She is also an instrument for the achievement of such union and unity."[11] The vocation of the Church to work for the greater unity of the peoples of the globe meets an especially urgent need in the nuclear age. This vocation does not mean that Christians can naively ignore the profound threats to their

---

11. Vatican Council II, Lumen Gentium (Dogmatic Constitution on the Church), no. 1, in Abbott and Gallagher, op. cit.

own nations and to the world as a whole that nuclear armaments have created. Rather, it means that we have a duty to take a stand which promotes the safety of all nations, including our own, by working for the rejection of these weapons of destruction.

I have reached into my conscience, as I pray you are reaching into yours, and I find that such a stand is the only and ultimate response that holds any promise of breaking the spiral of mutual fear which is driving nations into ever greater peril. It is my personal belief that this is a realistic response to our situation and the only response, at present, that is an expression of hope for the human family on our planet.

The Question of Deterrence

The conviction that nuclear weapons must be banished from the earth should press us to the utterly urgent issue of how to prevent their use from occurring while we still have them. The moral legitimacy of the production and development of nuclear arms in order to deter an adversary from using its nuclear force against us has become one of the most controverted questions in the nuclear debate in our day. Even if there were agreement on the unacceptability of any use of nuclear weapons, that agreement could co-exist with disagreement about the morality of possessing nuclear weapons for purposes of deterrence.

There are at least two kinds of deterrence, deterrence by pain and deterrence by denial. The deterrence theory by pain is built upon the supposition that a nation can prevent another's use of nuclear weapons by itself possessing such massive destructive force that only an adversary bent on suicide would dare launch an attack against it. It seeks to prevent nuclear war by creating a situation where no one could rationally consider starting such a war. There is another deterrence, the deterrence of denial, predicated on the idea that the possession and placement of more sophisticated low-yield nuclear weapons aimed at strategic military targets involving only those few civilians who are working in the nuclear field, can in fact deter an enemy because it denies the possibility of first strike capability (either of a conventional or nuclear nature) with impunity.

In following a deterrence strategy, nations threaten and prepare to take actions which can have catastrophic effects upon life in this world. At the same time the intention which leads to such threats and preparations is the intention to prevent nuclear war.

The danger and ambiguity of any deterrent strategy are immediately evident when one considers the possibility of an accidental initiation of a nuclear exchange. On the other hand, there are many persons who maintain that the possession of nuclear arms by each of the superpowers has in fact deterred any nuclear attack upon one by the other. These persons also suggest that an atomic attack would never have been launched against Hiroshima and Nagasaki if Japan had possessed an atom bomb and the United States was convinced that Japan was ready to use it.

In any case, the dilemma is real: does a system which seeks to prevent nuclear war by threatening nuclear attack truly prevent the use of these weapons, or does it make nuclear war more probable? If a concrete policy and strategic posture are actually means to the prevention of war and to the development of arms control, then the ambiguity inherent in the possession of nuclear weapons can be tolerated, even though not approved as a desirable situation.[12] On the other hand, if such a policy and posture are judged to make nuclear war more likely and the goal of abolition of nuclear weapons less attainable, then this policy would be difficult to justify on moral grounds.

Whatever the ambiguities about deterrence may be, one thing I believe is certain: the only way to prevent nuclear war for the children of today and for unborn generations to come is the abolition of nuclear weapons from the earth and the cre-

---

12. See John Cardinal Krol, "Testimony before the Senate Foreign Relations Committee. September 6, 1979. *Origins 9* (September 13, 1979), pp. 195-199.

ation of a world order and a civilization of love that will insure that they are not again produced, much less used.

The Cost of the Nuclear
Arms Race in Human Resources

Dearly beloved in Christ, when considering the nuclear arms race and nuclear war, we cannot ignore the immense cost in human resources. This factor has moral implications. The combination of deterrence theory, strategies which prepare for actually fighting nuclear wars, and sophisticated technological innovation in weapons programs constitute an immensely costly mixture. The total of the world's present conventional and nuclear military expenditures is $550 billion per year.[13]

This outlay is the equivalent of the total annual income of the poorer half of the entire population of the earth. In a world of over four billion human beings, where one-third of all people lack the necessities of life, the huge amounts of money that prevailing strategies have driven us to expend on weapons are an outrageous affront to human life, to the rights of the poor and therefore to God himself.

As the Holy See declared at the U.N. Special Session on Disarmament in 1976: "The obvious contradiction between the waste involved in overproduction of military devices and the extent of unsatisfied vital needs (both in developing countries and in the marginal and poor elements in rich societies) is itself an act of aggression which amounts to a crime, for even when they are not used, by their cost alone, armaments kill the poor by causing them to starve."[14] Moreover these expenditures for arms are not only a threat to the poor. They reduce the resources available for housing, medical care, human services and education of all of us and all of our children. The immense drain of human resources represented by the

---

13. Ruth Leger Sivard, *World Military and Social Expenditures 1981* (Leesbury VA: World Priorities, 1981), p. 5.

14. *The Holy See and Disarmament* (Vatican City: Tipographica Poligotta Vaticana 1976).

unprecedented arms build-up now underway robs the whole of God's family of possibilities for social and intellectual development and fulfillment. Indeed the economics of present arms policies around the world in itself raises serious moral questions.

An Appeal to the Leaders of Nations

Dearly beloved in Christ, the drift toward destruction must end! And so, in the name of God, in the name of the risen Christ in whom we place our hope, in the name of humanity, I ask you to join with me in raising an urgent appeal to leaders of nuclear nations, and to all citizens of these lands to turn back from the strategies of death.

Together let us call on the United States and the Soviet Union to consider carefully the wisdom of bilateral and even multilateral negotiations leading to a mutual halt on testing, production, and deployment of nuclear weapons and of missiles and aircraft designed primarily to deliver nuclear weapons. Serious consideration of this action I believe to be the minimal moral response to the present highly dangerous circumstances. I realize that this is a complex matter and falls far short of the goal of disarmament, but it could hopefully have the effect of breaking the spiral of fear and hostility which daily carries us closer to disaster. Obviously the process would have to be verifiable in order to yield trust and remove fear. We make a similar ugent appeal to the scientific and technological communities involved in the discovery, development, and production of nuclear weapons. After all, without them, the weapons would not have come into existence and could not be developed and produced.

More importantly, let us call on the leaders of all nations possessing nuclear arms, including our own, to heed Pope John Paul's appeal for peace, as enunciated in his message of January 1, 1982, and enter into negotiations which seek in all good faith to bring about an actual reduction in arms. Because of the utterly grave threat posed by nuclear arms, arms control and disarmament negotiations should not, in my judgment, be made dependent on previous resolution of the other serious differences which divide us. Indeed let us call on our government as well as the governments of other lands to approach the conflicts between us in a way which protects the integrity of negotiations on genuine arms control and reduction.

In a world threatened with nuclear catastrophe, do the superpowers dare risk any other way of dealing with their differences? As I have noted above, Pope John Paul II has wisely pointed out that the nuclear threat leads us to recognize "that war is the most barbarous and least effective way of resolving conflicts. More than ever before, human society is forced to provide itself with the means of consultation and dialogue which it needs in order to survive and therefore with the institutions necessary for building up justice and peace."[15]

I believe then that a positive appeal for negotiation, consultation, dialogue and for the strengthening of international institutions which foster a peaceful and just world order should accompany our call for the abolition of nuclear weapons from the earth.

Seeking Peace: The Task of All

In the exercise of my responsibilities as Archbishop of Boston, I ask all members of the Catholic community to consider carefully and conscientiously the course of action each of us should take in light of the teachings and of the concerns set forth in this letter. Above all, we need to pray together at all times, but especially in this Easter season that the Lord of life will give us the wisdom, the courage, and the hope to act on the basis of our commitment to Jesus Christ and to all our brothers and sisters in the human family.

The peace we seek is God's own peace. Without God's help it is beyond our power to attain it. But the Easter message is God's promise that this help is constantly offered to us by the Holy Spirit, the comforter. So let us pray daily that the Spirit will strengthen us in the bonds of peace. Let us pray that through the risen Christ, who is our peace, every dividing

---

15. Pope John Paul II, *1982 World Day of Peace Message*, no. 12.

wall of hostility may be broken down (cf. Ephesians 2:14). St. Paul has assured us that "to set the mind on the Spirit is life and peace" (Romans 8:6). So let us turn our minds and hearts to God and ask for peace and hope with all our being.

The good news of Easter also calls each of us to examine our own attitudes toward conflict and violence. Have we allowed ourselves to slip quietly into a kind of despair, a state of mind that accepts the inevitability of nuclear war? Easter challenges us to renewed hope and to renewed commitment to peace, both as individuals and as nations.

As shepherd of the flock, I have tried in this letter to let the message of Christ's resurrection renew and deepen my own service of the God of peace. I call on all the priests, deacons and religious of the Archdiocese to consider how the Easter proclamation can bring true renewal of your ministries in a nuclear world. I invite parents and families to let the hope of Easter become the foundation of your lives together so that the children of the next generation may have greater hope in their future. I ask that all of us examine how the labor of our hands and the work of our minds might become not only a means of earning our livelihood but a real contribution to the peace of the world.

The area of the Boston Archdiocese is a center of scientific, technological, medical, financial and artistic achievement which is second to none in our country. In all these areas of human creativity, we need to examine how we can direct our talents to the service of life, peace and hope rather than the spiral of fear and nuclear despair. And finally, I call on teachers and educators from kindergarten to the most advanced levels of learning to look at the future which awaits your students as you pursue your noble task. Let the words of Isaiah become your own: "They shall not learn war anymore" (Isaiah 2:4).

A Response of the Archdiocese to the Appeal for Peace and Life

In order to help the Catholic community of Boston deal with these urgent questions and needs, the Archdiocese plans to take a number of specific steps in the months ahead. An Archdiocesan conference on the response of Christians to the issues raised by the arms race will be convened on June 26. Its purpose will be further examination of questions dealt with in this letter and exploration of concrete ways for the Boston Catholic community to respond to them. In September we will begin organized programs on these questions in the parishes of the Archdiocese. Also in September educational programs in Catholic schools and parish religious education programs will begin.

It is my hope that this letter and these specific steps will be a source of renewed faith and hope that war can be avoided and that we can truly live as peacemakers in a fear-ridden world.

Conclusion: Prayer for Peace and Life

Before I bring this letter to a close, I wish to address all those who believe in God and who respect life with the words of Moses to God's people: "I set before you life or death, blessing or curse. Choose life then, so that you and your descendants may live, by loving the Lord your God, heeding his voice and holding fast to him. For that will mean life for you, a long life for you to live on the land, which the Lord swore he would give to your fathers, Abraham, Isaac, and Jacob" (Deuteronomy 30:19-20).

Because we choose life we choose peace, peace which is ultimately God's gift to us; and for this gift we must pray according to the mind of His Holiness, Pope John Paul II:

"Yes, our future is in the hands of God, who alone gives true peace. And when human hearts sincerely think of work for peace it is still God's grace that inspires and strengthens those thoughts. All people are in this sense invited to echo the sentiments of St. Francis of Assisi, the eighth centenary of whose birth we are celebrating: Lord, make us instruments of your peace: where there is hatred, let us sow love; where there is injury, pardon; when discord rages, let us build peace.

"Christians love to pray for peace, as they make their own the prayer of so many psalms punctuated by supplications for peace and repeated with the universal love of Jesus. We have here a shared and very profound element for all ecumenical activities. Other believers all over the world are also awaiting from Almighty God the gift of peace, and, more or less consciously, many other people of good will are ready to make the same prayer in the secret of their hearts. May fervent supplications thus rise to God from the four corners of the earth! This will already create a fine unanimity on the road to peace. And who could doubt that God will hear and grant this cry of his children: Lord, grant us peace! Grant us your peace!"[16]

I leave you with the words Jesus addressed to the two women who came to the tomb on the first Easter morning: "Peace! Do not be afraid" (Matthew 29:9-10). And in the words of the liturgy in which we celebrate our hope, I pray for all of us and for our world: "May the light of Christ, rising in glory, dispel the darkness of our hearts and minds. Christ yesterday and today, the beginning and the end, Alpha and Omega, all time belongs to him and all the ages; to him be glory and power through every age forever. Amen."[17]

Mary, Queen of Peace, pray for us.

A peace-filled Easter to all.

16. Pope John Paul II, *1982 World Day of Peace Message,* no. 13, pp. 20-21.

17. Liturgy of the Easter Vigil, *The Sacramentary of the Roman Missal.*

PART THREE

ECUMENICAL STATEMENTS

The Christian Church
(Disciples of Christ)

[1] From Resolution "Concerning Ending the Arms Race," adopted 1979

WHEREAS, the militarized world of the twentieth century is an insecure and unstable one, where international tensions threaten to erupt into wars that could quickly escalate into nuclear annihilation; and

WHEREAS, the arms race, by provoking an upward spiral of development and acquisition of weapons and technology in response to advances made by others in war-making capability, does not increase world security but tends to undermine it; and

WHEREAS, real security can never be achieved by a balance of terror in a heavily armed world, but depends on international peace and justice, with conflicts resolved through mutual understanding, negotiation, and law; and

WHEREAS, the United States military budget is being increased at a time when programs for human resources (education, employment, health-care, adequate nutrition) and physical resources (land use, environment, community development) are being reduced; and

WHEREAS, the Christian Church (Disciples of Christ) over the years in International Convention and General Assembly actions has strongly stated its opposition to war as a method of settling disputes between nations, and has called into question the nuclear arms race and high military expenditures to develop systems of death and destruction, thus diverting energies and funds from domestic and foreign programs for humanitarian, life-giving purposes; . . .

THEREFORE, BE IT RESOLVED, that the General Assembly of the Christian Church (Disciples of Christ) meeting in St. Louis, Missouri October 25–31, 1979 call upon President Carter and the Congress of the United States:

1. to question the role of the United States as the world's largest producer and exporter of arms and to intensify their efforts to reverse the dangerous and burdensome arms race;
2. to pursue with urgency a comprehensive ban on nuclear testing and effective limitations on the development, production, and sale of arms;
3. to seek seriously the development of peaceful ways to resolve conflicts between nations and to plan expeditiously for conversion to a healthy economy based on production for non-military purposes.

BE IT FURTHER RESOLVED, that the General Assembly suggest that the members of the Christian Church (Disciples of Christ), recognizing the possibility of cataclysmic destruction,

1. request materials from the Division of Homeland Ministries and undertake the responsibility of becoming more informed about the issues;
2. consider joining Disciples Peace Fellowship, a fellowship of members of the Christian Church (Disciples of Christ) who reject war as a method of settling international disputes and work together toward the elimination of war and the creation of conditions of peace among people and nations; and
3. set about, in their congregations and communities,

the essential task of seeking imaginative and reconciling ways to improve the human condition in a world of peace.

[2] Resolutions adopted by the General Assembly meeting in Anaheim, California, July 31-August 5, 1981

Resolution Concerning the Establishment of a Designated Peace Sunday in the Christian Church (Disciples of Christ)

WHEREAS, Luke's Gospel describes Jesus' ministry as one of peace (Luke 1:79), and Jesus himself pronounces God's blessing on the peacemakers (Matthew 5:9), and

WHEREAS, increasing military budgets, nuclear proliferation, and mistrust among nations are setting a spiritual tone of our times which is a denial of the Good News which Jesus taught and lived, and

WHEREAS, our heritage of witness for peace articulated by Alexander Campbell, Peter Ainsley, and others calls us to faithfulness to the gospel of love, and

WHEREAS, many members of the Christian Church (Disciples of Christ) long to affirm and express more fully the biblical vision of peace, and

WHEREAS, the concentrated attention of the whole Church will offer support and encouragement to the ministries of church school teachers, worship leaders, pastors, and all who share hopes and dreams for wholeness in the human family.

THEREFORE, BE IT RESOLVED, that the General Assembly of the Christian Church (Disciples of Christ) meeting in Anaheim, California July 31–August 5, 1981 urge that the Division of Homeland Ministries give careful consideration to the establishment of a specific Sunday in the church program calendar of the Christian Church (Disciples of Christ) to be designated as Peace Sunday and to be celebrated annually, and that the Division of Homeland Ministries and Disciples of Peace Fellowship jointly develop possible program resources, content and funding, and

BE IT FURTHER RESOLVED, that each congregation of the Christian Church (Disciples of Christ) be encouraged to focus worship, preaching, and study that day on peace issues, and

BE IT FURTHER RESOLVED, that each congregation of the Christian Church (Disciples of Christ) be encouraged to gather and make available to its members information on organizations which foster the cause of peace, and

BE IT FURTHER RESOLVED, that each congregation of the Christian Church (Disciples of Christ) be encouraged to utilize the established Peace Sunday as a focal point each year for launching or renewing one or more ongoing study groups on peace.

Resolution Concerning Nuclear Arms

BECAUSE GOD is Creator and Christ is Lord of all life; and in Christ God affirms and enlarges the freedom we experience in creation; and

BECAUSE this planet, Earth, is in the particular care of human beings by God's providence; and all life and the creation itself is fully valued by God, and so is sacred;

FUTHERMORE, since the tens of thousands of nuclear weapons now in existence and ready to be used are a daily threat to this Earth and all its inhabitants; and the "first-strike" strategies now the goal of military planners of the U.S.A. and the U.S.S.R. further threaten the Earth's too-wobbly stability so much that informed scientists now believe nuclear war to be inevitable before this century ends; and

BECAUSE there is widespread ignorance and willful avoidance of the realities of nuclear war; and the threat of these armaments and their continued increase saps the hope of our youth and blights the future of our children, being a major cause of the pervasive unrest and anxiety so characteristic of our times; and

BECAUSE the continuing expenditures for these armaments is a major source of the economic inflation that hurts us all; and the poor of Earth pay that price first; and the material and energy put into these weapons and their delivery systems and their complex auxiliary systems of detection, guidance, and protection wastes these limited resources; and many of our most able minds are used for these destructive enterprises;

THEREFORE, BE IT RESOLVED that the General Assembly of the Christian Church (Disciples of Christ) meeting in Anaheim, California, July 31–August 5, 1981, voice our deep conviction that this most heinous obscenity of the continuing nuclear armaments research, development, and production be brought to an immediate end; and we call upon the leaders of the nations to stop this madness and get on with those things that make for peace.

TO THAT END, we make this urgent plea that the governments and peoples of Earth stop producing these weapons and systems, and begin reducing those now in existence, and eventually abolish them altogether.

AS A MEANS, to get this underway, and building upon the first Strategic Arms Limitation Treaty (SALT I) we reaffirm our conviction that a negotiated, orderly and verified nuclear disarmament process is indispensable. We call upon the President and the Senate of the United States to make a new national commitment to join with all nuclear powers in the drafting and ratification of subsequent treaties to assure the progressive reduction and ultimate elimination of nuclear arms.

FURTHERMORE, we strongly encourage our congregations and their members to become informed about the realities of nuclear war, and to encourage groups in all communities to learn of these threats and to study ways to make peace the goal of governments.

IN ADDITION, we ask for a deeper commitment in the faith we share—that all persons are equally and fully valuable in God's sight, and therefore in ours; and that the attitudes of national, regional, and cultural superiority, which are roots of distrust and of war-making, be uprooted and replaced with care and respect.

IN CONCLUSION, we ask that this matter of the threat

of nuclear arms and their elimination be among the highest priorities for our church in the terms of education and action.

Resolution Concerning Support for the Conscientious Objector to War

WHEREAS, human rights are basic to our Christian faith and to the Christian Church (Disciples of Christ), and

WHEREAS, the right to refuse to participate in war is a basic human right, and

WHEREAS, the Christian Church (Disciples of Christ) is called to support the rights of conscience for those who are conscientious objectors as they do those who by conscience feel compelled to serve, and

WHEREAS, our churches are also called to support the peace testimony of the Christian Church,

THEREFORE, BE IT RESOLVED, that the General Assembly of the Christian Church (Disciples of Christ) meeting in Anaheim, California, July 31–August 5, 1981, call upon all our members and churches to support fully all our members and non-members who are conscientious objectors to war, with our prayers, our love and with any other support we can give these young people of draft age, and to encourage our churches and communities to offer opportunities for youth who are unsure and who wish to explore their alternatives.

Resolution Concerning a Nuclear Arms Freeze

WHEREAS, the Bible calls us to relate to all people as members of God's family and to be faithful stewards of God's earth, and

WHEREAS, the United States of America and the Union of Soviet Socialist Republics already possess nuclear arsenals which are sufficient to kill hundreds of millions of people and to destroy the life-sustaining resources of the earth, and

WHEREAS, new forms of technology encourage a "first strike mentality" among military planners and discussions of "limited nuclear war" among political figures, and

WHEREAS, this drift toward so dangerous a future is contrary to the position of the General Assembly of the Christian Church (Disciples of Christ) stated in resolutions such as #7936 "Concerning Ending the Arms Race."

THEREFORE, BE IT RESOLVED, that the General Assembly of the Christian Church (Disciples of Christ) meeting in Anaheim, California July 31–August 5, 1981 endorse the following position: To improve national and international security, the United States and the Soviet Union should stop the nuclear arms race. Specifically, they should adopt a mutual freeze on the testing, production and deployment of nuclear weapons and of missiles and new aircraft designed primarily to deliver nuclear weapons. This is an essential, verifiable first step toward lessening the risk of nuclear war and reducing the nuclear arsenals.

BE IT FURTHER RESOLVED, that congregations of the Christian Church (Disciples of Christ) be urged to engage in study related to a nuclear arms freeze, and through 1982 collect individual signatures in support of this position, signatures to be sent to the Department of Church in Society, Division of Homeland Ministries, and

BE IT FURTHER RESOLVED, that the Division of Homeland Ministries be requested to develop resources and programs to support these efforts, and

BE IT FURTHER RESOLVED, that the General Minister and President of the Christian Church (Disciples of Christ) send copies of this resolution and subsequent signatures in support of it to the President of the United States of America and the President of the Presidium of the Supreme Soviet of the Union of Soviet Socialist Republics. A Russian translation of this resolution has been prepared and is on file in the General Office of the Christian Church (Disciples of Christ).

Resolution Concerning a National Peace Academy

WHEREAS, there are military academies in our country where young men and women learn the art and skills of warfare;

WHEREAS, these centers are financed and controlled by

the Congress of the U.S.A. with the tax revenue of the citizenry for the express purpose of preparing young people in the military expressions and conflict resolutions;

WHEREAS, these military academies serve as training centers for military personnel from other countries as well as our own nation in the use of weapons, tactics and other destructive measures in combat situations;

WHEREAS, we have experienced the futility and cost of war and armed conflict as a means to peaceful settlement of international problems;

WHEREAS, we who are of the Judeo-Christian tradition, have become aware of options other than armed combat for the resolution and/or management of conflict; and

WHEREAS, this awareness causes us to advocate peaceful measures for the resolution of conflict as opposed to violent means;

THEREFORE, BE IT RESOLVED, that the General Assembly of the Christian Church (Disciples of Christ) meeting in Anaheim, California July 31 to August 5, 1981 endorse the advocacy of the formation of a National Peace Academy for the purpose of training persons to work for peaceful solutions to national and international problems.

FOR MORE INFORMATION: Division of Homeland Ministries, Christian Church (Disciples of Christ), 222 South Downey Avenue, Box 1986, Indianapolis, IN 46206 *or* Disciples Peace Fellowship, Box 1986, Indianapolis, IN 46206

Church of the Brethren

[3] From a resolution adopted by the Church of the Brethren Annual Conference, 1977

... Peace with Justice

We place a high priority on changing political structures in order to reverse the present spiral of violence, militarism, and the armaments race. The Church of the Brethren must be decisive in shaping its own programs and calling all Christians and other persons of good will to encourage the United States to:

- cease immediately its sale of arms to other countries
- pledge not to use nuclear weapons
- *dismantle its nuclear arsenal*
- strengthen global institutions that facilitate non-violent means of conflict resolution and the process of disarmament
- curtail foreign military aid and training
- refuse to sell nuclear fuels and technology to any state not agreeing to the Non-Proliferation Treaty and inspection by the International Atomic Energy Agency
- end its secret intelligence gathering and its political intervention in foreign countries

[4] From a resolution adopted by the Church of the Brethren Annual Conference, 1980

Times of crisis in the life of the religious community often create landmarks along the pilgrimage of faith . . .

Events and tensions at the outset of the new decade point up that this is also a time of crisis. Ever greater quantities of national and global resources are being diverted into an increasingly more devastating war machine. Hope for justice and peace becomes more remote. Those persons who are least able to bring about change—the poor, the aged, the young—are suffering the most.

. . . We also join our voice with those who call for a nuclear moratorium and cry out "Enough." Yet we recognize how limited this action would be since the current nuclear overkill capacity of ten or twenty or more times is already too much.

To break this mad cycle we call for bold and creative initiatives such as a unilateral decision by our government to terminate all nuclear tests and the production of all nuclear weapons and their delivery systems. In turn, we appeal to the Soviet Union to reciprocate in order to halt the rush toward a nuclear holocaust.

... We find our security in God, not in weapons, and would point those around us to that security.

FOR MORE INFORMATION: Church of the Brethren General Offices, 1451 Dundee Avenue, Elgin, IL 60120 *or* Brethren Peace Fellowship, Box 145, New Windsor, MD 21776

Episcopal Church

[5] "Christian Attitudes to War in a Nuclear Age," statement of the Primates of the Anglican Communion, 1981

The church in former ages justified war in certain circumstances by recourse to the theory of the 'just war'. This theory was never intended to commend war, but to limit its frequency. There have always been Christians who repudiated any legitimising of war. Today many others would join them believing that the very conditions for a just war themselves condemn not only the actual use of nuclear weapons, but also their possession as a deterrent.

Whilst justifying the legitimacy of such a unilateralist pacifist position, not all of us believe that the Church corporately ever has adopted or is likely to adopt such a stance. This does not mean that we are either indifferent or uncommitted. We strongly identify with the Final Document of the United Nations Special Assembly Session on Disarmament of 1978, especially when it calls for a comprehensive nuclear test ban; a halt to conventional arms procurement and trade; the development of an alternative system of security to the accumulation of weaponry and the mobilization of public opinion to counteract the armament race. We also strongly commend the proposal by Dr. Kurt Waldheim, the U.N. Secretary General, that all national governments set aside 0.1% of their defense budgets for disarmament research and education.

We pledge ourselves to work for multilateral disarmament, and to support those who seek, by education and other appropriate means, to influence those people and agencies who shape nuclear policy. In particular we believe that the SALT talks must be resumed and pursued with determination.

The Archbishop of Canterbury in a speech in Washington said: "We have made a great advance in technology without a corresponding advance in moral sense. We are capable of unbinding the forces which lie at the heart of creation and of destroying our civilization ... It is vital that we see modern weapons for war for what they are—evidence of madness." As Christians we recognize a demonic element in the complexity of our world, but we also affirm our belief in the good will and purpose and Providence of God for his whole creation. This requires us to work for a world characterized not by fear, but by mutual trust and justice.

"MANKIND IS CONFRONTED BY A CHOICE: WE MUST HALT THE ARMS RACE AND PROCEED TO DISARMAMENT, OR FACE ANNIHILATION." (Final Document of the UNSSD)

[6] From the "Pastoral Letter," House of Bishops, 1980

Since nuclear armaments here and in the Soviet Union have created a world in which the whole can nowhere be protected against its parts, our own national security has reached the zero point. The issue is no longer the survival of one nation against another. We stand now in mortal danger of global human incineration.

[7]   Statement on the arms race signed by 60 U.S. Episcopal bishops, 1980

We, the undersigned bishops of the Episcopal Church in the United States of America:

BELIEVING that war is contradictory to and inconsistent with the Gospel of our Lord Jesus Christ who calls us to be peacemakers, and

REAFFIRMING all the statements about war, peace, and violence in the past century by the General Convention, House of Bishops, and Lambeth Conference, and

OBSERVING the Faustian proportion of the international arms race, and the paralyzing effects—personal and economic—resulting from the fear in which it is based, and

QUESTIONING the validity of the theory of mutual deterrence which underlies the nuclear arms race, hereby

JOIN other persons throughout this nation who are requesting the President of the United States to propose to the Soviet Union a mutual nuclear weapons moratorium by which the United States and the Soviet Union agree to halt immediately the testing, production, and further deployment of all nuclear warheads, missiles, and delivery systems.

[8]   Resolution of the General Convention, 1976

WHEREAS, Today all mankind lies under the threat of nuclear destruction, and

WHEREAS, The devastation possible through even limited use of nuclear weapons is incalculable; and

WHEREAS, The U.S. having led in the development of nuclear power should also lead in its effective utilization and control; therefore be it

RESOLVED, The General Convention of 1976 commend the efforts made at the SALT talks to limit the number of nuclear weapons and delivery systems in the arsenal of the major powers; and be it further

RESOLVED, That the General Convention express its hope for a time when we may end our dependence on the use of nuclear weapons as a deterrent to war and may use nuclear power exclusively for peaceful purposes.

FOR MORE INFORMATION: Episcopal Peace Fellowship, Hearst Hall (Room 232), Wisconsin Avenue and Woodley Road NW, Washington, DC 20016

Lutheran Church in America

[9] From "Social Statement on World Community," adopted in 1970

It is clearly time for a rethinking of the meaning of national security. In view of the overkill capacity now possessed by the superpowers, national security can no longer be defined in terms of either nuclear superiority or even nuclear stalemate. The common threat which such weapons hold for all mankind teaches that their continued development can only undermine security. It is now necessary both to create an international legal framework within which arms control can be brought about and to help nations perceive that their safety must be conceived in more than military terms.

A beginning has been made in the construction of the legal framework. This effort should be intensified, should include all weapons of mass destruction. In the meantime, the United States should be encouraged to undertake such *unilateral initiatives* as may contribute to a climate more hospitable to the limitation of arms.

FOR MORE INFORMATION: Lutheran Peace Fellowship, John Backe, Coordinator, 168 West 100th Street, New York, NY 10025

National Council of Churches

[10]   Resolution on a Nuclear Weapons Freeze, adopted by the N.C.C. Governing Board, 1981

WHEREAS, The Strategic Arms Limitation Talks (SALT) between the Soviet Union and the United States are in abeyance as a result of events of the last two years; and

WHEREAS, heightened international tension is leading to sharp increases in the armament program of the Soviet Union and the United States as well as other nations with a consequent increase in the danger of war; and

WHEREAS, the National Council of Churches has long held that all the earth's resources are gifts of God, the Lord of Creation, and that men and women have a responsibility to preserve and enhance the created order, not to abuse and destroy it; and

WHEREAS, the National Council of Churches has consistently stressed the value of human life and God's activity in creation through the reconciling act in Christ whereby we are called to be agents of reconciliation; and

WHEREAS, representatives of the Orthodox and Protestant Churches, in a joint statement on March 27–29, 1979, entitled "Choose Life" "confessed that true security can be found only in relationships of trust;"

THEREFORE BE IT RESOLVED, that the Governing Board of the National Council of the Churches of Christ in the U.S.A.:

1. Urges both the United States and the Soviet Union to halt the nuclear arms race now by adopting promptly a mutual freeze on all further testing, production, and deployment of weapons and aircraft designed primarily to deliver nuclear weapons;

2. Until such time as a nuclear freeze by the United States and the Soviet Union may be agreed upon,

supports initiatives by either or both that would demonstrate good faith and make it easier for the other to take similar steps; and

3. Encourages all program units of the National Council of Churches to examine their responsibilities and opportunities in providing educational materials and other resources regarding the nuclear freeze to constituent communions; and

4. Calls upon affiliated denominations, their judicatories and congregations and related councils of churches to consider supporting this call for a nuclear freeze by:
   a. Making available to their membership speeches, printed resources, and audio-visual materials about the reasons for and importance of such a freeze;
   b. Supporting financially and by direct involvement the movement for a nuclear freeze;
   c. Calling upon their senators and representatives to provide congressional support for implementing such a freeze; and
   d. Urging the President and the Department of State to pursue initiatives leading toward a mutual freeze on the testing, production, and deployment of all nuclear weapons and delivery vehicles.

Presbyterian Church in the United States

[11] From "Resolution on Nuclear Weapons and Disarmament," adopted 1978

WHEREAS, the world is spending an estimated $400 billion annually on an unresolved arms race; and

WHEREAS, nuclear weapons pose an increasing threat of utter destruction if ever used, and the spread of nuclear weapons beyond the nations now known to have them is almost a certainty unless there is a reversal in the nuclear weapons competition; and

WHEREAS, President Carter, in his inaugural address on January 20, 1977, expressed the conviction that "the ultimate goal of this nation should be the reduction of nuclear weapons in all nations of the world to zero"; and

WHEREAS, the General Assembly of the United Nations is now meeting in a Special Session on Disarmament (May 23–June 28, 1978);

THEREFORE, the 118th General Assembly of the Presbyterian Church in the United States:

A. Reiterates its conviction that multilateral and comprehensive disarmaments is the goal toward which the United States should strive;

B. Supports a halt in further production of nuclear weapons multilaterally and a rollback of existing nuclear weapons;

C. Urges the United States government to continue to work for major strategic arms reduction through negotiation;

D. Again urges the United States government to continue to work for a multilateral agreement to halt all nuclear tests; . . .

E. Calls upon our members, in the light of our Christian vocation as peacemakers, to confess that we Christians in the United States have not been serious enough in our work for disarmament. We seek the help of Jesus Christ and call upon him for guidance that in all our congregations and program agencies we may commit ourselves anew to the Biblical vision of *shalom* by allocating more human and financial resources for education and action on the disarmament agenda;

F. Requests that the General Assembly Mission Board give leadership to our churches in educational efforts designed to increase awareness

among our church members on the dangers of the
continued arms race.

In response to the declaration "Choose Life" ... The 199th
General Assembly adopted the following statement: ...

That this General Assembly communicate to the
President of the United States and to each United
States Senator our respectful urging that they be
guided only by the aggressive and forthright pursuit
of peace in the handling of the SALT II treaty. We
urge on our great nation, in the spirit of the Lord Jesus Christ, a prudent willingness to risk in the quest
for a reduction of arms, and we urge a rejection of any
competitive quest for national superiority as an extension beyond the nation's reasonable defense. We
assure these elected officials of our prayers for them
in the pursuit of a just peace, and the consequent glorious opportunity to redirect resources from arms to
the nurture and feeding of the hungry.

[12] "Peacemaking," The Corporate Witness of the General Assembly, Public Policy Statements of the 121st General Assembly (1981)

I. Peacemaking: The Believers' Calling—An Affirmation of Policy and Direction

Twenty centuries ago, "in the fullness of time," God sent
Jesus the Christ. Now there is a special time in history—a season (kairos)—summoning the faith and obedience of God's people. For Christ has gathered and deployed his people around
the earth, across political and economic lines, in places of pow-
erfully protected affluence, and among the poorest of the poor.
The body of Christ responds to the world's pain with empathy
and anguish, one part for another, in our time.

Ominous clouds hang over human history. There are frightening risks in the continuing arms race and looming conflicts over diminishing energy resources as centers of power struggle for control. Our fear for safety has led us to trust in the false security of arms; our sin of war has led us to take life; and now we are in danger of taking our own lives as well. Furthermore, economic systems fail to allow a quarter of the world's population full participation in their societies, creating recurrent patterns of starvation and famine in Asia and Africa as in the 1970's.

But we believe that these times, so full of peril and tragedy for the human family, present a special call for obedience to our Lord, the Prince of Peace. The Spirit is calling us to life out of death.

The church must discern the signs of the times in the light of what the Spirit is revealing. We see signs of resurrection as the Spirit moves the churches to call for peace. We are at a turning point. We are faced with the decision either to serve the Rule of God or to side with the powers of death through our complacency and silence.

In these days we know that Jesus was sent by God into all the world. As we break bread together, our eyes are opened and recognize his living presence among us—Christ crucified by the tragic inequities of the earth—calling us together.

We are Christ's people, compelled by the Spirit and guided by our creeds to listen to a gospel that is addressed to the whole world. We are gathered around the Lord's Table with people from North and South and East and West. A new integrity is required of us: integrity in worship, integrity in secular life, integrity in relationship with Christ and Christians everywhere.

There is a new sense of the oneness of the world in our time. Humankind's initial forays into space have created a new perspective, a dramatic sense of the earth—the whole earth—as home. The era of satellite communication systems and the migration of millions of people from continent to continent have produced a new awareness of conditions of life everywhere on the globe.

It is not possible, in such a time, to avoid awareness of the economic disparities and political oppression besetting the human family. It is not possible to escape the knowledge of human suffering, and it is not possible to ignore the incongruous juxtaposition of affluence and arms on the one hand, and poverty and oppression on the other. The futility of nuclear war on a small planet as a solution to human problems is apparent.

We know that there can be no national security without global security and no global security without political and economic justice. As God's people, we will not cry "Peace, peace" without the fullness of God's shalom. As God's people, we will seek the security of the whole human family—all for whom Christ died. As God's people, we will celebrate the dignity of each of God's children.

We know that peace cannot be achieved by ending the arms race unless there is economic and political justice in the human family. Peace is more than the absence of war, more than a precarious balance of powers. Peace is the intended order of the world with life abundant for all God's children. Peacemaking is the calling of the Christian church, for Christ is our peace who has made us one through his body on the cross.

How will peace be achieved? By disarmament? Certainly, but not only by disarmament. By global economic reform? Certainly, but not only by global economic reform. By the change of political structures? Basically, at the heart, it is a matter of the way we see the world through the eyes of Christ. It is a matter of praying and yearning. It is an inner response to God, who loves the whole world and whose Spirit calls for and empowers the making of peace.

With repentance and humility and the power of hope, let us tend to our task.

To that end the 121st General Assembly (1981) affirms peacemaking as the responsibility of the Presbyterian Church, U.S. and declares:

(1) The church is faithful to Christ when it is engaged in peacemaking. God wills shalom—justice and peace on earth.

"Blessed are the peacemakers, for they shall be called children of God," said our Lord, the Prince of Peace. Those who follow our Lord have a special calling as peacemakers. In our confessions of faith the church has recognized this vocation, yet in our life we have been unfaithful to our Lord. We must repent. Our insensitivity to today's patterns of injustice, inequality, and oppression—indeed, our participation in them—denies the gospel. Christ alone is our peace. As part of his body in the whole church, we experience the brokenness of this world in our own life. Today we stand at a turning point in history. Our structures of military might, economic relations, political institutions, and cultural patterns fail to meet the needs of our time. At stake is our future and our integrity as God's people.

(2) The church is obedient to Christ when it nurtures and equips God's people as peacemakers. The church expects the gifts and guidance of the Holy Spirit in this task. (Eph. 4:16) Where the church is obedient to Christ, congregations will come alive in peacemaking. In worship we recognize the presence of God with us in our poor fragile lives. We live by the faith that God alone has cosmic dominion, that Christ alone is the Lord of the church and history, that the Holy Spirit alone empowers us here and now. We realize afresh that we are engaged in spiritual struggle.

In the proclamation of God's word of judgment and promise we are freed from guilt and paralyzing fear; at the Lord's Table we discover our brothers and sisters around the world; in baptism we are united in solidarity with the whole body; in prayer we lift our concern for the victims of injustice, oppression, and warfare; in praise we celebrate the gift of life, the Prince of Peace; in study we focus on foreign policy subjects in light of biblical and theological considerations.

The General Assembly has established positions on many subjects related to peace and justice, providing directions to facilitate the study and action necessary to equip God's people for the ordering of the church's life and the establishment of public policies in support of peacemaking. Interaction at the congregational level raises consciousness and transforms sensitivities about other peoples and their needs, about justice, and about the directions of United States foreign policy. Contact with other members of the worldwide Christian community enhances our growth as peacemakers.

Through worship and study we are miraculously strengthened by God's grace, and find new energy for action and a new sense of vocation crucial to peacemaking and the buoyant Christian life.

(3) The church bears witness to Christ when it nourishes the moral life of the nation for the sake of peace in our world. The church's faithful obedience to its calling means active participation in the formation of the values and beliefs of our society. It means seeking peace in the personal and social relationships of our culture and exercising our citizenship in the body politic to shape foreign policy. It is of strategic importance for us to nurture changes in public attitude and to raise public consciousness.

By God's grace we are members of a world community and can bring our global insights and peacemaking to our particular settings. By God's grace we are freed to work with all people who strive for peace and justice and to serve as signposts for God's love in our broken world. To deny our calling is a disservice to the church and the world. To affirm our calling is to act in "faith, hope and love." The love of Christ constrains us. The choices may be difficult but there is no substitute for acting as a church on the specific foreign policy problems affecting peace in our world today. Our strength is in our confidence that God's purpose rather than human schemes will finally prevail.

FOR MORE INFORMATION: Office of Corporate Witness in Public Affairs, Division of Corporate and Social Mission, General Assembly Mission Board, Presbyterian Church in the U.S., 341 Ponce de Leon Avenue NE, Atlanta, GA 30308. Southern Presbyterian Peace Fellowship, c/o Genevieve Yancy, Chairperson, 1808 Stokes Lane, Nashville, TN 37215

Reformed Church in America

[13] From "Christian Faith and the Nuclear Arms Race: A Reformed Perspective," A Theological Commission study recommended for distribution to the churches by the General Synod, 1980

God is the ultimate subject of theological reflection. The nuclear arms race may well be regarded as the penultimate subject of our time. There is no greater affront to the Lord and Giver of life, no more convincing evidence of human enslavement to the dark powers of this age, and no more urgent cause for the church's prophetic witness and action...

The General Synod of 1979 accepted eight specific recommendations which constituted a "Call to Action" concerning the nuclear arms race and disarmament. We note especially the second and sixth of those recommendations:

- to call for a full and general prohibition of: nuclear arms testing; development and deployment of new nuclear weapon systems; production and accumulation of chemical and radiological arms as well as other weapons of mass destruction;
- to urge our churches in their teaching and preaching to emphasize the biblical vision of peace and to stress the devastating social and personal consequences of the arms race.

...The nuclear arms race is first and foremost a false religion. It is, to be sure, also bad politics, bad economics, bad science, and bad war. It can and should be opposed on all these fronts. To confront the motivating power of the arms race, however, to confront its vital nerve, the church must come to understand it theologically. Only with a biblical discernment can we unmask this threat to life, expose its evil nature, and name its many names.

[14] From "Christian Imperatives for Peacemaking," a statement approved by the General Synod, 1981

The ominous threat of militarism demands that Christians prepare themselves intellectually and spiritually to fill the role of peacemakers in a sinful world. The secular world teaches that our primary security against that which threatens us is to be found in ever-increasing military might. We cannot deny that there are many forces threatening the *shalom* (peace and justice) of people around the world. It is the responsibility of those who would be called peacemakers after the style of Jesus Christ to develop the critical capacities and spiritual roots that allow them to question both the sanity of the arms race and its consistency with biblical values. . .

The General Synod of the Reformed Church in America has several times voiced its concern about the arms race and the growing militarism in the world. In response to these concerns, the Christian Action Commission calls upon the General Synod:

- to urge each congregation to engage in a serious study of the meaning of Christian peacemaking in today's world.
- to urge each congregation to be diligent in corporate and individual prayer for peace.
- to urge each congregation and individual member to engage in acts of Christian peacemaking as the Spirit leads them, and to support one another in this witness.

FOR MORE INFORMATION: Office of Social Witness, Reformed Church in America, 18th Floor, 475 Riverside Drive, New York, NY 10015

United Church of Christ
Office for Church in Society

[15] "Peace Priority Voted at General Synod 13," Excerpts from UCC NETWORK, July, 1981, Volume 4, Number 7

General Synod 13 issued a strong challenge to the current mood of the country and the direction of national leadership. Reflecting a different set of values and listening to a voice other than that of the latest popularity polls, General Synod reaffirmed its prophetic and faithful leadership of the United Church of Christ.

Meeting in Rochester, New York, June 27–July 1, the 705 delegates to General Synod voted overwhelmingly to place the search for world peace at the top of the whole church's agenda for the next four years.

The selection of priorities for the next four years was perhaps the key decision made by the Synod. A priority selection process had presented the Synod with four options: faith, family life, peace, and youth. The Synod could select up to two at this Synod and will select up to two more from a new list at the next General Synod in two years.

The Synod first voted to choose two priorities. Ballots were then passed out to the 705 delegates, who could vote for one or two priorities.

Peace was the overwhelming choice, with 588 votes, 83% of all potential voters. Family Life was second with 365 votes, 52% of the total. Faith had 265 votes, 38%, and Youth had 100 votes, 14%.

Local churches, Conferences, and church-related groups are now asked to accept the two priorities of Peace and Family Life within the next 12 months.

The Goal Statement for the Peace Priority, which was strengthened on the Floor with amendments by the Christians for Justice Action, a new caucus group, is as follows:

Peace Priority Goal Statement

To enlist all parts of the church, as witnesses for Christ and humanity, in *study and action* to the end that:

- the Biblical and theological role of the church and its members as peacemakers be explored and implemented;
- policies and programs be developed to resolve global tensions and create a peaceful world;
- the dependence of the United States and world economies on the production of armaments be reversed to the end that human and material resources be used to promote the quality of life for all persons;
- the arms race be reversed;
- the development and use of nuclear and biochemical weapons be recognized as completely contrary to the Gospel of Jesus Christ.

Broken Arrow

WHEREAS, nationalism historically has been a universal passion of people, and patriotism an emotion which can be aroused to war; and

WHEREAS, nuclear armaments have been perfected in great number and with such explosive power that nuclear war would mean the end of life as we know it; and

WHEREAS, the money spent for nuclear weapons deprives our world of financial resources for basic human needs; and

WHEREAS, the biblical mandate of the prophets and the gospel of Jesus Christ is the foundation of our faith and action, declared in the Good News, "Blessed are the Peacemakers . . ."

NOW, THEREFORE, BE IT RESOLVED, the Thirteenth General Synod of the United Church of Christ affirms a commitment to nuclear disarmament through negotiation with all existing and developing nuclear powers and communicates this commitment to the President of the United States of America, and the secretaries of state and defense, through the

Office of the President of the United Church of Christ; and

BE IT FURTHER RESOLVED, that the United Church of Christ's President express to national leaders our forthright desire for nuclear disarmament even if this process must begin with unilateral initiatives on the part of the United States.

Peace and the Resolving of Conflict

OBEDIENT to the Commandment to love one another;

MINDFUL of our belief that all of us are brothers and sisters and of our covenant to struggle for peace and justice;

RECALLING that throughout history there have been Christians who have abhorred war and who have sought the ways of peace and that this responsibility is now ours;

RECOGNIZING that much violence in the world is related to the age-old conflicts among religious communities;

CONCERNED that economic, social and political conditions in the world are creating many situations which may result in disorder, destruction and armed conflict;

AWARE that such conflict may escalate to the use of nuclear weapons and global war;

BELIEVING that a deterrent effect of nuclear arms is lessened as sophistication of weapons makes nations unsure that they can anticipate, detect and effectively counter a nuclear strike;

THE THIRTEENTH GENERAL SYNOD

CALLS UPON all Christians and particularly the members of the United Church of Christ to gather within their churches for a disciplined study of the causes of conflict and of peaceful action to prevent or resolve it;

SEEKS to build, in our Christian communities, new foundations for our nation's dedication to peace;

SUPPORTS efforts toward peace through the political institutions of our country and international agreement for progressive arms limitation called for by the Twelfth General Synod and which, as means for peaceful resolution of conflicts are found, can lead to general reduction of arms with all of its concomitant social and economic benefits;

NOTES with satisfaction that a National Commission was established to study proposals for the National Academy of Peace and Conflict Resolution, recommended by the Twelfth General Synod; and we ask that the President of the United Church of Christ and congregations and individual members of this church inform the President of the United States and members of the Congress that we consider the establishment of the Academy a matter of high priority;

STRIVES to prevent the worldwide increase and spread of nuclear weapons and delivery systems;

RECOGNIZES the need, in the world's present circumstances, for defense forces well-chosen, well-equipped, well-trained, well-led and well-rewarded.

However, we call for the most careful deliberation and public consensus that there is a compelling necessity before major steps are taken toward national mobilization or toward the introduction of new weapons systems which may, by their uncertain intent and unpredictable use, be provocative rather than deterrent;

CALLS upon the local congregations, conferences and instrumentalities to provide leadership in efforts toward reconciliation among religious communities in conflict;

URGES a new awareness of the social, economic and political problems which may give rise to conflict and to responsible action to solve them, in the name of our Lord Jesus and in the spirit of love which He taught and exemplified.

Calling Upon the United Church of Christ to Become a Peace Church

WHEREAS, the Bible strongly directs us as Christians to work diligently to settle disputes peaceably, justly, and fairly; and

WHEREAS, the UCC responds positively as a body to scriptural direction from God; and

WHEREAS, the UCC has a history and tradition of love, acceptance, and inclusion that directs toward working for peace;

THEREFORE, the Thirteenth General Synod of the United Church of Christ:

1. Calls upon all segments of the UCC to become a peace church;
2. Encourages all nations to convert resources used for military purposes to peaceful uses for the benefit of humanity;
3. Calls upon the Office of Church in Society to make this known to the world and to work in concert with other peace organizations toward these ends;
4. Calls upon the OCIS to develop and distribute resources on the biblical foundations for peace and study materials appropriate for use within the local congregations of the UCC for the purpose of education and consciousness raising on the fundamental element in our faith;
5. Encourages all governments to settle disputes through peaceful diplomacies; and
6. Calls upon the UCC to work positively toward making Isaiah's vision from God a reality on earth, "... and they shall beat their swords into plowshares, and their spears into pruning hooks; nation shall not lift up sword against nation, neither shall they learn war any more." Isaiah 2:4 RSV.

In Opposition to the Resumption of the Weapons of Chemical Warfare by the United States Government

WHEREAS, over 1,300,000 casualties were caused by chemical agents during World War I, including 100,000 deaths—over half Russian—and 100,000 incapacitations. The 1925 Geneva Protocol—not ratified by the United States until 1975—bans first use of chemicals but does not prohibit the manufacture of stock. After World War II, in which chemical weapons were not used, the United States stockpiled a large arsenal of nerve gas and mustard gas, artillery projectiles, mines and bombs, much of which is still fully serviceable. Production stopped in 1969 when the Nixon Administration decided not to add to this supply.

WHEREAS, the production and possession of biological weapons was renounced unconditionally by the United States in 1969 and is banned by the Biological Weapons Convention of 1972. Biological weapons, based on germs or toxins, are distinguished from chemical weapons and are a separate matter.

WHEREAS, after an eleven year halt, the United States moved toward resuming the production of lethal chemical weapons in 1980 when Congress appropriated $3.15 million for a factory in Arkansas. Although an additional $19 million for equipment was denied, the issue is being considered again this year. On May 21, 1981, the United States Senate, by vote of 50 to 48, approved the appropriation of $20 million to equip the new binary weapons facility. Research further indicates that the Administration intends to lift the 1975 ban on production of chemical weapons, declaring them essential to the national defense, and to request supplementary funding later this year, for the inclusion of production of binary nerve gas in the budget for the 1982 Fiscal Year. Over a period of several years, the cost of chemical weapons procurement could reach $4 billion.

WHEREAS, the nerve gas weapons to be produced at the Pine Bluff, Arkansas plant are called binary because each weapon contains two sealed containers of relatively non-toxic chemicals which react to make lethal nerve gas when mixed in flight in an artillery shell or bomb. The nerve gas weapons now stockpiled contain the same lethal chemical in a single unit. While in principle binary weapons are safer than existing weapons, there has, in fact, been no serious accident in the manufacturing, transporting, or storage of the existing stockpile since procurement began about 30 years ago.

WHEREAS, there is also a question about how safe the binaries really are. Although the production of binary chemical weapons is supposedly safer than past methods of production, the two components used in the proposed binary are, in fact, individually quite toxic. One component, DF, is as toxic as strychnine; the other, QL, causes gastric distress, breathing difficulty, and skin rash.

WHEREAS, the Central Pacific Conference, at its 1980 Spring Assembly, passed a resolution opposed to the production, research and development, stockpiling and use of all forms of lethal or permanently debilitating war gas, including the "binary weapon."

THEREFORE BE IT RESOLVED, the Thirteenth General Synod of the United Church of Christ 1) calls upon the United States Congress to defeat any attempts to appropriate funds for equipping the binary chemical weapons production facility at Pine Bluff, Arkansas, or any other facility, and expresses its opposition to the resumption of lethal chemical weapons production; 2) directs the Office of Church in Society to continue to advocate this resolution to the President of the United States and to members of Congress; and 3) calls upon Conferences and local church members of the United Church of Christ to express their support for this resolution to the President of the United States and to their representatives in the Congress.

The United Presbyterian Church in the U.S.A.

[16] From "Peacemaking: The Believers' Calling," adopted by the General Assembly, 1980

Peace is more than the absence of war, more than a precarious balance of powers. Peace is the intended order of the world with life abundant for all God's children. Peacemaking is the calling of the Christian church, for Christ is our peace who has made us one through his body on the cross.

How will peace be achieved? By disarmament? Certainly, but not only by global economic reform. By the change of political structures? Basically, at the heart, it is a matter of the way we see the world through the eyes of Christ. It is a matter of praying and yearning. It is an inner response to God, who loves the whole world and whose Spirit calls for and empowers the making of peace.

With repentance and humility and the power of hope, let us tend to our task.

To that end the 192nd General Assembly (1980) affirms peacemaking as the responsibility of the United Presbyterian Church and declares:

1. *The church is faithful to Christ when it is engaged in peacemaking...*
2. *The church is obedient to Christ when it nurtures and equips God's people as peacemakers...*
3. *The church bears witness to Christ when it nourishes the moral life of the nation for the sake of peace in the world.* The church's faithful obedience to its calling means active participation in the formation of the values and beliefs of our society. It means seeking peace in the personal and social relationships of our culture and exercising our citizenship in the body politic to shape foreign policy. It is of strategic importance for us to nurture changes in public attitude and to raise public consciousness...

[17] Resolution on Nuclear Weapons Freeze, adopted 1981

The 193rd General Assembly:

1. Endorses the "Call to Halt the Nuclear Arms Race."
2. Directs the Office of the General Assembly to send copies of the "Call to Halt the Nuclear Arms Race" to all ministers, presbyteries, and synods, and five copies to each clerk of session; and to all commissioners of the 193rd General Assembly.

3. Requests the Peacemaking Project of the Program Agency to provide study and interpretive materials on the "Call to Halt the Nuclear Arms Race," such material to include background packets, speakers, posters, audio-visual aids, and resources for Bible study and worship.

4. Requests congregations, presbyteries, and synods to study the "Call to Halt the Nuclear Arms Race" prior to the 194th General Assembly (1982).

6. Directs the Peacemaking Project of the Program Agency to report to the 194th General Assembly (1982) on the actions taken by congregations, presbyteries, and synods; and

7. Sends to the President of the United States, to all members of the Senate and the House of Representatives, and to all appropriate persons in the Russian Orthodox Church copies of the "Call to Halt the Nuclear Arms Race" with a statement of our endorsement of the paper.

8. Sends a protest to the Secretary of the Navy on the naming of the latest nuclear submarine "Corpus Christi" because it is improper and offensive to have a nuclear submarine so named.

[18] From resolution, adopted by the 193rd General Assembly, 1981

WHEREAS, the church is seeking peace according to Christ's command when it summons the nation to take realistic first steps in reducing the prospect of nuclear war; and

WHEREAS, there is a growing body of Christians in this country, some of whom oppose the use of nuclear weapons under any circumstances while others reluctantly approve their use in response to enemy nuclear attack, but all of whom look upon the idea of their nation's deliberately initiating nuclear war, regarding it as an act of singular and monstrous wickedness; and

WHEREAS, in the opinion of experts a pledge never to make a preemptive strike with nuclear weapons would be an important first step in "delegitimizing" nuclear war, carrying the hope that such a pledge from the United States would lead to a similar one from the Soviet Union, thus opening the way to the establishment of more zones free of nuclear weapons and eventually to the reduction of existing stockpiles of nuclear arms;

THEREFORE, be it resolved that the Presbytery of Union request the forthcoming 193rd General Assembly (1981) to petition the President of the United States, the Secretary of State, and the Foreign Relations Committees of the Senate and House of Representatives that our nation make a solemn public commitment never again to be the first to employ nuclear weapons as an instrument of warfare.

FOR MORE INFORMATION: Peacemaking Project, United Presbyterian Church in the USA, 475 Riverside Drive, New York, NY 10015.

World Council of Churches
[19] **Statement on Nuclear Disarmament, adopted by the Central Committee of the World Council of Churches, 1980**

The Central Committee heard the message from the Melbourne Conference, which spoke of the "Clouds of nuclear threat and annihilation" and that from the Conference on Faith, Science and the Future, which reminded it that the gravest danger that humanity faces today is a nuclear holocaust. It is with great sense of urgency that the Central Committee makes this statement.

Developments in the recent period have brought the world closer to the brink of a nuclear war. Unless the present trends are immediately halted, a nuclear war is now a distinct possibility. Many scientists are convinced that in the past year the hands of the clock have moved closer to the midnight of nuclear war.

The tension between the USA and the USSR has increased. They have each developed and continue to develop new generations of ever-more devastating nuclear weapons. The dangers inherent in the deployment of these weapons within Europe have been heightened by the NATO decision to base new missiles possessing counterforce qualities and exceptional accuracy.

In August, 1980, the United States officially announced a new policy which contemplates a "limited" nuclear war. This has further raised the anxieties about a nuclear holocaust. The current weapon program of the major powers, if not stopped, will pull the nuclear trip-wire tighter. The development of "nuclear war-fighting capabilities" will increase the hair-trigger readiness for massive nuclear exchange at a time when political tensions are increasing all over the world.

Many years ago the USA, the UK and the USSR agreed to negotiate a treaty banning all nuclear tests. Regrettably no draft of such a comprehensive test ban treaty has been presented. Neither China nor France has indicated willingness to enter into such an agreement. The deliberations at the Second Review Conference on Non-Proliferation Treaty currently being held in Geneva have highlighted the fact that the nuclear weapon states that have signed the treaty have failed to fulfill their obligations under the treaty to start nuclear disarmament, thus undermining the credibility of the non-proliferation regime.

The Central Committee urges all nuclear powers to: (a) freeze immediately all further testing, production and deployment of nuclear weapons and of missiles and new aircraft designed primarily to deliver nuclear weapons; (b) start immediately discussions with a view to making agreements not to enhance the existing nuclear potentials and progressively reducing the overall number of nuclear weapons and a speedy conclusion of a comprehensive test ban treaty.

The Central Committee also urges an early ratification of the SALT II agreement.

In view of the possibility of nuclear war, the Central Committee urges the Madrid Conference (on European Security and Cooperation) to decide to start negotiations on nuclear disarmament.

FOR MORE INFORMATION: World Council of Churches, Dwain Epps, 777 U.N. Plaza, N.Y.C. 10017